THE
WEST
OF
IRELAND

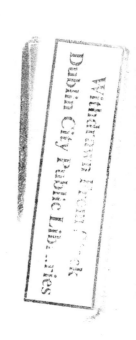

THE
WEST
OF
IRELAND
NEW PERSPECTIVES
ON THE NINETEENTH
CENTURY

EDITED BY CARLA KING AND CONOR MCNAMARA

The
History
Press
Ireland

First published 2011

The History Press Ireland
119 Lower Baggot Street
Dublin 2
Ireland
www.thehistorypress.ie

British Library Cataloguing in Publication Data.
A catalogue record for this book is available from the British Library.

ISBN 978 1 84588 705 6

Typesetting and origination by The History Press
Printed in Great Britain

CONTENTS

ACKNOWLEDGEMENTS

W E WOULD like to thank a range of people whose generosity with their time and knowledge has made this collection possible. We are indebted to all the members of the History Department of St Patrick's College, Drumcondra for their encouragement and collegiality. We should like to thank the St Patrick's College Research Committee for providing a grant to cover the cost of including photographs in the book and we are particularly grateful to Ciarán Mac Murchaidh, dean of research and humanities for his support. The staff at the Cregan Library have always been a model of professionalism and their library remains an inspiring place to work in, for undergraduate, research student and staff alike. We thank the Board of Trinity College, Dublin, for permission to quote from the Davitt Papers. Seán Lucey would like to thank the IRCHSS and the ESRC 'Welfare Regimes under the Irish Poor Law, 1851-1921' project for providing the funding to undertake his research.

The staff at the National Library of Ireland have been particularly helpful in locating new and uncatalogued material. The entire staff of the manuscripts Department, including Colette O'Flaherty, Colette O'Daly and Ciara Kerrigan, in particular, have at all times been enthusiastic and obliging and the expertise of Tom Desmond, James Harte, Nora Thornton and Maria O'Shea was always readily offered.

Ronan Colgan at The History Press Ireland was enthusiastic from the beginning and we are grateful for his support and encouragement over the past year. We were fortunate to have a number of talented people who read drafts of the manuscript and we are thankful to Patricia McVeigh for her editorial work.

We are most grateful to the contributors without whose talent, commitment and co-operation this collection would not be possible. We continue to be inspired and challenged by their research.

Conor McNamara and Carla King

PREFACE

Conor McNamara and Carla King

The idea of the west of Ireland as a place apart – somehow different and distant from the rest of Ireland – has long roots. Never extensively colonised by English or Scottish settlers in the early modern period, parts of the west retained traditional Irish customs and culture, including the Gaelic language, Gaelic modes of land usage and settlement, considerably longer than other, more economically developed parts of Ireland. However, the nineteenth century saw the advent of formative economic, social and political changes which profoundly impacted on rural communities, entailing transformations in traditional bonds of obligation and patronage and the obliteration of enduring systems of social organisation. Despite its chronic problems of economic backwardness, or perhaps because of the prevalence of dire poverty, Connacht was the point of departure for the seminal political movements which transformed rural Ireland, the Land League and United Irish League, and with the emergence of cultural nationalism came to be seen as the locus of the 'authentic' in Irish cultural identity.

These eight essays address aspects of transition in the west of Ireland over the course of the nineteenth century and how various social groups and political organisations mediated social and economic change. Topics examined include both governmental bodies charged with addressing the perpetual problem of poverty and representative associations formed to assert the economic and political interests of distinct social groups in the rural economy, such as herdsmen, agricultural labourers and tenant farmers. Over the course of the century the incremental modernisation of the functions and role of the state and the increasing commercialisation of the rural economy heralded the gradual encroachment of the state into the realms of authority traditionally exercised by the landed elite, in terms of law and order, education, the provision of medical care and the administration of relief, facilitating the increasing disengagement by the landowning classes from the common culture of their tenants. The poor, on the other hand, began to become incorporated for the first time into the wider conventional political arena as the advent of mass political mobilisation challenged perceived notions of deference, legitimacy and respectability.

There are myriad further aspects of change in the west of Ireland over the course of the nineteenth century worthy of academic attention which are not discussed in this collection including multiple issues surrounding the decline of the Irish language, the lives of women, the world of the town, the commercialisation of agriculture and many others. However, it is hoped that this short collection addresses some issues of importance and interest generally to academic researchers, students and the reading public alike. The overwhelming impression which emerges is that that there is no overarching meta-narrative of historical experience of the nineteenth century in the west of Ireland. The saliency of local identity, the complexities of contrasting social structures, linguistic and cultural diversity and contrasting social and economic realities, even within broadly comparable regions, make it highly problematic to talk about 'the history of the west' as other than a complex range of contrasting, distinct, and in many ways, completely separate historical experiences. Thus, while the notion of 'the west' retains evocative, even romantic connotations, it is of limited validity as a descriptive term to frame historical discussion of an inherently complex rural society.

The dire consequences of the Great Famine in the west, as elsewhere in Ireland, have been well delineated by a range of established historians including Cormac Ó Gráda, James Donnelly Jnr and Joel Mokyr. However, in this collection Conor McNamara explores a serious food shortage crisis that overtook nine western counties in May 1822, more than two decades before the cataclysm of the 1840s. His study examines the impact of the partial failure of the potato crop on both the urban and rural poor and analyses responses to the problem of food shortage on the part of Galway landowners who formed the 'Committee to Prevent Pauperism in North Galway' in 1824.

A number of essays in this collection focus on distinct social groups in the rural economy and their experiences in the face of increasing economic modernisation, agricultural commercialisation and popular political mobilisation. Pádraig Lane discusses the fate of agricultural labourers in the west throughout the course of the century. Always on the economic margins as a social group, the bitter struggles of seasonal migratory labourers, casual labourers and *spailpíns* are examined through the descriptions of contemporary commentators, foreign travellers and government reports. A portrait emerges of a people apart, perpetually on the periphery of a vibrant rural society as the economic and political agenda of the small tenant farmers became gradually absorbed into the logic of Irish nationalism.

In terms of the evolution of modes of popular political participation, a significant aspect of modernisation in nineteenth-century European society was the emergence of mass associational culture as nationally co-ordinated political movements steadily replaced smaller regional and communal organisations as conduits for ordinary people seeking redress for perceived social or economic injustice. While Daniel O'Connell pioneered mass political participation in the early 1820s, a succession of political movements of varying size and sophistication representing the economic grievances of tenant farmers emerged from the mid-century onwards and pressed for sweeping land reform. In this respect Andrew Shields examines the tenant right movement in the west in the immediate post-famine period, examining why it faced particular economic and social obstacles to expansion amongst ordinary rural tenants. Analysing the leadership of the movement in the west, Shields discusses the failure of the organisation to garner popular support amongst poverty-stricken tenants and the relative absence of grass roots local leadership. In a complementary chapter, Gerard

Moran explores the experience of a single tenants' organisation in east Galway during the years 1876-80. As a precursor of the Land League and led by the indomitable Matthew Harris, the Ballinasloe Tenants' Defence Association was an early example of a formative cross-sectional coalition of nationalists, small farmers, tenants and townspeople. His study provides an early example of the formidable political potential inherent in broad alliances of seemingly disparate sections of rural society, a model that was to prove crucial to the later success of the Land League, the single most important political organisation in modern Irish history.

While both Protestant and Catholic landowners were often strident in their response to tenant organisations such as the Land League and United Irish League, Miriam Moffitt's exploration of the experience of Protestant tenant farmers addresses a lacuna in our knowledge of the tenants' struggle for the land. On the one hand, Protestant tenants' economic interests prompted some to seek common cause with land reform movements, while at the same time, their shared communal sense of separateness as a religious minority and concurrent solidarity with landlord co-religionists negated any lingering class conscious solidarity for many others. Moffitt traces a complex pattern of divided loyalties and experiences, as some Protestant tenants supported land reform movements, particularly the UIL, whereas others suffered boycotting by their Catholic neighbours, not on account of their religious identity, but Moffitt argues, because they held tracts of grazing land coveted by their neighbours.

John Cunningham examines the important role of a distinct social group that has attracted little attention from historians heretofore. Herdsmen and shepherds traditionally formed something of 'an aristocracy of labour' among the agricultural workforce in late nineteenth-century rural society. Despite enjoying higher social status than many other agricultural workers and benefitting from the extension of pasture in the post-famine years, herds struggled, through their own representative organisations, to defend their customary 'freedoms', including access to land, housing and grazing rights. The liminal position of herds in rural society, being neither farmer, tenant or labourer, and the hereditary nature of their craft, saw them occupy a unique and highly specialised role in the agricultural economy.

Two chapters in this collection address aspects of the state's response to the perpetual problem of poverty and chronic economic underdevelopment in the west. Recent work by historians such as Virginia Crossman and Laurence Geary have reassessed poor law and medical provision in Ireland and in this collection Seán Lucey utilises a case study of the Westport Poor Law Union to examine the development of the care offered in its infirmary and the institution's gradual evolution toward providing the facilities akin to those of a general hospital. Due to the fact that under the workhouse system medical and other provisions had to be paid for primarily from local rates, the impoverished nature of many western districts limited the services they could provide. In her contribution, Carla King looks at the evolution of governmental development strategies from short-term relief measures to combat specific food crises to the more comprehensive provision of wide-ranging policies in the closing years of the nineteenth and early twentieth century and the rationale behind the founding of the Congested Districts Board in particular. She examines the approaches adopted by the state and traces the influence of social improvers such as Michael Davitt and James Hack Tuke and the Board's relationship with the nationalist political establishment and the United Irish League.

1

'THIS WRETCHED PEOPLE'

The Famine of 1822 in the West of Ireland

Conor McNamara

THE GREAT Famine of 1845–8 was the single worst catastrophe to befall the west of Ireland, decimating the lowest ranks of rural society and drastically accelerating the relentless progress of complex inter-connected social and economic processes of unremitting structural transformation characterised by the proliferation of farm amalgamation, the rise of mass emigration and the decline of the Irish language. An Ghórta Mór has justifiably attracted a formidable body of academic work placing the disaster firmly within the larger nexus of complementary structural processes transforming the social and economic character of rural Ireland throughout the nineteenth century. However, as Mary Daly has pointed out, the Great Famine was not an isolated event and rural society in the west was characterised by consistent and profound food shortages for several decades before the crisis of the 1840s; yet this aspect of rural society has failed to attract sustained academic attention.[1]

In nineteenth-century rural Ireland, the crucial social relationship was that between landlord and tenant and the occupation of agricultural land was separate from its ownership with the occupier of a piece of ground rarely holding his land in fee.[2] This chapter examines the vulnerability of the rural poor in the west to food shortages in the pre-famine period and the response of landowners to the crisis in the context of contemporary political and economic orthodoxy.[3] Joel Mokyr has concluded in relation to food scarcity in nineteenth-century Europe, that poverty did not inevitably lead to disaster and disasters did not require a necessary pre-condition of poverty.[4] Food consumption in the west had historically been different from that in England, France and even parts of the east of Ireland, with an overwhelming reliance on potatoes responsible for a peasant population who were comparatively well off as far as energy levels and physical strength was concerned but conversely, were both poorly housed and badly clad.[5] While in a European or British context the rural poor throughout Ireland were notable for their physical strength and the relative abundance of turf meant they were generally well heated, the backward nature of the rural economy in the west meant the western poor were inherently vulnerable to periodic bouts of extreme food shortage during the 'hungry months' of June, July and August, which marked the transition between the exhaustion of the annual supply of potatoes and the arrival of the new crop in late August and September. K.H. Connell has concluded that there were nineteen partial failures of the potato crop between the Great Frost of 1741 and the famine of 1845, with food scarcity increasing in severity from the early 1820s onwards.[6] James Donnelly Jnr has observed that in Cork distrust and acrimony very often poisoned relations between farmers and labourers during the period, noting, 'this is scarcely surprising in view of the grossly exorbitant rents farmers charged for cabins and gardens'.[7] Thus, while Cormac Ó Gráda has asserted that the nutritional and horticultural advantages of the potato resulted in the Irish, 'being better fed, better heated, and perhaps even happier than has been suggested', Mokyr has highlighted the intense vulnerability of the Irish poor and has argued that structural changes to the rural economy led to a sharp decline in the living standards of the poorest rural classes between 1815 and 1835.[8]

The famine of 1822 resulted in severe distress in nine western counties for a number of months in the late spring and summer following the earlier-than-usual exhaustion of the potato harvest. The crisis represented one of the worst periods of Irish food scarcity of the nineteenth century, with government figures indicating over one million people in severe distress in July 1822 alone.[9] Extreme food scarcity lasted from May until August and was confined to nine western counties with widespread distress occurring across counties Limerick, Sligo, Leitrim, Roscommon, Cork and Kerry, with deaths from starvation concentrated along the western seaboard in counties Clare, Mayo and Galway. The crisis represented the *nadir* of an eight-year period of distress in many parts of the west as 1817 saw a fever epidemic raging across the west and south with Connemara and west Mayo particularly badly affected.[10] Limerick was the worst affected county in the south of the country with the medical inspector for Munster estimating that one-fourth of the inhabitants of Limerick city contracted fever with one-seventh of those infected eventually dying from illness.[11] Food scarcity remained a serious concern for the authorities until 1825 with severe distress persisting along the western seaboard for the remainder of the decade. In 1829 a government select committee concluded, 'It is almost impossible in theory to estimate the mischief attendant on a redundant, a growing and unemployed population... the tendency of such a population to general misery must be rapid... leading to the boundless multiplication of human beings satisfied with the lowest condition of existence.'[12] While the majority of the Irish poor were well fed for most of the year, they were vulnerable to even small shocks to the rural economy and their plight was exacerbated by their want of cash, which, combined with their uncertainty of tenure, meant the spectre of eviction continually haunted 'the lower orders'. As potato supplies kept for less than a full year, in times of crisis exhausted stocks could only be replenished by purchasing potatoes at markets, a transaction requiring the exchange of money, something the majority of the landless poor in the west simply did not possess.

'This Wretched People': Rural Distress

The European wars that raged between 1789 and 1815 created an extraordinary economic boom for the Irish economy with the volume of agricultural exports to Britain rising by unprecedented levels.[13] Extraordinary economic growth concealed many of the inherent flaws in the rural economy, however, and the conclusion of the European conflict produced an unprecedented period of sustained economic depression across all agricultural sectors in Ireland.[14] War in Europe led to a sharp rise in Irish corn prices for a sustained period of almost two decades and facilitated a significant increase in grain acreage as landowners sought to cash in on the export market with land traditionally used for pasture increasingly ploughed for grain.[15] The rise in tillage exports also facilitated rapid growth in the size of the rural labour force as labour intensive wheat crops required a considerably larger labour force than pastoral farming. Following the conclusion of the Napoleonic Wars, the agricultural boom which saw a dramatic rise in prices, rents and the number of working men, came to a shuddering conclusion with dramatic and traumatic consequences for the rural economy, and the rural workforce in the west, hardest hit of all. A government committee set up to investigate the state to which the poor had been reduced in 1830 was told that rural Ireland had entered a state of transition following the end of the economic boom of the previous decades. The report noted:

> Such was the state of things so soon as a fall in prices occurred after the peace. A change then began to take place in the system of managing lands. The great decline of agricultural produce prevented many of the middlemen, as well as occupiers, from paying their rents, an anxiety began to be felt by the proprietors to improve the value of their estates and a general impression was produced in the minds of all persons that a pauper population spread over the country...[16]

The Irish rural population increased at a phenomenal pace during the last two decades of the eighteenth century, with the preference for early marriages and the dominant position of the potato sustaining a culture of large family units reinforced by the cheapness of rearing children and their value as free labour.[17]

The tendency towards the sub-letting of already inadequate plots aggravated by the increasing preference of landowners to sublet large sections of their estates, the absence of a Poor Law until 1838 and the concurrent necessity for several generations to live together in cramped cabins which were often shared with the family's cow or pig, contributed to the often wretched lives of the typical rural family in the west.[18] The fear expressed by many landowners in 1830 that a relentlessly rising population placed unendurable demands on a rural economy which remained in dire need of modernisation was underpinned by the rapid expansion of the lowest social class in the west. As Table 1 outlines, the decade before 1822 saw the population of county Galway alone increase by almost 145,926 people to 286,921. These official government figures must be treated with scepticism, however, as the rise in population for Galway, Limerick and Cork is unrealistic. During the same decade, in counties Clare and Cork combined, the population increased by over a quarter of a million people and in county Limerick the number of houses more than doubled from 17,897 to 36,089.[19] Economic growth, however, had a positive impact for landowners only so long as it was accompanied by economic prosperity and the end of the Napoleonic Wars reversed the economic boom and initiated a period of weakening demand for exports, falling prices for produce and a general restriction of the money supply.[20] As the economy deteriorated, it became more and more difficult for tenants to pay their rents, middlemen struggled to balance their accounts and owners of land started to accumulate unprecedented losses.

Table 1: Population increase from 1813-22 in the nine counties affected by the famine of 1822

County	Houses 1813	Houses 1822	Population 1813	Population 1821	Population Increase, 1813-21
Clare	29,301	36,312	160,603	209,595	48,992
Cork	91,447	n/a	523,936	702,000	178,064
Galway	21,122	51,484	140,995	286,921	145,926
Kerry	31,749	34,612	178,662	205,037	26,415

County	Houses 1813	Houses 1822	Population 1813	Population 1821	Population Increase, 1813–21
Leitrim	17,899	19,123	94,095	105,976	11,881
Limerick	17,897	36,089	103,865	214,286	110,421
Mayo	43,702	53,940	237,371	297,538	60,167
Roscommon	30,254	38,289	158,110	207,777	49,667
Sligo	n/a	24,246	n/a	127,879	n/a

Source: *Abstract of the Population of Ireland According to the Late Census Viz. The Return of the Number of Houses and Inhabitants in the Several Counties of Ireland as Collected by the Enumerators' Periodical Returns of Progress and from the Reports of Magistrates: Together with a Comparative View of the Number of Houses and Inhabitants in 1813*, p. 2, HC, 1822, (HC; 36), vol, xiv, p. 737.

The first national reports of extreme distress in the west appeared in early May 1822, when the *Freeman's Journal* reported that in counties Galway and Mayo, 'such misery at so early a period was never witnessed', and in parts of county Roscommon the poor were reported to be slaughtering their lean cattle in order to eat their carrion carcasses.[21] The paper reported that on the west coast of Connemara, 'due to the failure of their crops, they [the poor] are now sent destitute to roam in search of feed and hundreds die along the coast from the effects of eating shellfish and a species of seaweed which they endeavour to exist on.'[22] The immediate cause of the calamity was the partial failure of the potato crop in the autumn of 1821 due to unseasonably wet weather earlier in the year. Consequently, a reduced potato crop began to run out earlier than usual in many western counties and in April the inability of the poor to purchase food stuffs after they had exhausted their supply of potatoes began to create widespread alarm. The inability of small tenants and the landless to purchase food had two principal causes with a dramatic rise in the cost of potatoes due to the prevalence of speculation, exacerbated by the dire shortage of money amongst the very poorest rural class, most of whom subsisted largely outside of the moneyed economy. At least half of all transactions between labourers and farmers in rural Ireland in the first half of the nineteenth century are estimated to have been of the nature of barter deals, with agricultural labourers typically working 230-300 days a year in return for rent allowances and payment in kind.[23] This figure was considerably higher in the west, with the vast majority of landless tenants paying their rent with their labour and growing their own food on very small plots of rented land - known as conacre or garden plots. The government was later informed by a committee set up to investigate the state of the poor that, 'the nature of the late distress in Ireland was peculiar... the potato crop which furnishes the general food of the peasantry had failed: but there was no want of food of another description for the want of support of human life. On the contrary, the crops of grain had been far from deficient and the prices of corn and oatmeal very moderate.'[24] The *Freeman's Journal* agreed with this analysis noting 'that there is plenty of nutritious food in the country the stocks in the hands of factors declare, but the want of employment and no money in circulation, prevents the poor from obtaining any relief.'[25] As the crisis unfolded, speculation in potatoes became increasingly rife and in Roscommon prices for potatoes became so high that the *Roscommon and Leitrim Gazette* predicted 'if these prices are maintained, thousands of the poor must perish for want of food.'[26] The lack of money rather than the absolute lack of food was also highlighted as the main source of distress by the *Connacht Journal* which pondered whether 'the abundance of provisions in neighbouring counties is but tantalising them [the starving poor]'.[27] In Roscommon it was reported 'It does not seem that there is any absolute scarcity of provisions, but the potatoes being consumed, they can only be procured in the market and there is no money to purchase them – it is scarcity of money, not food, which distresses the poor.'[28] The government committee of 1823 agreed, noting, 'they [the rural poor] are unaccustomed to have recourse to markets and indeed they seem rarely to have the means of purchasing.'[29] For landowners and large farmers, however, the rise in prices provided a welcome boost and in north Galway, land agent Henry Comyns noted, 'the markets are much better than they have been in consequence of some people who are buying in speculation.'[30]

The west coast was the scene of the worst deprivation during the crisis and in June the special reporter of the *Freeman's Journal* recorded; 'I am not able and have not language to describe the deplorable state to which this wretched people are reduced, many of them subsisting on a weed gathered on the sea shore and carried many miles on their backs.'[31] In the Castlebar district of Mayo, Revd W.R. Smyth wrote to the London Tavern Committee, decrying, 'the pale and emaciated look of our peasantry, [which] speaks in a language that cannot be misunderstood.' Likewise, Revd John Jagoe wrote that in Skibbereen, he knew of 'twenty or so families who have been subsisting on scarcely anything except nettles and weeds which they pick up in the corn fields.'[32] During the same month in the remote parish of Ballinahinch, Revd Charles Seymour reported that fifteen people had died in his parish in two days and four times that number were afflicted with cholera and were past recovering.[33] In July, Revd Thomas Loftus reported that in his isolated parish of Ballinakill, forty-seven people had perished from hunger, twenty-nine more from typhus and seventeen from dysentery and 'crowds assail me in every direction looking for assistance'.[34] In June, with the average wage for rural labourers set at eight pence per day, women were walking from Connemara to Galway town to be hired to transport turf on their backs for three halfpence per day. The *Freeman's Journal* noted that women were:

> ...daily employed drawing down turf from the bogs in the neighbourhood of Galway town upon their back and for as great a load as they can carry. They obtain but three half pence, performing a journey of six miles barefoot in the burning sun; but such is the scarcity of money that they hesitate not to perform this arduous undertaking for so small a pittance.[35]

The government's response to the crisis was heavily influenced by the fever epidemic of 1817-19 when enduring public and private mechanisms for distributing charitable relief were centrally co-ordinated by a five-man Government Relief Board. Centralised government relief operated alongside two main voluntary charitable organisations – the London Tavern Committee and the Mansion House Committee. The Government Relief Board held its first meeting on 13 May but their efforts were pre-empted by English philanthropy which saw the London Tavern Committee, composed of London merchants, MPs and landowners, establish their own relief committee on 7 May, followed by a similar enterprise in Dublin where the Lord Mayor called a public meeting in the Mansion House on 16 May. These three central bodies donated money and foodstuffs, which were in turn distributed by centralised county committees which co-ordinated aid distribution to baronial committees composed of land-owners. These in turn organised relief schemes, implemented by parochial committees organised by Catholic and Protestant clergymen, landown-ers and their agents. The London Tavern Committee donated a total of £304,180 in aid during the crisis with grants of potatoes, rice and meal accounting for the bulk of the aid, along with direct grants of money to central county committees.[36] The efforts of the London Committee were universally acclaimed in the distressed districts and at a meeting of the gentlemen and clergy of Kerry in May, a resolution was passed noting, 'a strong impression has been made in the hearts of our peasantry, by so munificent an act of strangers, doing honour to the national character of England.'[37] Landowner Daniel Coghlan of Crookhaven, county Cork, assured the committee, 'the humane liberality of the sister Kingdom to this unfortunate country never can be forgotten by an Irish heart, possess-ing the smallest spark of any humanity.'[38]

The three committees acted along similar principles in that all money raised for relief was intended to aid local contributions, with gratuitous relief to be avoided and aid distributed through employment in public works. Both Protestant and Catholic clergy were involved at a local level, with money to be used by local committees to provide provisions and seed potatoes at a reduced cost which did not interfere with prevailing prices for basic commodities. Small works were preferred to large schemes as it was hoped that this would encourage landowners to contribute and in this respect the Mansion House Committee preferred parish committees to county committees, as smaller schemes avoided the scenario of large num-bers of desperate people gathering at single schemes.[39] As well as money, the committees also sent potatoes which were distributed at a reduced cost at public works schemes.

The government appointed three senior engineers, Alexander Nimmo, Richard Griffith and John Killally, to supervisor major schemes of public works in nine counties. Griffith supervised public works in Limerick, Cork and Kerry and spent a total of £17,043; Alexander Nimmo supervised works in Galway, Mayo, Leitrim, Sligo and Roscommon, spending £26,893; John Killally supervised road works totalling £14,725 in county Clare and south Galway.[40] While priests and Protestant ministers were prominent on parochial committees, government relief schemes were generally overseen by leading members of the country's most prominent gentry families.[41] Various members of the extended Blake, D'Arcy and Daly families acted as principal overseers on eight schemes in county Galway with Charles Le Poer Trench personally overseeing eight schemes and Lord Clonbrock overseeing three.[42] In Kerry the formation of relief schemes was hampered by the failure of parochial committees to produce statistics on distress but Griffith supervised the employment of over 7,000 persons on private relief schemes in county Limerick alone with £6,999 distributed to thirty-eight individual parish committees employing men on road repair schemes.[43] In Cork Griffith estimated that between 25,000 and 30,000 people were daily employed between July and August on the creation of forty-three miles of new road, with repairs carried out on 460 miles of existing roads.[44] In Connacht Alexander Nimmo oversaw the largest number of public work schemes with £12,953 spent in county Galway, £6,034 spent in Mayo, £3,147 spent in Sligo, £2,682 spent in Roscommon and £165 spent on one public scheme in Leitrim.[45]

In county Clare and south Galway, John Killally estimated that there were 26,845 persons 'unfit by age or disease to procure sustenance', with a further 90,000 in dire need but capable of labouring on government schemes.[46] It was reported by the *Clare Journal* in April that, 'to mitigate the extreme wretchedness to which the poor are reduced has hourly exercised the ingenuity of every benevolent man'.[47] By early June, 'fever and dysentery [were] rapidly extending their ravages amongst the famishing peasantry… with external relief [proving] wholly inadequate'.[48] As the crisis reached its peak in late June, 13,795 families, comprising 77,680 people, were reported by baronial relief committees to be in dire want of food. These figures represent only six of the ten Clare baronies, however, and as Table 2 indicates, distress was at its most extreme in the barony of Upper Tulla with 13,637 people reported as being in dire need. In June the MP for Ennis, William Vesey Fitzgerald, informed parliament,

'If any persons supposed that the charity of England, even added to the sums already voted by parliament, would be sufficient to meet the calamities of Ireland for the next six weeks, such persons deceived themselves.'[49]

Table 2: Persons in need of daily outdoor relief in county Clare, June 1822

Barony	Families	Persons
Upper and Lower Bunratty	2,473	16,260
Clonderalaw	2,960	16,200
Ibrickane	583	3,007
Inchiquin	1,616	9,384
Islands	1,907	14,335
Upper Tulla	2,385	13,637
Total	11,924	72,823

Source: Figures compiled by the County Clare Central Organising Relief Committee and printed in the *Clare Journal and Ennis Advertiser*, 20 June 1822.

Miserables Craving Relief: Urban Distress

The urban poor were severely affected by the rising cost of basic food stuffs during the sporadic food crises which characterised the pre-famine rural economy and throughout the summer of 1822 many thousands of working people generally considered to constitute 'the respectable poor', including tradesmen and skilled labourers, were forced to seek outdoor relief in the towns of Galway, Limerick and Ennis. Urban distress was further exacerbated by the arrival into towns of thousands of starving families fleeing rural districts in search of food, spreading typhus amongst the respectable classes and the poor alike. In urban areas the need to prevent the eruption of violent disorder and the spread of contagious diseases governed attitudes towards charity. The editor of the *Limerick Chronicle* warned of 'the disregard of social restraint and good order to which the excess of famine may, it is feared, excite a large portion of the peasantry.'[50] As the fear of being besieged by the sick and dying from remote rural districts became overwhelming amongst the respectable classes in Galway, magistrates took measures in both Ballinasloe and Galway town to prevent the rural poor from entering in search of aid. During the fever crisis of 1817 Galway town had been ravaged by typhus, which the rural poor inevitably transported with them and the *Connacht Journal* reported in May 1822 'once again the wretched hovels of our Liberties are absolutely crowded to excess with half-famished and famished beings, oppressed and broken down for want of the common necessities of life.'[51] Fear of the rural masses continued to haunt the respectable classes in Galway throughout the period and in 1823, the paper urged town magistrates to avail of existing legislation to prevent 'strange beggars' from entering towns, stressing the 'expediency of not admitting into our towns those hordes of poor strangers who, driven by distress, seek relief amongst us, and carry with them the seeds of infection, which are ever attendant upon distress.'[52] 'Strange beggars should be kept out of the town and we call upon our magistracy to put the powers, with which the government has vested in them, rigorously into effect, to drive all vagrants from our towns. We expect this as an act of justice, we demand it as a measure of paramount necessity.'[53] As Table 3 indicates, charges for vagrancy across Ireland declined rapidly following the crisis to almost one-third of the 1822 level.

Table 3: Charges brought for vagrancy in Ireland, 1822-28

Year	1822	1823	1824	1825	1826	1827	1828
Charges	623	486	419	345	312	324	234

Source: *Criminal Commitments Ireland: Summary Statements of the Numbers of Persons Charged with Criminal Offences Committed to the Different Jails in Ireland for Trial at the Assizes and Sessions Held for the Several Counties, Cities, Towns, and Liberties Therein During the Last Seven Years*, p. 7, HC, 1829, (HC; 256), vol. xxii, p.427.

Noting in April 1822 that thousands of poor people were reduced to a single meal of oatmeal and water per day in county Clare, Sir Edward O'Brien, believed 'if they were to commit all the persons who took provisions for their support, no gaol in the country could hold them; nay, farther, that the parties so arrested, if they could get their families around them, would think that they had made a happy exchange in getting into prison.'[54] The threat which the rural poor posed to respectable members of society often informed public comment on the crisis, and the *Connacht Journal* noted in February 1823 'scenes of poverty and wretchedness which have been witnessed on every side are beyond description... What is to become of this starving population, hopeless and desperate? They will be driven from their homes by pestilence and famine and bearing contagion along with them, will turn towards Galway to beg relief at our doors.'[55] The paper proceeded to publish details of starving families in the vicinity of the town, noting on one occasion, 'several starving families have taken up in our suburbs and strange to tell, no effort has been made to dislodge them, the sooner, this was done, the better'.[56] These measures, the editor assured readers, 'would prevent false hope and discourage others' and 'it is with considerable reluctance that we have been forced by a sense of duty to recommend any measure of harshness or inhospitality towards our fellow countrymen in distress but self preservation, the first law of nature, demands it of us.'[57] 'Matchless charity it would be to feed and foster them for sure destruction... this would be charity with a vengeance.'[58]

A public food kitchen was opened in the town of Ennis in mid-April 1822 with food dockets distributed by Relief Committee members amongst the poor with the provision that 'street mendicants' were not included.[59] The crisis affected even the respectable ranks of the town's tradesmen and skilled workers and at the end of April, it was reported 'the streets of Ennis were lined with labourers and trades people who stand leaning against the walls, their arms folded and despair in their countenances... they have with their families become wanderers through the country.'[60] The outdoor kitchen distributed over 5,000 pints of soup in the first thirty days, feeding 100 people daily with the number of applicants in May reported to be 'beyond the means of the institution'.[61] Likewise in Limerick city, the crisis mirrored the situation in Galway and Ennis but on a much wider scale and in June almost 20,000 people were returned on a 'list of miserables craving relief' and in the city's poorest parish of St Mary's 'so wretched a population is not to be found in the whole of Munster'.[62] The city's relief committee could only afford to employ a small number of men on relief schemes with 150 men working for a rate of eight pence per day clearing the Shannon river basin and whitewashing cabins, 'as fever and dysentery rapidly extended their ravages amongst the famishing peasantry'.[63] Later in the month the paper declared, 'the overseers of the works will do well to direct their attention to the opening of graves in the burying grounds most convenient in the city'.[64] The situation in Limerick replicated the distress in Ennis with the ranks of the sturdy poor including unemployed tradesmen, reported by the local press to be 'unable to conquer their feelings of shame as far as to send their wives or children to crave, perhaps in vain, a little porridge... in their habitations you will find neither a table, chair or stool to sit on, not even a straw bed... I shall not shock the public delicacy and feeling by relating the various species of misery which I witnessed.'[65] By early July, the county Limerick Central Committee had raised a total of £8,011 locally for the distribution of relief with average grants to local committees of between £50 and £100 distributed to clergy and landowners around the county.[66] By the end of July, 1,700 persons were being employed in the city with the price of labour reduced from eight pence to seven pence per day for men, three pence for boys and two pence for horses.[67]

The Limits of Landlord Paternalism

In pre-famine Ireland poverty and pauperism were perceived as distinct phenomena; the former being presented as inevitable and in some ways beneficial with the latter derived from the choices of individuals. As Virginia Crossman has explained, 'poverty was presented as an inevitable and in some ways beneficial aspect of civil society, and one that it was neither possible nor necessary to eliminate. Pauperism on the other hand derived from the choices of individuals and represented a threat to society by disrupting social and economic relationships based on the operation of a free labour market.'[68] The indolence of the rural poor was believed by many landowners to be the primary cause of the backwardness of the rural economy in the west which was portrayed by some commentators as inextricably linked to the horticultural demands – or the lack thereof – of the potato. According to the editors of the *Roscommon and Leitrim Gazette*, the relative ease with which potatoes flourished and the relative lack of manpower required to reap a large harvest left the poor with too much free time:

> The ease of the potatoes, both in sowing, reaping and preparation left the peas-
> ant in too much leisure to contract bad habits and have evil communications;
> or in idleness they will sit roasting their legs at the fire, during a large portion
> of the day and many of them are kept thus in a state of barbarity. In compari-
> son to this way of life, the hunter (though ferocious) is active and manly.[69]

Noting the starvation which prevailed across the county in April 1822, the same newspaper noted that the giving of alms should never be permitted to disturb the existing social order, as 'no person maintained on charity should be raised above that rank which he held in the period of health and industry. On the contrary he should descend at least one step below the station which he then occupied.'[70] The government committee to enquire into the state of the people in 1830 came to a similar conclusion, noting the prevalence of:

> A numerous and almost naked population, whose utmost industry extends
> to the raising of sufficient potatoes for their daily food and saving turf for a
> supply of fuel. These objects accomplished, they have little further motiva-
> tion for exertion, since employment in the service of others seldom presents
> itself. No wonder then that such families exhibit many proofs that idleness is
> the mother of mischief.[71]

In July 1822 the dire human consequences which food shortage entailed for the lowest tiers of rural society in the west threatened to contradict the traditional paternal role of the gentry and the mounting anxiety that rural society was gradually being overwhelmed by the escalating destitution of an increasingly desperate rural population initiated a protracted debate

regarding the human cost and the economic necessity of agricultural modernisation. As external aid was predicated on supplementing local efforts,
the endeavour of landowners was the formative factor in governing the
response to distress in local districts. Irish landlords' economic position
weakened in the pre-famine period and the general rise in rents which the
economic boom stimulated before 1815 precipitated a concerted attempt
by landowners to sustain abnormally high levels of income from 1815
onwards while simultaneously curtailing investment in their properties.[72]
Landlords' increasing economic curtailment coincided with the decline
of the traditional paternal role of the gentry as the popular democratic
character of the movement for Catholic Emancipation saw landowners
become ever more conservative in their social and political outlook. The
growing influence of O'Connell's constitutional crusade, combined with
the expansion of the role of the state in providing remedial relief for the
poor, the administration of the law and the maintenance of the peace,
steadily exacerbated the growing cultural chasm between landlord and
tenant throughout the 1820s. In terms of the evolution of popular political aspirations, Galway MP, Anthony Richard Blake observed in 1825, that
ordinary Catholics had become 'bound together by a sense of common
grievance'[73] and MP Denis Browne of Westport complained, 'with my
own agents, and with people that I thought would never feel, except with
me, with those very people that I thought would care as little for those
political questions as anyone, those people show me every minute that
they think against me.'[74]

The dread of an emerging social crisis posed a range of moral dilemmas
for landowners and provoked a re-examination of the relationship between
the duties of Christian charity and the necessities of political economy.
William Trench of Cangort Park, King's County, was a land agent on the
Clonbrock and Mahon estates comprising over 15,000 acres in north
Galway and south Roscommon and his 'Plan for Bettering the Conditions
of the Poor Permanently in Ireland' was approved by the newly formed
'Committee for the Prevention of Pauperism in North Galway' at a series
of meetings attended by local landowners from the barony of Kilconnell in
February 1824.[75] The board began its work by appointing a series of 'gentle-
men deacons' to undertake a census of the parishes of Killian and New Inn

with the number of persons, their age and sex in each townland recorded, along with the details, circumstances and 'conduct' of the families visited. The deacons were asked to 'care to make themselves intimately acquainted with such circumstances, intending to transmit at a future period their remarks to their landlords.'[76] Following their initial survey, the board concluded that the lethargy of the rural poor was chiefly responsible for the backwardness of the rural economy and resolved that the unreasonably high rate at which labour was set and the lack of industry amongst the labouring classes retarded the rural economy.[77] The committee lamented that agricultural labourers preferred 'dilatory employment about a small farm, which by the way, they do not cultivate, rather than work for such hire as they can get, but a steady adherence to the principles laid down for this committee will, it is not doubted, soon convince them that their true policy will be to work for such hire as they can get, rather than be idle and to be active when at home.'[78]

The board was 'more convinced than ever that the male population in many instances were without labour because they do not see fit to offer themselves at such hire as the persons likely to employ them are willing to find it in their interest to give – they do not see that it is in their interest to be always engaged with every member of their family able to earn.'[79] Noting 'the evident anxiety on the part of poor females to earn their support in any manner within their reach', the committee stressed the role of young women in alleviating poverty.[80] The board's proposed solution was predicated on the stimulation of a local linen industry by encouraging women and young girls to become involved in the spinning of yarn in their homes through the subsidisation of flax seed, spinning wheels and looms which would be facilitated by their landowners and co-ordinated by the committee. The price of labour could then be reduced by setting out strict criteria for the families they were willing to assist and the board vowed not to give assistance to any families, 'the heads of which being able to earn by labour and where children are able to earn by industry'.[81] A system of incentives and bonuses was created with the committee proposing to act as agents, purchasing finished material from the producers at a set rate, selling it at the market in Ballinasloe and repaying the sums contributed by individual landlords.

The Galway committee's conclusions regarding the causes and exigencies of rural poverty were greatly at odds with the findings of the government report to enquire into the state of the people in 1825. In relation to rates of pay and employment in the west, Denis Browne of Westport, first cousin of the chairman of the Galway committee, Ross Mahon, told the board of inquiry that while 'the price of some articles is three times what it had been, there is a great deficiency in that respect [employment]... we have generally employment at very low wages.'[82] Likewise, a government committee concluded in 1830, 'want of demand for labour necessarily ensures very severe distress among the labouring classes. This, combined with the consequences of an altered system of managing land, is stated to produce misery and suffering which no language can possibly describe and which it is necessary to witness in order fully to estimate.'[83] The Galway committee's assertion that rates of labour were prohibitively high was absurd and while the average rate of pay for a day's labour without food in the west of Ireland was ten pence per day, Ross Mahon, who was chairman of the Galway committee paid his labourers eight pence per day, while his cousin, Denis Browne paid six pence per day – half the average rate in many other counties – and labourers were reported to be working for four pence per day in north Roscommon in April 1822.[84] The committee made no recommendations regarding the nature of the land tenure system despite the government board of enquiry concluding that high rents for conacre generated during the economic boom of the early decades of the nineteenth century left tenants unable to meet their demands and led directly to the prevalence of sub-letting and ultimately to over-cultivation and dire poverty:

> Lands rose greatly in value from year to year and leasees were tempted to realise profit-rents by sub-letting their farms. In this way a system previously existing was continued and extended and one or more mesne tenants were interposed between the owner and the occupier... the tendency on the part of the tenant was either to sublet or subdivide among his family...[85] The poor living on a farm so sub-divided, cut it up, destroy it, abuse the land by bad tillage, and do not leave so much as a bush or tree but they cut them all down. The cabins they live in are the most miserable and wretched to be seen, enough to give them fever and sickness, which it does in many cases.[86]

Anthony Richard Blake MP concurred that high rents generated untold misery, telling the government committee, 'their pride, and there is a sense of pride amongst the lower orders, as among the higher, is wounded by the sense that they belong to a degraded class'.[87] 'Arrears lay as an encumbrance upon them, pressing them down, and discouraging them altogether.'[88] If the Galway committee's conclusion regarding the relationship between labour rates and poverty was patently incorrect, their commitment to stimulating a local linen industry through an elaborate system of rewards and incentives was naive. While most homes in the district possessed a spinning wheel, a dearth of technical expertise meant that only the coarsest material could be produced in very small quantities which fetched the lowest prices at the market in Ballinasloe and was bought primarily by the poor themselves. The expertise, investment and entrepreneurship necessary to successfully compete in the linen market demanded a protracted investment over a number of years, involving a degree of technical sophistication which did not exist in rural Galway.[89] A demand for linen did exist in western towns but the coarseness of western material made it unsuitable for the wider market. In respect of linen produced in the west, Dublin linen merchants, Nolan and Taafe, noted in 1823 that Galway manufacturers, 'do not spin their flax enough, for this is the thing that has kept the manufacture of the town of Tuam backward for twenty years… If they cannot be got to spin their flax fine enough for manufacture, the demand will be fluctuating, wavering and uncertain.'[90]

While the achievements of the various relief committees in feeding large numbers of people on outdoor relief over a number of months in 1822 were not inconsiderable, western newspapers were consistently critical of the response of the gentry to the crisis and the *Roscommon and Leitrim Gazette* issued a stinging rebuke to landowners in east Connacht: 'How shocking it is to see dogs fed in gentleman's houses with bread, milk, stir-about, meal and soup, whilst poor Christian inhabitants are dying for want of food – whilst on the very same person's table lie newspaper accounts of human creatures, not many miles distant eating dead horses, diseased beef, wild weeds and eagerly catching cows' blood.'[91] Extensive coverage was given in the western press to the distribution of relief at Boyle, county Roscommon, where it was alleged that the starving were working for four pence per day building a private road for a landlord with money donated by the London Tavern Committee. The situation was compounded by reports that meal intended for relief of the starving poor was being fed to horses towing gravel.[92] The *Connacht Journal* believed that relief efforts in the county were inadequate and called for a public meeting to discuss the situation and an immediate 'communion' to be opened with the government on the crisis.[93] The paper noted in March 1823 that there was still upwards of 100 tons of oats intended for distribution during the previous summer in store in Galway town. The editor speculated, '[the donors] never could have supposed that while men were starving, their meal would have been reserved to be the food of rats.'[94] Other reports were equally critical of both landlords and tenants, with one speculating, 'if the proprietors [of land] were obliged to contribute to the maintenance of the poor, they would more strictly watch over their conduct. They would either find work for them or they would diminish their numbers by discouraging improvident marriages.'[95] In relation to the use of publicly raised funds for the provision of private relief schemes in Limerick, it was reported, that 'strong feelings of discontent prevail relative to the disposal of the different liberal donations from England... [with] gentlemen putting money into their own pockets... It was never contemplated by any Englishman giving money to relieve the distress of the poor in this country that such uses should be made of it.'[96]

Irish representatives at Westminster were also consistently critical of the government's relief efforts and in June John Smith MP noted that in Cork alone there were 132,000 individuals 'who must perish with hunger if they did not receive relief. In one barony of the county of Clare, many persons had actually perished from famine. It was for the government to say what, under such circumstances, it meant to do... Enough had not been done, and therefore government ought to take more decisive measures.'[97] Thomas Spring Rice, MP for Limerick city, believed 'however great the sums placed at the disposal of the London Committee, it was impossible, even if they trebled their amount, that they could do more than relieve the present suffering, and that only in a very slight degree'.[98] No less a figure than Peel himself acknowledged that the exceptional nature of the crisis warranted a more pragmatic approach from the state, noting 'the Irish government were endeavouring to give relief in every possible way, not with strict regard to the principles of political economy, for unhappily the case was one that compelled them to set all ordinary rules at defiance'.[99]

Conclusion

From 1815 onwards landowners in rural Ireland increasingly resisted demands for rent abatements, reduced the number of leases on their estates and took legal action against tenants in arrears more readily, while working towards removing insolvent occupiers from their properties in order to minimise the losses incurred because of the economic downturn. As Samuel Clark has argued, 'by the 1820s the traditional exchange of benefits between landlords and tenants had become severely strained because both sides were faced with actual or potential losses that could only be minimised at the expense of the other.'[100] The 1822 famine illustrates several of the key themes pertaining to rural society in the west during the period of economic decline which commenced in 1815 and culminated in the Great Famine of 1845-8. The increasing vulnerability of the rural poor to even partial crop failures, the inability of the state to co-ordinate a comprehensive response to food shortage and the sustained criticism of the reaction of landowners to the crisis characterised a society in which distress was increasingly viewed as the inevitable, albeit regrettable, consequence of economic backwardness and in which the role of charity was in merely tempering the suffering of the rural poor in times of excessive misery. The dearth of comprehensive statistics regarding deaths during the crisis has resulted in a reluctance on the part of historians to comprehensively label the crisis a famine. However, a broad survey of a wide range of contemporary reports reveals the prevalence of deaths, dire hunger and intense distress in both rural and urban settings. The failure of contemporary authorities to produce comprehensive statistics reflected the reluctance of landowners to acknowledge the scale of the crisis and many leading landlords were severely criticised for their slow response to the crisis, including Ross Mahon, chairman of the 'Committee to Prevent Pauperism in North Galway', who was singled out for particular condemnation by local clergy.[101]

Severe distress continued to be a defining characteristic of life for the lowest classes of rural society in the west throughout the period with the government sanctioning £50,000 for local and temporary relief in early 1831 and a further grant of £30,000 issued in August 1835, with smaller sums approved in 1836, 1837 and 1839.[102] In this respect, the 'Committee to Prevent Pauperism in North Galway' was a retrospective attempt by land-owners to re-assert their moral stature in the face of mounting criticism of their failure to adequately respond to the crisis amidst the increasing usur-pation of their traditional paternal role by various agencies of the state. The organisers of the committee were members of a social group in decline, retrospectively seeking to justify their own failure to respond to rising pov-erty exacerbated by the structural changes transforming the failing rural economy. The decision of the Whately Committee in 1833 to recommend the establishment of a system of Poor Law relief adapted from the English and Scottish models fundamentally exposed the paternal pretensions of landowners. In this context, the Galway committee was a short-lived initia-tive, reflective of the social and political values of the landowning classes which recognised the undesirability of destitution rather than the neces-sity of addressing 'ordinary' poverty. Their endeavours were primarily born out of a desire to control responses to, and interpretations of, extreme distress which inevitably had negative repercussions for all social classes. By applying a rigid distinction between deserving and undeserving poor, the criteria for financial support justified the exclusion of practically the entire spectrum of the poorest classes of rural society. Underlying their deliberations was an effort by landowners to reinstate themselves into a position of moral authority in the face of increasing misery and the grow-ing diminution of the moral and political stature of land owners as a group. In this context, distress was a regrettable but necessary by-product of agri-cultural modernisation and the role of charity was in merely tempering the excessive zeal of improving landlords as one landowner explained to a government committee in 1830, 'the risk to be apprehended is not that the proprietors of land should be insensible to these considerations, but that they should, in some cases, proceed with too much rapidity.'[103]

2

POOR CRAYTURS

The West's Agricultural Labourers
in the Nineteenth Century

Pádraig G. Lane

I N NINETEENTH-CENTURY Ireland, rural people made a
sharp distinction between those who held land and those who did not,
and relations between farmers and their labourers were often bitter.[1]
While divisions between rural social groups were complex and not easily
delineated, Samuel Clark has argued that 'we should think of the agrarian
class structure as formed by a gradation in levels of power and wealth, from
the landless labourer to the very large farmer, with infinite distinctions in
between.'[2] The landless constituted the least respectable tier of rural society,
frequently regarded as being outside the conventional standards of decency,
living amongst their extended kin, marrying and fraternising within their
own class. Clark has noted that on the eve of the Great Famine in 1841,
70 per cent of the adult male agricultural workforce consisted of labourers with the landless 'forced to seek employment where ever they could
find it... the farmer might keep a tally of wages owed to the labourer and
at the end of the season deduct the sum from the total amount of rent
that was due.'[3] The social cleavage between farmers and labourers remained
vast throughout the century and rents charged for cabins, garden plots and
related privileges were often beyond the means of casual labourers, forcing

many to squat on the property of middlemen or occupy tiny sub-divisions of their relatives' potato ground.

The inexorable decline of the poorest class in rural society, those surviving on very small, economically unviable plots of land, often supplemented by seasonal or migratory labour, and the equally large class of landless people who sought a precarious livelihood by proffering their labour at casual rates to farmers, was the single most remarkable human catastrophe of the nineteenth century in Ireland. There was never any shortage of compelling images of the rural poor, whether sought in fiction, in the observations of the passing stranger, or in weighty and worthy reports of parliament. This chapter examines depictions of the labourers and landless men of the west, and how the struggles of the *spailpíns*, casual labourers and seasonal migratory workers evolved throughout a century characterised by the relentless structural transformation of the rural economy, the prevalence of periodic bouts of food shortage and a declining demand for the labour of the rural poor in an Ireland, increasingly transformed by the commercialisation of the rural economy.

Pre-Famine Images of Rural Labourers

In pre-famine rural society, as Oliver MacDonagh has explained, 'farmers were quite outnumbered by a vast army of labourers. Just as the Irish farmer of these years was a very different sort of being from his English counterpart, so too, and for the same reason, was the Irish labourer.'[4] Population growth, however, had positive consequences for landowners only so long as it was accompanied by economic prosperity and the end of the Napoleonic Wars in 1815 initiated a period of weak demand for Irish agricultural produce, making it more difficult for tenants to pay their rent, while evictions became an increasingly attractive strategy for landlords seeking to reform the management of their estates.[5] The economic plight of the landless became increasingly severe in the thirty years before the onset of the Great Famine and with rents for small garden plots rising, demand for labour decreasing and the reliance of the poorest on the potato increasing, a steady multiplication of a landless class living precariously on the edge of economic desperation pushed rural society toward the catastrophic famine of the 1840s.

Even by the standards of pre-famine Ireland, the poverty of the cottier class in the west was remarkable and staggering accounts of their misery abound in government reports, newspapers, literature and travellers' accounts, as the desperation of the western poor inevitably contributed to the willingness of landless men to hire their labour at rates far beneath those paid in the north and east of the country. While the consensus of contemporary landowners was that cottier and day labour in Connacht was generally unproductive,[6] a government committee tasked with enquiring into the state of the labouring poor in 1823 found, 'far from being uniformly inactive and idle, the peasantry of Ireland have a considerable anxiety to procure employment'.[7] The same committee noted, 'the peasantry of the south and west quit their homes at certain times of the year in search of employment... many hundreds of the peasantry of county Kerry hire themselves in the neighbouring county of Limerick at four pence per day... offering work for the merest subsistence that can be obtained, at the lowest possible rate of wages, for two pence per day, in short, for anything that would purchase food enough to keep them alive during the ensuing twenty-four hours.'[8] A respondent to the same committee noted, '[the landless] live in a state of misery of which I could have formed no conception, not imagining that any human beings could exist in such wretchedness. Their cabins scarcely contain articles that could be called furniture... there are no such things as bed clothes... they slept in their working clothes, yet, whenever they had a meal of potatoes they were cheerful...'[9] Irish Under-Secretary Thomas Drummond drew attention to the particularly severe levels of poverty amongst the rural poor in 1838, which he believed distinguished the people of the western counties from those of the south and midlands. Noting the degree to which the population of Connacht was dependent on the potato, resided in wretched mud walled hovels and relied on casual wages that on average did not exceed 6*d* per day, he observed, 'poverty and misery have deprived them of energy, labour brings no adequate return, and every motive to exertion is destroyed'.[10]

Maria Edgeworth, in *The Absentee* (1812), cast a sympathetic eye on those 'poor crayturs', the womenfolk of the migratory Connacht farm workers.[11]

She caught their images as they set out to beg on the country roads while their men folk went with their scythes to the harvest fields of England. She depicted the wretched hovels from which they emerged and described the meitheals of labourers awaiting the estate steward of an evening, their tally sticks to hand, 'it being the way the labourers do keep an account of the day's work'.[12] These were the cottiers whom Lady Morgan saw as bartering the sweat of their brow to earn shelter for their families in Sligo.[13] Charles Lever presented a more sombre image of the violence begotten by the labourers' misery and in his *St Patrick's Eve* (1845) and *The Martins of Cro' Martin* (1856), just as in Lady Morgan's Sligo story, *Mount Sackville* (1833), the want and misery that had eaten into the cottiers' nature made them prey, when evicted from their hovels, to the agrarian societies and rural insurgencies invariably controlled by their masters, the farmers.[14] Anthony Trollope captured the vulnerability of the cottier labourers to eviction and the contempt in which they were held in *The Kellys and the O'Kellys* (1859) where his leading character, Barry Lynch, offered the prospect of a tenancy of a large holding to a famer on condition of the clearance of the multiplicity of cottier occupants who had no security of tenure other than traditional conacre agreements for potato ground: 'If you've a mind to be a tenant of mine, Colligan, I'll keep a lookout for you. The land's crowded now, but there's a lot of them cottier devils I mean to send to the right about. They do the estate no good, and I hate the sight of them.'[15]

The rural poor in the west were notoriously badly clad and J.B. Trotter, describing a busy harvest in September 1817 in Galway, could not help noticing the wretchedness of the casual labourers,[16] while Thackeray, on the eve of the Great Famine, could only marvel in horror at the 'multiplicity of rags' that marked the scene before him.[17] The misery of the agricultural labourers was perennially remarked upon by strangers to the west, such as the German visitor, Pükler Muskau, who, while traversing Galway and Mayo in 1828, observed that the poor were marked by 'poverty, beggary and whiskey', unable to buy sufficient food and only surviving, 'because the poor alone could survive the privation of necessaries'. Another German traveller, J.G. Kohl, noted on the eve of the Great Famine, the miserable appearance of seasonal migrant reapers and farm labourers on the Connacht roads as they made their way home from England, working for wages of between 6*d* to 8*d* per day in the months between May and October, compared to rates of 1*s* to 1*s* 6*d* a day which they could earn toiling for prosperous English farmers.[18]

By 1830 milk had practically disappeared from the diet of the poorest rural class and while pig rearing was on the increase, they were bred strictly for sale at market and the extraordinary growth in potato cultivation represented an index of declining living standards.[19] The extreme poverty of rural labourers, whether cottiers surviving on potato ground provided by their employers, or the still more woebegone day labourers, forcibly struck traveller, Jonathan Binns in the 1830s. Expressing his horror at the wretchedness he witnessed in the west, Binns recorded the western labourers' lack of food and clothing in districts across counties Sligo and Mayo, their subsistence for nine months of the year on dry potatoes and their habitation in wretched cabins with scarcely a chimney or proper ceiling, many, he believed, driven to drink to escape their misery.[20] In 1831 Binns observed that employment opportunities for rural labourers had steadily decreased in the years since the Napoleonic Wars, with wages no higher than 6*d* to 8*d* a day, and conacre, even stubble, increasingly difficult to obtain.[21] Similar conditions prevailed in the less economically depressed districts of east Connacht, and in the east Galway hinterland between Ballinasloe and Aughrim. Binns observed that labourers frequently had to cease work owing to hunger and in times of distress when the lumper potato became scarce, potatoes had to be purchased at inflated prices, a problem frequently arising between Garlic Sunday – the first in August – and September, when the first crop of potatoes were ready for eating. So insufficient were their wages of 5*d* per day and yet so fierce the competition that existed for them, Binns noted, labourers' families often consumed a day's earnings before night was over.

Traveller, Asenath Nicholson, recorded a western labourer's testimony on the eve of the Great Famine that Connacht landowners had the wisdom to see that the landless could subsist on potatoes and had therefore reduced them to servitude.[22] For all their poverty, however, labouring men traditionally married early, placing blind trust in the yield of their crowded potato gardens to support large families. In the 1830s, the prominent letter-writing family, the Blakes of Connemara, remarked upon the light-heartedness of their labourers after their day's work, with a sufficiency of turf, milk, potatoes and meal, but it was an idyll overshadowed by the dire lack of regular employment which left them vulnerable to intense periods of food shortage.[23]

On the eve of the Great Famine, the Devon Commission provided graphic evidence of the high levels of poverty in districts considerably more economically advanced than the chronically impoverished coastal districts of the extreme west. In places such as Dromore West and Tubbercurry in county Sligo, Swinford and Ballina in county Mayo, Boyle in county Roscommon and Mohill and Drumshanbo in county Leitrim, references to the continuing dependence of the landless on conacre ground and complaints regarding the absenteeism of landlords who may have provided employment, organised relief or addressed the fitful nature of employment and inadequate wages, continued to abound.[24] In Swinford, the lack of employment and regular wages was complained of with day rates for labour cited as remaining, at best, at a rate of 6d to 8d – the same level of wages which prevailed twenty years previously, and which contributed, according to Swinford man, G.V. Jackson, to the migration to England of 'nine-tenths of the men' of Killeaden, county Mayo in the spring 1845[25] – a tragedy mirrored in similar testimony taken at Dromard, near Mohill, and at Port, near Drumshanbo.[26] At Curry and Dromore West in county Sligo, want of conacre ground at a rent bearable to the labouring class, reflected the hardship of those forced into buying provisions from the shopkeepers of the villages and towns, frequently on long-standing lines of credit, with the relatively high price of provisions resulting in serious financial hardship, exacerbated, many claimed, by the lack of resident landowners or strong farmers who might have been expected to provide work and wages.[27]

James Donnelly Jnr has concluded that in pre-famine rural Cork, 'careless, inefficient estate administration in general and the middleman system in particular, furnished a hospitable framework within which the forces of population explosion and the expansion of tillage farming brought about a striking and extremely dangerous increase in small holdings.'[28] In the west, as landlords sought to clear their estates of unprofitable tenants, they were especially concerned to dislodge landless squatters occupying property without paying rent or seeking the permission of the landowner, and the holdings of middlemen or absentee landlords were often overrun with landless squatters and their extended kin.[29]

The popular perception that dreadful poverty was the preserve of the extreme west is misguided, however, and widespread distress persisted across east Connacht throughout the century, reflecting the continuing saliency of economic desperation even in areas where farming was considered relatively commercialised. While clearances on estates such as the St George property in Connemara and in the Erris district of Mayo represented a catastrophe for the landless people involved, it was the refusal of landowners in Roscommon to make sufficient conacre plots available – potato ground that would have held body and soul together for labouring families, which reflected the intensity of labourers' exclusion from the commercial market despite the relative advancements in the rural economy across east Connacht.[30]

For labourers in the north east, an end to the decencies of human behaviour was reached when many Sligo farmers shed their workers *en masse* in response to a decline in prices at the onset of the Great Famine, while in north Leitrim farmers refused to pay their poor rates on the pretext that outdoor relief made farm workers idle.[31] Likewise in Rathibarren, county Sligo in 1845, labourers complained they could barely survive on the one pound of Indian meal that was their daily portion, while in Roscommon only the influx of troops prevented seizure of food from the depots and a group of labourers in Mayo were prevented by the intimidation of other labourers from taking work on exploitative terms.[32]

Labourers and the Famine

As in all human calamities, exploitation of the poor by the rich during the Great Famine in Ireland was compounded by exploitation of the poor by the marginally better off and as Mary Daly has argued, the potato blight destroyed a complete socio-economic system in rural Ireland.[33] In this respect, Cormac Ó Gráda has concluded 'traditional interpretations of the Irish Famine emphasise the divisiveness central to famines everywhere but they have tended to let farmers off the hook in their condemnation of government and landlords.'[34] The Irish Famine was fundamentally different, even in the context of the horrors of modern African humanitarian disasters, in terms of the proportion of the population directly affected and the duration of the crisis.[35] While relatively few people died directly of hunger, conditions such as dysentery, typhoid fever and typhus, as well as other hunger-induced diseases, accounted for the majority of the one million or so who perished. While people of all social rank died, deaths were socially and geographically concentrated amongst the poorest classes in the west and in this respect Ó Gráda has found that Karl Marx was at least broadly correct in claiming that the Irish Famine killed 'poor devils only'.[36]

The number of agricultural labourers employed during the Irish Famine plummeted as many cottiers who worked for farmers had to abandon their employment to seek relief on public works where higher wages and better conditions were available. As they were paid in land only for their labour and that land was now useless, owing to the blight, it was illogical for labourers to continue to toil for farmers for effectively no reward. By March 1847, over 700,000 labourers were employed on public works but as Daly has noted, farmers and their sons also went in search of relief, sometimes motivated by sheer greed.[37] The crisis for labourers was compounded as the disaster intensified and farmers began to dispense with their remaining labourers as they could no longer afford to feed them and the landless were replaced by the multiple ranks of farmers' sons and their extended kin. For larger farmers, however, the higher cost of labour, brought about by the improved rates of pay provided by relief works, were more than offset by escalating grain prices.[38]

The tendency for farmers to thin the ranks of their labourers was not a short-lived phenomenon and the 1847 Poor Law Extension Act left Irish ratepayers carrying the full cost of famine and poor relief, with each electoral district responsible for supporting its own poor, thus heightening the motivation for farmers to employ as few labourers as possible.[39] In this respect, the reliance on mass emigration to alleviate the economic pressure on rural families in the decades following the Great Famine was not a universal panacea for poverty. The lack of economic resources amongst the landless resulted in their immobilisation as a social class, which, unlike the sons and daughters of their employers – the sturdy small holders – prevented them from escaping the poverty which was their lot by leaving

for England or the United States. The passage for those who did manage
to leave was usually made possible by the considerable sacrifice of a relative who had previously emigrated and managed to save the price of the
ticket for a member of their extended family, often a younger sibling,
niece or nephew. Even where limited assisted emigration was facilitated
by landlords, such as on the Palmerston and Gore-Booth estates in Sligo,
the primary motive was not humanitarian but to rid their estates of their
labourers in order to amalgamate their plots and stock them with heifers, leaving a legacy of mixed emotions for both the departed and those
prevented by old age from leaving, watching on mournfully as their family
plot was occupied by a local farmer.[40]

Through sheer endeavour and the sacrifice of their extended kin, many
landless people did manage to escape, however, and not until 1851 did the
attractions of further shores weaken for the labourers of Sligo, as the economy began to show signs of recovery and wages and employment increased
in the county.[41] The census of 1851 revealed the decimation wrought by
the Great Famine on the cottier class, an outcome which would have been
welcomed by those who argued that the disappearance of cottiers was a
sine qua non for the economic progress that would in theory be generated
by an injection of new capital and an end to the domination of the older,
frequently improvident gentry.[42] By 1850 a shortage of labourers in the
rural workforce, partially facilitated by successive generations of clearances
and emigration, was exacerbated by the annual migration of harvesters to
England. In the spring of 1853 and 1854, this created problems for farmers
looking to hire labourers at low wages in the Connemara, Loughrea and
Athenry districts of Galway and in Tyrawley and Ballina in Mayo.[43]

The demand for workers in the Newport and Castlebar districts of
Mayo and the Ballinasloe district in Galway in 1853 presented considerably
improved economic conditions for labourers and what both the *Western
Star* and the Poor Law Commissioners both termed the opportunity for a
'more continuous state of employment'.[44] Whereas in 1850 the *Roscommon
Journal* had spoken of the need for adequately remunerative wages, and
one observer questioned whether the landlords of encumbered estates in
Connacht had the wherewithal to pay proper wages, by 1853 wages of 1s
to 1s 6d per day were reportedly being paid in the Tuam district of north

Galway where hitherto as little as 8*d* to 10*d* per day had been the norm.[45] While historically there had been scepticism amongst landowners as to whether a Connacht labourer was willing to do purposeful labour, it was accepted by landowners that careful direction of labourers was always necessary. In 1853, one Connemara landlord had to go to the unprecedented lengths of importing labourers from outside the local district, such was its scarcity.[46] In September 1854, harvest wages reportedly stood at 1*s* 4*d* in west Galway, while in the area around Galway town, a daily rate of 1*s* 8*d* to 1*s* 10*d* was obtained.[47] By mid-decade, the Poor Law Commissioners were estimating that wages in Connacht had risen by anything from 25 per cent to 80 per cent, with the greatest increase having occurred in hitherto distressed areas of the province.[48]

Such a surge in employment and wages, however, was a transitory phenomenon and apart from exceptional cases and benevolent landowners, in the long term, labour would remain casual, seasonal and poorly paid, and turning cottiers surviving on potato ground into a wage-paid rural proletariat would prove to be problematic.[49] The rise in labourers' wages following the Great Famine was a short-lived phenomenon. In Galway and Mayo and more widely throughout the province, Poor Law Commissioners reported a dearth of employment available to labourers by the end of the 1850s and that 10*d* a day paid at Bunowen, near Clifden was a more representative rate than the 1*s* 6*d* per day generally considered the average rate in the province, with the adverse affects of absentee ownership regularly commented upon by the commissioners throughout the period.[50]

Across Galway, in the Clifden, Oughterard, Glenamaddy and Ballinasloe districts, a serious shortage of employment for the labouring population persisted, while in the Ballinrobe, Swinford and Ballycroy districts of county Mayo, the absence of employment remained a central feature of reports. Commenting on the Connemara estates of the Law Life Insurance Company, the former properties of the Martin family, agriculturalist Henry Coulter criticised the poor wages and employment provided in 1862 when there was so much by way of land improvement that could have been undertaken so as to benefit the labourers of the region, noting that a policy of providing employment on a relief basis only in response to distress exacerbated the chronic state of crisis facing the rural poor.[51]

The economic recession of the 1870s made conditions for labourers even grimmer, with falling wages and reduced employment in tillage, compounded by rising food prices. In parts of east Galway in 1881 wages fell from 1s 6d per day to 1s 2d per day with the price of potatoes rising to 10d per stone at Clonfert, making mutton or fowl prohibitively expensive as labourers were reported to be unable to afford to buy milk or butter.[52] While it is estimated that the 5,000 to 7,000 migratory labourers who travelled annually from Mayo to Britain brought back some £5 to £8 in wages, with similar figures noted for other counties, poor housing remained a major problem for labourers.[53] Housing conditions naturally ranged depending on the nature of a particular labourer's economic situation, but generally fell into one of four categories: the number of labourers who occupied garden plots on their employers' farms declined as the century progressed; full time and seasonal boarded servants living in the homes of sturdy farmers continued to predominate in east Connacht; *spailpíns* or migratory workmen, often Irish speakers from the western seaboard who were taken on for seasonal work in east Galway and other commercial agricultural regions and who frequently occupied makeshift outhouses in or near their employers farmhouse; and urban labourers, who, due to the declining availability of conacre had been forced to move to the towns, and were often wretchedly housed as 'weekly tenants' on exploitative terms in the property of landlords and middlemen who were often merchants or famers.

The Labourers' Act of 1883 was intended to provide affordable homes for agricultural labourers with 'labourer' defined as 'a person who habitually works for hire, in agricultural work upon the land of some other person and includes a herdsman…'[54] The building of small slated houses composed of one and two bedrooms with one acre of land cost local authorities an average of £100 each, and were repaid by an average annuity of around £5 per year, but the stipulation to provide such plots was in the main resented by many local authorities in the west.[55] Michael Davitt believed the Act represented an opportunity for social progress where labourers were concerned; however, there was little enthusiasm or implementation of the Act across Connacht as ratepayers and local nationalist representatives inevitably tended to resent the stipulations which imposed additional rates on property owners.[56] A typical view expressed at Boyle was that only labourers in long-term employment should be considered and an 'at-will settling' of town labourers 'on the land' be precluded.[57] In December 1883, the first returns of schemes proposed under the Act highlighted the poor take-up of its provisions, and an 1893 report on Agricultural Labourers, referring specifically to the Westport Union, indicated the absence of resident landowners as a significant factor which made the burden of schemes on the rates insuperable, and proposed the maintenance of the existing housing stock as an alternative.[58] The immediacy of the issue was brought home by the publicly reiterated intention of farmers in county Roscommon to resist the implementation of cottage schemes in 1883; by a member of the Portumna Board of Guardians, who was also a farmer, passing on to his family land earmarked for sites so that the Board's plans could be scuppered in 1884; by farmers at Claremorris who were told that they would not be re-elected to the Board of Guardians if they defaulted on schemes.[59]

Labourers and Nationalist Ireland after the Famine

The emergence of the Land League in 1879 and the social revolution which it instigated in the decades following the Land War created an Ireland in which the economic agenda of the victorious 'sturdy small holders' increasingly framed nationalist expectations concerning wider notions of social progress, political legitimacy and national identity based on an exclusive idealisation of the peasants' connection with the soil in a resolutely rural Gaelic idyll.[60] The historical importance of the League's achievements is unquestionable. However, the degree to which the revolutionary social reforms initiated by successive generations of land purchase represented a modernising form of 'people's war' or an exclusive form of historical regression, based on the economic expectations of an anti-urban, small tenant class intent on promoting the glorification of their own status as the ultimate repository of all things authentically Irish, is open to historical debate.[61]

Agricultural labourers were historically reluctant to assert themselves in wider associational collectivities and there was only fitful and uncoordinated resistance to changes in their conditions in the 1850s, as the rural workforce became increasingly alienated from a prospering farmer class and labourer agitations such as those at Ballinakill, Tuam and Creggs in county Galway and at Castlebar in county Mayo, remained isolated, localised events.[62] Champions of the cause of the landless such Fr Patrick Lavelle in Castlebar in 1869 and Fr Patrick Kelly in Strokestown in 1870, occasionally presented compelling cases for the rural workforce, but they remained exceptions. Whereas Fr Lavelle linked their plight to that of tenant farmers under the common yoke of landlordism, Fr Kelly decoupled the workers' lot from that of farmers who had gained from rising livestock prices, as well as from the cottiers' misfortunes, noting the wretchedness of labourers who had been driven off the land into rural towns and forced to live in hovels, dependent upon casual employment, cut off from access to potatoes and milk as food prices rose and denied any hope of amelioration of their conditions.[63] Fr Kelly's analysis was supported by several reports from the Poor Law Commissioners which highlighted 'the continuous rise in the cost of provisions' from which the urban poor suffered disproportionately. Noting the 'high price of food and other necessaries,' the commissioners pointed to the workhouse index of prices which rose from 1s ½d in 1851 to 2s 7¼d in 1870.[64]

The Land War initially seemed to hold out the prospect to the landless of a dramatic improvement in their circumstances. Initially masked as a united struggle of rural labour against landowner capital, the initial meetings of the League at Irishtown, Westport and Castlebar and the rhetoric of the League's leaders bespoke rural workers' right to the necessaries of life, security and happiness.[65] Speeches by Michael Boyton in Mayo, Matt Harris at Cong and Thomas Sexton at Keadue emphasised the lack of employment in places such as Kilmovee in Roscommon, Dromore West in Sligo and Gallen, county Mayo, and with references to 'the daily bread of the tillers of the soil', and 'landless farmers', their overtures to labourers and the landless was overt.[66] In October 1880, P.J. Sheridan at Sligo and Thomas Brennan at Carrick-on-Shannon, similarly evoked the spirit of a united struggle against a parasitic landlord class and summoned up the prospect of better times for labourers when the great estates were taken over.[67] Even Parnell was not immune from promising better housing and increased employment at higher wages that would result from the land struggle and at Aughrim and Gort in Galway, and at Kilcoo, county Leitrim in 1881, the material improvement in labourers' conditions was declared an imperative for the Land League.[68] Likewise, at a mass meeting at Kiltyclogher, county Leitrim, the housing of labourers by farmers was complained of, and at Tulsk, it was agreed that the term 'master' was to be replaced by the terms 'employer' and 'employed'.[69]

It is ultimately unsurprising that divisions between the expectations of competing social groups in rural society found expression within the League's discourse as competing notions arose over entitlements to scarce resources and exactly what constituted a just settlement of the land question. In this respect, J.J. Lee has argued, 'tension between labourers and farmers was widespread before the Great Famine and rural class relations would presumably have been far more strained in 1880 had the proportion of labourers to farmers remained at its pre-famine level.'[70]

Paul Bew has highlighted that while the League was above all a class alliance of the rural bourgeoisie, middle and poor tenants and the landless, class struggle within the peasantry was an important part of its experience and the movement's strategies remained fundamentally in the interests of the more substantial tenantry, making it unpopular with sections of the rural poor and the agricultural proletariat.[71] Ultimately, successive Land Acts left the landless unrewarded and the feeling amongst the landless that the small farmers had won their economic emancipation off the backs of the labourers persisted, despite the fact that the landless as a social group in Connacht overlapped closely with the small farmer class. Arguably, the advent of small tenant proprietorship left the landless in a worse position than previously, shut out from the opportunities for social advancement and economic improvement open to the small holders, the social gulf between the landless and the small tenants remained as wide as ever.

Conclusion: A People Apart

As the nineteenth century drew to a close the social conditions of the rural poor in the west had undoubtedly been transformed. However, the amelioration of the lot of the landless reflected wider social and economic advances rather than any concerted effort by the nationalist establishment or the state itself to address the specific grievances of the landless. Yet there remained vibrancy and vigour amongst even the most economically oppressed, tempered by a looming sense of disaster reflected in a new dependency which the reliance on poor rates, remittances and emigration created. The improvement of the lot of labourers remained illusory when the persistence of the casual nature of their work, the prevalence of exploitive wages, poor working conditions and the persistence of their social exclusion as a distinct social group is concerned.

The absence of significant political or popular support for remedial land or welfare legislation, and unrewarded by the land struggle despite the Land League's rhetoric of inclusivity. Political neglect and social inertia regarding the plight of the landless, manifest in the belated implementation of the Labourers' Acts, reflected the failure of rural society to fundamentally recognise the validity of the economic plight of rural labourers as a social group. The decline of mud-cabins and the improvement of their housing attested to the prevalence of clearances as well social improvement. Employment for most landless people remained casual and sporadic, confined to particular periods of the year, with regular agricultural recessions, a surplus of labour, and the lack of collective organisation amongst labourers themselves, negating the prospect of a genuine amelioration of their conditions.

At the end of the century, the image remains of labouring people as a group apart, distinct and outside of the boundaries of respectable society, holding nonetheless, to a stoical, defiant, image of themselves. As the twentieth century opened, many labourers remained, like their forefathers before them, all too weary of the rising sun in the Spiddal district of Connemara, cursing, *'Horaí dhuit a ghrian, Mar is fada thú a goil siar'*, or in the Gort district of south Galway, stoically awaiting the passing of the mail car when he would be called to his midday meal.[72]

3

'SERVING THE FARMER'

The Tenant Right Movement in the West, 1848-57

Andrew Shields

Introduction

THE TENANT League of the 1850s, unlike the Land League later
in the nineteenth century, made, at best, only tentative inroads in
the west. Although the role of the Tenant League was not quite as
negligible as some subsequent commentators have suggested, the movement made far more headway in the rest of Ireland than it did in the west.[1]
This chapter explores the reasons why this was the case and examines the
factors which rendered it extremely difficult for the Tenant League to gain
any real impetus in the province. This chapter will explore the progress of
the agitation for tenant right in Connacht and delineate the differences
that existed between the character of the movement in the west and that
which it assumed elsewhere in the country. In this respect, this chapter will
look at the way in which ecclesiastical politics came to play a key role in
determining the character of the tenant right agitation in Connacht. The
first section of the paper will briefly outline the history of the national
movement for tenant right in the late 1840s and early '50s, before explor-
ing the history of the movement in Connacht and the reasons for its

relative weakness. The final part of the paper will explore the legacy which the movement for tenant right left in terms of the evolution and development of subsequent mass agrarian movements such as the Land League.

The agrarian agitation of the late 1840s and early '50s arose primarily as a result of the increasing insecurity felt by tenants in the course of the famine years. A profound sense of insecurity amongst the rural poor had been accentuated by the prevalence of large-scale evictions throughout the previous decade. In 1849 alone, over 72,000 persons were permanently evicted from their holdings and it has been estimated that, in total, close to a quarter of a million persons were evicted between 1849 and 1854.[2] The rate of evictions was particularly high in the west. Between 1849 and 1854, over 26,000 tenants in Mayo were 'permanently dispossessed'. In the district around the town of Ballinrobe alone, the local landowner, Lord Lucan, permanently demolished over 300 cabins and evicted close to 2,000 persons between 1846 and 1849.[3] While eviction rates were somewhat lower in the other Connacht counties, they were still high in comparison to most other parts of the country. Connacht also suffered the highest levels of excess mortality during the famine. Some 40.4 per cent of the total number of excess deaths in Ireland occurred there in the years between 1845 and 1851, in contrast to the 8.6 per cent which occurred in the province of Leinster.[4] The number of excess deaths during the period in Mayo alone has been estimated at between 100,000 and 120,000 persons, the highest rate of any county in Ireland.

The high level of deaths there was directly related to the prevalence of smallholders in the county. In the period before the Great Famine, over 75 per cent of Mayo tenants had occupied holdings valued at £4 or less.[5] Similarly, in east Galway over 60 per cent of the tenants who held land on the Gregory estate, which straddled the border with county Clare, had holdings of less than ten acres.[6] As K. T. Hoppen has shown, only 9.6 per cent of holdings in the province of Connacht were rated at £10 or above for Poor Law purposes in 1841, as opposed to 32.6 per cent in the same category in the province of Leinster and 33.3 per cent in the province of Munster.[7] Given these circumstances and the fact that the Tenant League was to appeal primarily to the better-off classes of sturdy small holders and middling farmers, it is unsurprising that it eventually struggled to achieve any real impetus in the west. Furthermore, the high rates of evictions, emigration and excess mortality in Connacht during the Great Famine years rendered it extremely difficult for the League to initiate or maintain a successful popular agitation. The Great Famine greatly exacerbated the extremes of poverty in the province, demonstrated by the fact that no less than twelve of the twenty-two Poor Law Unions in Ireland recognised as 'distressed' in the winter of 1846-7 were in Connacht. A further demonstration of the extent of the distress was the fact that in the year 1847 alone, 920 inmates died within the walls of Loughrea workhouse.[8]

The Beginnings of the Tenant Right Movement

As a result of the post-famine agricultural depression and the insecurity generated during the famine years, tenants in some parts of the country began to organise to seek an improvement in their conditions. In October 1849, a Tenant Protection League was established in Callan, county Kilkenny, and between October 1849 and June 1850, twenty-eight similar societies were established across the provinces of Munster, Leinster and Connacht. Of these twenty-eight, however, only a handful, including those in Tuam and Castlebar, were in the west.[9] In general, these tenant associations campaigned for the lowering of rents and the introduction of 'fixity of tenure', which essentially meant that tenants could not be evicted so long as they paid their rents. They were strongest in the province of Leinster, which contained some of the most prosperous regions of the country. Large farmers in the east had, however, been seriously affected by the rapid fall in wheat prices which had declined by up to 35 per cent between 1847 and 1849. Broadly speaking, the Tenant League can be seen as a movement composed of relatively prosperous tenant farmers, who had a long experience of production for the Dublin market and the export market to Britain.[10]

At the same time as agitation was beginning in Leinster and Munster, there was a largely separate tenant agitation taking place in Ulster. Relations between landlords and tenants in Ulster had traditionally been better than those elsewhere in Ireland. In the late 1840s, however, Ulster tenants began to face many of the same insecurities as tenants elsewhere in the country. In particular, they were afraid that landowners would use the agricultural depression to attack the traditional operation of the 'Ulster custom'. As well as providing for fixity of tenure, the 'custom' involved incoming tenants making payments to outgoing tenants when they left their holdings. These payments generally covered both the costs of any improvements that tenants had made to their holdings and their 'interest' or 'goodwill' invested in them. This practice represented a tacit recognition that, over time, a tenant had acquired a kind of 'property' in his holding. As K.T. Hoppen has pointed out, the chief peculiarity of the Ulster custom was the implication 'that tenants somehow possessed property rights in land they did not own'.[11]

Unlike the agitation in the rest of the country, tenant agitation in Ulster was principally directed at achieving legal recognition for the prevailing custom and was strongest among Presbyterian tenants, attracting the support of a large number of Presbyterian ministers.[12] The problem for Ulster tenants and for tenants elsewhere in Ireland where the custom sometimes existed in 'attenuated form', lay in the fact that it had no legal standing and its operation was dependent on the individual landlords' consent.[13] Many landlords were, in fact, prepared to sanction the custom in practice, as it meant that outgoing tenants could use the payments they received to clear off any arrears of rent they might have owed. Landowners were generally opposed to the custom being converted from a customary into a legal right, however, and many of those who favoured the modernisation of the rural economy were ambivalent in their attitudes towards the custom. It was frequently argued that it drained the financial resources of incoming tenants and prevented them from undertaking necessary improvements. For many smallholders in the west, however, the impact of the Great Famine meant that such debates remained theoretical, having little direct relevance to the precarious conditions in which they found themselves.

The Tenant Right Movement in Connacht

It was only after the tenant right movement became well established elsewhere in the country, particularly in the provinces of Leinster and Ulster, that it gained its first footholds in Connacht. It is doubtful whether the movement would ever have developed in the west but for the precedent set by tenant associations in other parts of the country. In this respect, it was significant that an anonymous correspondent to the *Freeman's Journal* felt compelled to apologise in April 1850 for the apathy which, the writer claimed, prevailed 'in this province on the great question of tenant right'. The writer went on to attribute the passivity on the part of western tenants to the 'extent' and 'intensity of the hardships they had endured' over the previous five years. According to the correspondent, those in the province who had any access to capital were intent on emigrating, while 'no amount of energy' could be expected from poorer tenants 'in favour of a popular course of agitation'. As a consequence of this, the writer concluded, it would be necessary for a number of prominent individuals, probably clergyman, to first give an impetus to the agitation in the province, before it could attract a wider popular support. The writer also criticised the western clergy in particular, for their failure to take a more active role in this regard.[14]

In late April 1850 Fredrick Lucas, who was to become one of the leading figures in the tenant agitation, wrote to John MacHale, the Archbishop of Tuam, informing him that all those involved in the preparation of the national conference of the various Tenant Defence Associations were agreed that it was 'most important' that there should be 'a strong expression of opinion from the west' in favour of the new agitation. This would best be achieved, Lucas suggested, if MacHale himself were to attend their conference or induce a senior clergyman from his archdiocese to do so.[15] Writing to the Archbishop soon afterwards, Lucas accepted that 'the pressing duties' of his archdiocese meant it was unlikely that he would be able to personally attend the conference. At the same time, however, he insisted that it was desirable that there should be 'some western voices' at the proposed conference to ensure that its proposals did not 'lag behind the necessities of the west'.[16]

By this time, MacHale, who had been a leading member of the Catholic hierarchy since the mid-1820s and Archbishop of Tuam since 1834, had developed a personal popularity unrivalled by any other Church leader in the country.[17] He had been notable for his involvement in Irish political life, particularly through his strong support for Daniel O'Connell's movement for repeal of the Union. His involvement in the campaign for repeal led Donal Kerr to describe MacHale as being O'Connell's 'staunchest and most important clerical supporter'.[18] He was also notable within the Catholic hierarchy for his strong nationalist sympathies and his genuine concern for the condition of the poor in his archdiocese generally. MacHale's own background, as the son of a comparatively prosperous farmer and innkeeper, resembled that of many of the leading figures in the Tenant League. During the Great Famine he wrote a number of public letters to Lord John Russell, calling his attention to the appalling conditions in which much of the western tenantry were suffering. He had also recommended the immediate introduction of some form of fixity of tenure and compensation for improvements.[19] In May 1850, MacHale reasserted his belief that the land question was the 'paramount' outstanding grievance in Ireland and that it was essential that 'the primitive right of man to enjoy in security and peace the fruits of his labour' should be firmly established there.[20] His interest in the agrarian question meant that MacHale was to prove the most vocal and consistent supporter of the Tenant League among the Catholic hierarchy. He played a key role in the early days of the movement, in giving an impetus to the movement in Connacht. As we shall discover, however, even his advocacy of the movement was not enough to override the numerous unique social and economic obstacles which the organisation faced in the west.

It was no coincidence that the first recorded meeting in favour of tenant right in the west took place shortly after Lucas had written to MacHale to seek his support. The meeting took place in the court house in Castlebar in May 1850, with the attendance described in a contemporary report as 'most numerous and respectable'. The 'respectable' character of the meeting was further demonstrated by the fact that Frederick Cavendish, a son of one of the leading Anglo-Irish politicians of the late eighteenth century, Sir Henry Cavendish, played a prominent role. Cavendish had founded the *Connaught Telegraph* in 1828 and despite his own comparatively privileged background had been a strong supporter of Daniel O'Connell's movement for the Repeal of the Union.[21] Cavendish's appearance at the meeting was also in line with the high profile which other prominent journalists like Gavan Duffy and Frederick Lucas had already taken in the movement. Another prominent figure at the meeting was Fr James MacHale, the parish priest of Eglish, who was a close friend but not a relative, of his more illustrious namesake. He had earlier been involved in the abortive attempts to establish a tenant league in county Mayo in late 1847.[22]

Broadly speaking, those who spoke at the Castlebar meeting came almost exclusively from among the Catholic clergy and middle class of the district. In this respect, the meeting bears out K.T. Hoppen's depiction of the League as primarily an alliance between the comparatively prosperous tenant farmers in the countryside and the Catholic bourgeoisie in the towns.[23] Along with Fr James MacHale, other Catholic priests present included Fr Michael Curley, one of his curates, Fr Peter Geraghty, the parish priest of Beccan, Fr Peter Ward, the parish priest of Turlough and Fr Michael Joyce, a curate on the Aran Islands. Among the lay speakers were Thomas O'Dowd, a local solicitor, and Henry Murphy, a grocer in the town. The meeting was also notable, however, for the emphasis that speakers placed on the immediate cessation of evictions in the district. One resolution asserted that in no other part of Ireland had 'extermination been so generally, so recklessly, and so cruelly carried on' as in the west. The meeting also followed the pattern set by other Tenant Association meetings held elsewhere in the country with resolutions being passed supporting the extension of tenant right throughout the country and calling for the payment of compensation for improvements to tenants who had undertaken them at their own expense.[24] The meeting also declared its support for the proposal made by a number of the leaders to hold a national conference to bring together representatives of all of the various tenant associations across the country. Such a conference, it was hoped, would then draw up a programme of demands which they would campaign to have implemented at Westminster. The Castlebar meeting resulted in the formation of the Castlebar Tenant Right Association, with membership open to all who paid a subscription of a shilling per annum. The subscription was set sufficiently high to exclude the more impoverished smallholders and labourers in the district from membership.

The meeting at Castlebar was followed soon afterwards by a similar meeting at Westport which like the former meeting, was held at the court house in the town. Unlike the Castlebar meeting, however, no landlords attended the Westport meeting, leading one of the speakers to complain that they had abandoned their tenants 'in their hour of need'. There was also a strong anti-landlord tenor to many of the speeches delivered at the meeting. An example of this type of rhetoric was provided by Fr Peter Ward, the parish priest of Aughagower, who claimed that the number of families in his parish had fallen from 1,662 before the Great Famine to only 754. He attributed this to the smallholders there being 'swept away by famine, by emigration and by extermination from the face of the country'. He was also critical of the British government for its failure to adopt any measures favourable to Irish tenants. This lack of support from both government and landlords, Ward suggested, meant the Catholic clergy was the only group left that was in a position to defend the smallholders of the county. Only they, he claimed, could 'assert their rights… or proclaim their wrongs'. Significantly, Ward's speech suggested that he had little hope for a successful outcome to any attempts to persuade the British parliament, as it was then constituted, to introduce a measure extending tenant right throughout the country.[25] There was a radical tinge to his speech, reminiscent of the flavour of those later given by his fellow Mayo priest, the indomitable Fr Patrick Lavelle.[26]

Despite Ward's populism, however, both meetings indicated a core weakness of the early tenant right movement in the west. This lay in the fact that it was essentially a top-down movement rather than a genuinely grassroots organisation. It was also operating in a situation where the potential economic bargaining power of the western tenantry had been profoundly weakened by successive years of intense hardship. In consequence, the majority of the smallholders there and even some of the better off farmers were more concerned with mere survival than the co-ordination of a mass agitation. In this sense the movement had little to offer the landless and agricultural labourers in general. This fact may account for the rather cryptic document found on a Sligo Ribbonman in August 1850, which stated: 'What is your opinion of this bill? What bill do you mean? I mean the tenant right. It will serve the farmer.'[27] In this context, it was significant that the figures for agrarian outrages recorded by the constabulary for the province of Connacht at this time were comparatively low, unlike in the 1870s, when figures for violent unrest were the highest in the country.[28] In 1850, for example, the Royal Irish Constabulary reported 174 agrarian outrages in the province, as opposed to 403 in Ulster and 408 in Leinster.[29]

The high proportion of chronically impoverished smallholders, cottier tenants and labourers in the west rendered it extremely difficult for a movement like the Tenant League, which remained fundamentally farmer oriented, to gain any real mass impetus. Unlike the Land League, which succeeded (albeit temporarily) in appealing far beyond this narrow social group, the Tenant League never succeeded in broadening its support base beyond more prosperous sturdy small holders.[30] While the Land League could be seen as a mass movement with some clerical support, the Tenant League in the west remained very much a clerically dominated organisation and had very limited success in developing the mass base necessary to pursue successful agrarian agitation. Despite its weakness in the west, however, MacHale's backing gave the organisation at least a superficial vitality in the spring and summer of 1850.

Following the Westport and Castlebar meetings, the movement gained its first foothold in counties Galway and Roscommon in June 1850, when meetings in support of the extension of tenant right were held at the town house in Tuam and at the court house in Roscommon town.[31] As with earlier meetings, the Catholic clergy played a significant role at both events and Archbishop MacHale was among the signatories of the requisition which led to the holding of the meeting at Tuam. The requisition was also signed by John MacEvilly, at that time a professor at the Catholic college, St Jarlath's, but later to succeed MacHale as Archbishop of Tuam.[32] It was also significant that one of the principal speakers at the Tuam meeting was Fr Patrick Duggan, then a curate in the parish of Kilmoylan, but already showing signs of the abilities that would later lead to his becoming Bishop of Clonfert.[33] Frederick Lucas, who had met Duggan earlier in the year in Dublin, told MacHale that he was 'delighted with his frankness and intelligence' and was extremely keen to secure his support for the League.[34] At the Tuam meeting, Duggan was careful to distinguish between the programme of the Tenant Associations and what he described as 'communism or socialism'. 'As a minister of religion,' he insisted, 'he could be no party to spoliation nor to the slightest infringement on the just rights of any man.'

In line with this disavowal, Duggan's speech concentrated on defending the principle of compensation for improvements in cases where tenants had undertaken these at their own expense. He claimed that the comparative rarity of improving tenants in Connacht was a direct product of the fact that they had no security for any capital which they might invest in their holdings.

Duggan spoke from personal experience, as his own father was to be evicted from his holding in the course of the 1850s. In the years that followed, he was to be a consistent supporter of the Tenant League with Lucas occasionally using him as an intermediary between the leadership of the League and its supporters among the Catholic hierarchy. At the Tuam meeting, the parish priest of Headford, Fr Richard Walsh, struck a more radical note than Duggan and most of the other clerical speakers. Like Fr Ward at the Westport meeting, Walsh demonstrated a degree of scepticism about the prospects for the new agitation. Having outlined the catastrophic effects of the Great Famine on his own parish, he claimed there was little prospect the new movement would achieve its objectives. This was the case, he argued, because 'landlords and government were united in their desire to annihilate not only the entire Celtic race, but the Catholic religion'.[35] The tone of his rhetoric was indicative of the sectarian tensions that were later to undermine the Tenant League. In this respect, it was to prove extremely difficult to maintain an alliance between Catholic agitators and their Presbyterian 'allies'. As we shall see, this was to become increasingly clear after the introduction of the Ecclesiastical Titles Bill brought religious issues to the forefront of the agitation.

The Formation of the Tenant League

The purpose of early tenant right meetings was essentially to create local associations across the country in order to pave the way for a national conference to be held in August. Despite MacHale's support for the movement, he did not, however, as Lucas had anticipated, attend the national conference, sending instead, a message of support.[36] In the event, however, the attendance at the conference was heavily weighted towards local associations in Leinster and Ulster. The western attendance was particularly meagre, with only one representative attending from the entire province of Connacht, Thomas O'Dowd, a curate in the parish of Oughaval, which lay within MacHale's archdiocese of Tuam.[37] The conference brought together the northern tenant agitations with those in the rest of the country which up to this point had been two largely separate movements. The conference was attended by around 200 delegates including a number of Liberal MPs. The meeting led directly to the establishment of the new national Tenant League, which was designed to co-ordinate the activities of the various local tenant associations across the country. The conference also drew up a programme of demands, including fixity of tenure, the lowering of rents and the legalisation of the 'Ulster custom' in those areas where it already existed.

Unusually for an agrarian movement during this period, the conference also decided on the creation of a parliamentary party to agitate for tenants' demands. The main proponents of this step were Charles Gavan Duffy, a leading Young Irelander who edited *The Nation* newspaper and Frederick Lucas, an English-born convert to Catholicism who edited the Catholic newspaper, *The Tablet*. Both men believed the new party had the potential to become a national political organisation, which could succeed, where even Daniel O'Connell had failed, by uniting Irishmen across religious lines.[38] They also believed that the extension of the Irish electorate after the 1850 Franchise Act, which extended the vote to many strong farmers, gave the new party the opportunity to achieve considerable electoral success. The League's programme, however, as defined in 1850, went further than a mere legalisation of the existing 'custom', demanding that rents be based on a compulsory and independent valuation of land (fair rent), that tenants should be left undisturbed in the possession of their holdings so long as they paid their rent (fixity of tenure) and that tenants should have the right to sell their 'interest' in their holding to an incoming tenant (free sale).[39]

Compensation for improvements, however, never became a compelling or popular slogan for the smallholders and cottier tenants of the west, since to undertake improvements required surplus capital on the part of the tenant and, thus, was beyond the capability of most. Even the concept of 'fair rent' had little real meaning for impoverished smallholders living on the economic margins. As Roy Foster has pointed out, for such tenants the payment of 'any rent at all was probably too high.'[40] For this reason, a correspondent to the *Freeman's Journal* in May 1850 suggested that legislation should be introduced into parliament setting an upper limit on the levels of rent to be paid in the province; however, the writer conceded that there was likely to be very little support for such a provision among landowners.[41]

Shortly after the first national conference, the largest of the early tenant meetings in the west was held in Ballinrobe, county Mayo, on 19 August 1850. As with similar meetings, the speakers were drawn largely from the Catholic clergy. These were Fr Peter Conway, parish priest of Killursa and Killower and Fr Michael O'Donnell, parish priest of Kilmeena. A number of curates also took part these included Fr David Mylotte from the parish of Annagh and Fr James Waldron of Partry. Other speakers were described as 'tenant farmers' and 'independent electors' and were probably drawn from among the more substantial farmers in the county. Their relative wealth was indicated by the fact that one of the speakers claimed he saw 'many of the Poor Law Guardians from this union' and 'many of the wealthy tenant farmers, both Protestant and Catholic' in attendance. The audience at the meeting was drawn from a wide geographical sweep, taking in farmers 'not only from the parish of Ballinrobe, but also from Joyce's Country, Cong, Kilmolara, Neale, Kilmaine, Partry, Robeencross and Kilcommon'. Like MacHale's own archdiocese of Tuam, this attendance included regions of both north Galway and a wide swath of county Mayo.

A notable feature of the gathering was the strength of anti-landlord rhetoric employed. This was a product of the high rate of evictions in the county and the poor reputation which a number of the larger landowners, including Lord Lucan and Lord Sligo, enjoyed. One speaker referred to local landowners as being 'unholy oppressors and cruel exterminators', before describing those who had been evicted during the Great Famine years as 'martyrs to the acts of a despotic, grasping, profligate, idle and inhumane proprietary, who, with some honourable exceptions… [had] robbed them of the fruits of their honest industry and toil and mercilessly cast them on the highways to perish.'[42] A series of speakers subsequently heaped lavish praise on the recently elected MP for the Mayo constituency, George Gore Ouseley Higgins. Higgins had stood on a pro-tenant right platform and his return was seen as a major victory for tenants in the county. As a result, it had been opposed by the majority of the larger landowners, including Lord Lucan and Lord Sligo, who had strongly backed the Conservative candidate for the seat, Isaac Butt. During his election campaign, Higgins had identified himself closely with the tenant right movement,[43] and Hugh Connolly, a prominent tenant right activist from the north, had spoken at several of his election meetings.[44] Higgins also attracted a good deal of clerical support during the campaign, especially from priests like Fr James MacHale and Fr Michael Curly who were already closely associated with the agitation and his pledge to 'uphold the great cause of tenant-right' even secured the support of Archbishop MacHale.[45]

Although Higgins's commitment to tenant right was later to prove at best ambivalent, at this point both he and his parliamentary colleague, George Henry Moore, were perceived as being among its chief champions in the west. Higgins's identification with the movement was further strengthened in September 1850, when a large meeting was held on his estate at Trafalgar Lodge near Westport. Both Higgins and Moore had enhanced their reputation as landlords during the Great Famine and it appears to have had a radicalising effect on their political opinions. Ultimately, however, Higgins was to prove to be far more moderate in his politics than Moore, who subsequently became one of the leading figures on the more radical wing of the Independent Party. The gathering at Trafalgar was described by the local press as a 'monster' meeting (implying a comparison with O'Connell's 'monster meetings') and the attendance was estimated at close to 20,000 persons.[46]

Such meetings were as much social occasions as political ones and, in this instance, some 260 tents were set up in the grounds of Trafalgar Lodge. According to one local reporter, 'from each one the sound of the Irish bagpipe and violin were heard, while neatly attired lads and lasses – and of these the west can boast not a few – tripped it gaily on the light fantastic toe.'[47] Before the meeting commenced, a brisk trade went on in the selling of sheep and cattle, some reaching prices as high as £1 4s and the festivities included a boat race, organised by Higgins himself.

An indication of the general character of the day was the fact that of the forty persons named by the *Connaught Telegraph* as having been in the 'vicinity of the chair' at the meeting, seventeen were clergymen.[48] The remainder were either small landowners or professional men, including a number of solicitors, merchants, butchers and a small group of journalists. Furthermore, the fact that some of those attending arrived 'in gig carts' suggested that many came from among the sturdy small holder class of tenant farmers.

Despite the impressive attendance at the Trafalgar meeting, it did not, as its promoters hoped, lead to a sustained tenant agitation in the county or in the west more generally and in the long term the organisation proved incapable of maintaining a sustained agitation in Connacht, a failure reflected in the comparatively meagre sums raised in subscriptions.[49] This was a reflection of the fact that poorer tenants were simply not in a position to subscribe to the League, while better off farmers were adopting a 'wait and see' approach to the organisation. It also was significant that none of the tenant associations formed in the west at this time developed anything like the national profile achieved by some of their counterparts in other parts of the country. As Joseph Lee has pointed out, a movement whose appeal was primarily to 'prosperous, market-oriented wheat and barley growers in the east of the country, was always unlikely to succeed in a comparatively poor province such as Connacht.[50]

The Introduction of the Ecclesiastical Titles Bill and the Tenant Right Movement

At this crucial juncture in the movement's fortunes, developments occurred outside the province which were to further undermine its prospects. Shortly after the national Tenant League had been launched, another separate agitation, this time religious in character, broke out in Ireland. This arose as a result of the introduction of the Ecclesiastical Titles Bill by the Liberal government in Britain in February 1851. In September 1850, Pope Pius IX re-established a Catholic hierarchy with territorial titles in Britain. Up to this point, English Catholic archbishops and bishops had gone under the title of vicar apostolic. As a result of Pius IX's action, they now took on titles such as the Archbishop of Westminster and so on, putting them in direct competition with their Anglican counterparts. The Ecclesiastical Titles Act rendered this taking of territorial titles illegal and introduced fines for any members of the hierarchy using them in any public act. The Liberal government's introduction of the Act angered many of its Irish Catholic supporters, who decided to vote against it at every possible opportunity.

These MPs were a minority within the Liberal Party, comprising twenty-four out of the sixty-three Irish Liberal MPs sitting in the House of Commons. The most notable of these rebels were George Henry Moore, a large landowner from county Mayo and William Keogh, barrister and MP for Athlone. These MPs took a leading role in the Catholic Defence Association which was established at a meeting held in Dublin on 19 August 1851.[51] In the west, the tenant agitation was to be gradually subsumed into this 'Catholic' protest movement which swept across Connacht in late 1850. As a result, most of the protest meetings held against the Ecclesiastical Titles Act included demands that the British government introduce legislation favourable to Irish tenants. A tenant right meeting held in Tuam in February 1852 provides a clear example of this trend, with as much attention being given to issues such as the prevalence of proselytism by Protestant ministers in the town and the necessity for the disestablishment of the Church of Ireland as devoted to agrarian issues.[52] In the long term, however, the agitation against the Titles Act had the effect of diverting those clerical energies that had played such an important role in the early days of the tenant agitation in Connacht. The rise of the new 'Catholic agitation' accentuated the clerical dominance over the movement for tenant right in the west. While this may have strengthened it in the short term, in the long run, as divisions began to emerge within the Catholic hierarchy about the wisdom of continuing to support the agitation and as Archbishop Cullen moved towards withdrawing his support from it, it became a source of weakness.

In August 1851, the leadership of the Catholic Defence Association met with the leaders of the Tenant League to decide on a common platform for the next general election. Having agreed to join forces, the Independent Irish Party, the new party formed by the coalition between the two groups, went on to win forty-eight seats at the general election of July 1852. This represented the high point of the party's success, establishing it as a new and significant force in Irish politics. However, it failed to make much impression in the northern counties, where only one Independent Party MP was elected. This failure weakened the movement in Ulster and ultimately led it to distance itself from its national counterpart. The Independent Party's original stance had been that it would remain independent of both of the main British political parties. This position was based on an explicit rejection of O'Connell's policy of pursuing an alliance with the Whig-Liberal Party, a position that had been largely discredited within nationalist political circles during the Great Famine years.[53] The leaders of the Independent Party believed that this policy had failed to achieve its professed objective of securing material improvements for the majority of the Irish population. They also believed that it was only through maintaining its independence from the two main British political parties that the new party could hope to gain concessions from either of them. Like their counterparts in the later Home Rule Party, the Independent Party leadership believed their best hope of securing their objectives lay in holding the balance of power at Westminster. They also hoped that by maintaining an independent stance, they could increase the pressure on the leaders of both the main British parties to make concessions to their demands. It was essential that the leaders of the Liberal Party in Britain should not be allowed to take Independent Party support for granted, and that it should be made clear by Irish MPs that this would have to be earned. This policy of remaining independent from both major British parties, however, was always a difficult stance to maintain and was fatally compromised in 1853 when MPs William Keogh and John Sadleir, two of the leading members of the party, accepted office in the coalition government led by Lord Aberdeen.

Although the 1852 election was a successful one for the Independent Party, its subsequent history was to be marked by decay, disunity and decline. Despite this, the new party's candidates performed creditably in Connacht, with seven of its forty-eight MPs elected for constituencies in the west.[54] It was notable in this context that the election campaigns of successful candidates tended to focus more heavily on 'Catholic' questions than on the issue of tenant right. The nature of the election campaign in Connacht further reinforced the linkage between these issues which had been established from late 1850 onwards. This close connection also meant, however, that Catholic clerics were to play a particularly prominent role at the 1852 election. Archbishop MacHale, for example, endorsed Independent Party candidates not only in the Mayo constituency but also in the two neighbouring constituencies of Galway city and Galway county. The election in Mayo also reinforced the growing political closeness between Archbishop MacHale and George Henry Moore, who, by this point, was one of the leading figures within the Independent Party.[55] The defection of Sadleir and Keogh, however, further increased the fissiparous tendencies already present within it. As a result, many MPs who had taken the 'Independent pledge' reverted to their traditional support of the Liberal Party. In this context, it is important to note that many of the MPs elected under the Independent Party banner in 1852 had, in a sense, really been Liberals who had taken the Independent pledge in order to be elected. The gradual defections from the Independent Party meant that by 1853, only twenty-six of the forty-eight MPs elected in 1852 remained loyal to the Independent principle.[56] One of those MPs who defected from the party was Ouseley Higgins, who, as we have seen, was strongly supported by the Mayo clergy in 1852, but by 1854 was described by the Irish Chief Secretary, Sir John Young, as being 'a steady friend' of the government and 'always on the alert on our side'. In 1856, he was rewarded for his support by being appointed a colonel in the local militia.[57] One result of this apostasy was that he incurred the unremitting hostility of Archbishop MacHale, who, with the support of the majority of the local clergy, vigorously opposed his subsequent campaigns for election for the county.[58]

Higgins's defection to the Whig-Liberal camp won him the support of Archbishop Cullen, however, who used all his considerable influence to promote his candidacy at subsequent elections.[59] By this point, Cullen, a prominent supporter of the Independent Party in its early stages, had begun to distance himself from it. His principal political concern at this time was the extension of the Church's influence and in consequence, he was anxious to see Catholics taking up as many official positions as possible in an attempt to undermine what he perceived as 'Protestant ascendancy' monopoly of state offices. To this end, Cullen viewed an alliance with the Liberal Party as essential and as a result he soon lost his enthusiasm for the independent principle.[60] In 1854, his attempts to prevent other Catholic clerics from campaigning for the Independent Party seriously weakened the party and led to a bitter dispute between him and Frederick Lucas. This controversy eventually resulted in Lucas undertaking a 'mission' to Rome to protest against Cullen's unbending stance. The mission ultimately ended in failure and its effect was to further damage the credibility of the Independent Party, especially among Irish Catholics. Lucas himself died unexpectedly in late 1855, not long after the failure of his mission to Rome.[61] Early in the following year, disillusioned by the decline in popular support for the Independent Party and in pecuniary difficulties of his own, Charles Gavan Duffy retired from parliament and emigrated to Australia. The departure of two of its most prominent members from Irish political life further exacerbated the party's difficulties.

Unlike Cullen, however, MacHale's nationalist sympathies meant he remained a keen supporter of the independent principle throughout the party's existence and unlike most of the other members of the Catholic hierarchy he was to largely ignore Cullen's strictures with regard to clerical involvement in politics. Throughout the 1850s, he continued both to exert his influence in the party's favour and encouraged the clergy in his archdiocese to do the same, with the result that in its latter years, the clergy in Connacht took an increasingly prominent role in support of the party.[62] His support, however, represented a double edged-sword for the party, as while it undoubtedly strengthened it in the west, it resulted in the party becoming enmeshed in the growing personal and political rivalry that characterised the relationship between the dominant Church personalities of the era, Archbishops MacHale and Cullen.[63] These tensions within the party were further reinforced by the growing tendency of many of the MPs who had previously taken the independent pledge to revert to their traditional support for the Liberals. The divisions between its northern and national wings and among its leaders in parliament further exacerbated the party's difficulties. At the 1857 general election, only thirteen Independent Party MPs were elected and the party's threat to landlord influence, which in 1852 appeared so formidable, had largely evaporated. Its effectiveness was further diminished in 1859, when its remaining MPs split as a result of the Conservative government's Reform Bill.[64]

During this period, the Tenant League also fell into decline, largely as a result of a steady increase in agricultural prosperity. In the twenty-five years between 1851 and 1876, Irish wheat prices rose by 20 per cent, while barley prices rose by 43 per cent and beef and butter prices by 87 per cent.[65] These price rises principally benefited the more prosperous farmers in Leinster, particularly those in counties such as Kilkenny, Kildare and Meath. Farmers from these and similar agricultural areas in Munster had also provided the backbone of the Tenant League's campaign. As a result, the crisis in agricultural prices served to undermine 'the whole basis of the agitation' of the Tenant League.[66] Eviction numbers also fell dramatically in these years, as did the number of agrarian outrages.[67] In the province of Connacht, evictions fell from a high point of 3,278 net evictions in 1850 to 167 in 1859.[68] This improvement in the condition of farmers in Ireland was further facilitated by the increasing shift across all classes of farmers from tillage to pastoral farming, a transition largely fuelled by the rise in the price which farmers could receive for their beef and dairy exports on the English market. This structural transition of the rural economy was partially facilitated, especially in the province of Leinster, by the decline in the number of smallholdings brought about by successive decades of farm amalgamation.

While agricultural conditions in the west remained substantially different to those in other parts of the country, the tenant right movement, which had developed only shallow roots in Connacht, was unable to survive its decline elsewhere in the country. Although it maintained a shadowy existence in the province in the years between 1852 and 1857, its influence was fatally undermined when George Henry Moore lost his Mayo seat as a result of a petition brought against him by Ouseley Higgins, one of the defeated candidates.[69] In his petition, Higgins cited clerical interference as a key cause of his defeat and the election demonstrated the lengths to which Archbishop MacHale and his clergy were prepared to go in support of Moore's candidacy. Their willingness do so was largely a product of the fact that by this point, Moore had clearly demonstrated that he was the most politically capable leader of the tenant right movement in Connacht. While he had begun his political career as an extremely moderate liberal and proved capable of attracting a good deal of Conservative support, Moore appears to have been radicalised by his experiences during the Great Famine, when he played a prominent role in relief works in his native county.[70] Although a substantial land-owner, his experiences inspired his conversion to a belief in the necessity of some form of parliamentary intervention to secure the 'future amelioration of the condition of the Irish people,' leading him to become an early advocate for tenant right.[71] In July 1850, he pledged himself to support any measure which would give tenants 'fair and full' compensation for any improvements they had made on their holdings. Such improvements should also, he argued, be considered the property of the tenant who had undertaken them, rather than of their landlords, as had been the case legally up to that point.[72]

As a result of the large number of defections which took place within the Independent Party in the course of the 1850s, Moore gradually became one of the dominant figures within its ranks. However, his advocacy of the tenant cause meant he lost much of the landlord support on which he had relied for his electoral successes in the late 1840s. This made him increasingly dependent on the backing of the Catholic clergy, which ultimately led to his undoing. Moore's unseating in 1857 followed a parliamentary committee of inquiry into the manner of his election in which evidence from a series of witnesses provided detailed accounts of the extent of the clerical involvement on Moore's behalf. The most notorious example of this type of clerical intervention was that by Fr Peter Conway who told intending voters that his 'curse as a priest, the curse of God, the curse of the Church and people' would be upon them if they voted for Higgins.[73] The inquiry was also the scene of what could best be described as a *bravura* performance by Archbishop MacHale himself. In the course of his evidence MacHale strongly defended the rights of the clergy to take part in elections. He argued that the selection of 'worthy persons to fill important offices' was in itself 'a moral question, involving serious responsibilities with regard to the public will'. He also ridiculed Higgins's inconsistency in declaring himself a supporter of tenant right, while supporting a ministry which treated it, in MacHale's words, 'with derision'. MacHale was also unimpressed by Higgins's continued personal support for tenant right legislation, introduced in the House of Commons in the years after he had received office from the government. To vote for tenant right while at the same time supporting a Prime Minister who opposed it, was, MacHale argued, 'a mere mockery, a delusion and a snare'.[74] Despite MacHale's impressive performance, however, his intervention did not succeed in ensuring Moore's retention of his seat and the latter's loss of the seat represented the death knell for the movement in the west.

Conclusion

As this chapter has demonstrated, the tenant right movement in Connacht faced serious social and economic obstacles which were particular to rural society in the west. The prevailing social conditions remained unconducive to the launching of a successful agrarian agitation and it is questionable whether the movement could ever have succeeded given the prevalence of dire poverty and subsistence farming. The bargaining power of the majority of the rural population in Connacht was at a particularly low ebb during the period in which the Tenant League was active. Furthermore, many of the preconditions for a successful agitation, such as a well-developed transport network and a supportive newspaper press, were non-existent.[75] The Tenant League itself was based on too narrow a class basis to attract popular support in a province where so much of the population lived on or below the verge of subsistence. If, as K.T. Hoppen has argued, the Tenant League was primarily an organisation 'of those who not only believed themselves strong enough to be able to acquire further increments of strength but who feared that they had something substantial to lose' it was not a sentiment which had a great deal of resonance among the smallholders of the west.[76] In the long term, however, the Tenant League provided a model for mass agrarian movements such as the Land League. The leadership of both organisations was also to be dominated at a local level by a combination of the Catholic clergy, large farmers and shopkeepers. Many of the leaders of the Land League served their apprenticeships in the earlier movement. Perhaps in recognition of the exclusive character of its predecessor, the Land League made a far greater attempt to appeal to smallholders and agricultural labourers.

4

LAYING THE SEEDS FOR AGRARIAN AGITATION

The Ballinasloe Tenants' Defence Association, 1876-80

Gerard Moran

RESEARCH ON the agrarian campaign in the west of Ireland in the nineteenth century has mainly focused on the establishment and development of the Land League between 1879 and 1882, and the emergence of the United Irish League in the late 1890s. While studies of these agrarian movements have been undertaken by Paul Bew, Samuel Clark, Donald Jordan, Fergus Campbell, Philip Bull and others, their focus is on the history of these organisations' activities with little emphasis on the lead up to their formation and a minimal understanding of how the seeds for agitation had been laid out by local organisations and personalities.[1] Bull indicates that the Ballinasloe Tenants' Defence Association was an important vehicle for the establishment of the Land League, but no assessment or study of the organisation has been undertaken.[2] The role of James Daly and to a lesser extent Matthew Harris have in recent times been given their deserved recognition, but the contributions of individuals have to be studied in the broader context of the regions they lived in and the organisations with which they were involved.[3] While the Irishtown meeting and the Land League burst onto the scene in 1879, there were local organisations that helped pave the way for the mobilisation of the agrarian classes and for the eventual formation of the National Land League in October 1879. The importance and influence of these local organisations has been largely ignored or regarded as peripheral to the emergence of the agrarian campaign. The Ballinasloe Tenants' Defence Association, which came into existence in May 1876, played a major role in the mobilisation of the agrarian classes in the east Galway-south Roscommon region in the late 1870s and provided the foundations for the establishment of the Land League. Its aims, structure and personalities were afterwards to play an influential role in the furthering of the Land League agitation.

Irish agrarian society underwent a massive transformation as a result of the Great Famine; the agricultural emphasis changing from tillage to grazing and contributed to large scale evictions with an estimated 250,000 people being turned out.[4] Among those who cleared their estates were the Pollocks and Gerrards in east Galway. The clearances led to resentment and anger among the tenant farmers and while this was largely directed at the large landowners, underlying tensions existed between small farmers and graziers which eventually surfaced during the United Irish League campaign, but was also evident during the Land League agitation.

The importance of the Land League agitation of 1879-82 was that it brought together the different sections of Irish society into a collective action which eventually provided tenants with security of tenure. The work of Clark and others have shown how a coalition of urban and rural interests encompassing both militant and constitutional nationalists mobilised the population into an agitation which displaced the power of the landlords over their tenantry and eventually led to farmers becoming proprietors through successive land purchase acts between 1885 and 1909.[5] However, the seeds of agitation were put in place before 1879 through local organisations such as the Ballinasloe Tenants' Defence Association.

Local farmers' clubs and tenant defence associations were a feature of the Irish agrarian landscape from the late 1840s to the late 1870s. The establishment of the Callan Tenants' Protection Society in October 1849 was the first such organisation in Ireland and was quickly followed by the formation of similar organisations in the rest of the country. However, these clubs largely disappeared in the mid-1850s as a result of improving economic circumstances, the failure of the political establishment to secure redress of the tenants' grievances and the absence of local leadership. While some of the farmers' clubs continued in existence, they primarily catered for the needs and grievances of large farmers who were mainly graziers and were largely social organisations concerned with conviviality and in improvements in agricultural techniques, rather than with political agitation. The formation of new clubs tended to occur whenever major issues arose regarding the land question, as in late 1869 and early 1870, when Gladstone's land legislation was about to be introduced into parliament, or when local landlords were engaged in raising rents or carrying out evictions on their estates. Unfortunately, little research has been done on the history of these local farmers' clubs or tenant defence associations to enlighten us as to their formation, structures, organisation or activities. Some existed briefly and contributed little to the overall agrarian philosophy, while others drifted towards political agitation, eventually becoming the local organisations of the Home Rule movement, as with the Limerick and Clare Farmers' Club.[6] They were not homogenous groups in their aims, approaches and methods.

The Ballinasloe TDA came into existence in May 1876. This was a time of increasing tenant disillusionment over Gladstone's 1870 Land Act which promised security of tenure. Under pressure from tenant defence associations throughout the country, Isaac Butt, leader of the Home Rule Party, decided to introduce a bill to deal with the deficiencies of the 1870 Act. The main proposals of Butt's land bill, first brought before parliament in March 1876, were threefold: to extend the provisions of the 1870 Act to farms held under the Ulster Custom; to amend the Act which allowed landlords to compel a tenant to contract out of the provisions of the Act and thus reduce the tenant's claim for compensation in the event of their being evicted; to allow a tenant eligible for protection under the 1870 Act to demand a declaration of tenancy which would provide for the valuation of his holding to be set by arbitration and allow him security of tenure at an agreed rent.[7] The bill was largely a compromise; for some it did not go far enough, for others it was too radical. Mitchell Henry, MP for county Galway, was unhappy with the bill's provisions because it provided smaller tenant farmers with little security of tenure.[8] It was accepted by the tenant organisations, including the Ballinasloe TDA, as a step in the right direction, but from the time it was introduced in the House of Commons it was clear it had neither the necessary support in parliament nor even of a section within the Home Rule Party.

From the time of their election on the Home Rule ticket, the two Roscommon MPs, the O'Conor Don and Charles French, had been suspect on the basis of their attitudes towards Home Rule and it was believed that their involvement with the party stemmed more from a desire to save their seats than from any sense of allegiance. By 1876 their parliamentary activities indicated they had little sympathy for the tenants' grievances.

The Ballinasloe Tenants' Defence Association was ruled by a twenty-three man committee elected each May, which met on the first Wednesday of each month. Initially the meetings were held in members' houses, usually the residence of Patrick Madden of Dunlo Street, but in September 1877 rooms were rented at Church Street. The executive comprising the president, vice-president, treasurer and secretary, had the most power. Membership was open to any person on payment of an annual subscription, the minimum charge being one shilling and council members were exhorted to use their influence to enrol as many of their neighbours and friends as possible. The rules stipulated that a general meeting should take place on the first Wednesday of each quarter and at the end of each parliamentary session a general meeting was to be held to discuss and evaluate the parliamentary performances of the local MPs and call upon them 'to give an account of their stewardship'. The association at election time would also consult and consider the merits of the different candidates and advise as to who their members should support.[9]

An examination of the council make-up for 1877-8 gives a good indication of the geographical spread of the association. There were seven priests, four from Ballinasloe and one each from Taughmaconnell, Shannonbridge and Lawrencetown; six laymen from Ballinasloe, three from Shannonbridge and one each from Moore, Taughmaconnell, Killimore and Creagh. The council also included Alfred O'Hea from the *Connaught Telegraph*, John McPhilpin of the *Tuam News* and John Callanan of the *Western News*.[10]

The backgrounds of the officials who served as officers of the Ballinasloe TDA between 1876 and 1880 provide a good indication of the cross section of support it had within the community. Matthew Harris was a Fenian, a building contractor and a member of the council throughout the period and acted as secretary between 1878 and 1880. Although he had been brought up on a farm near Athlone, he inherited land but then gave it over to his sister.[11] Michael Malachy O'Sullivan was a Fenian and a local school teacher and was secretary between 1876 and 1878. William E. Duffy was a Poor Law Guardian in Ballinasloe union and held a farm at Kidlawn. He was president between 1876 and 1878. James Kilmartin, a native of Shannonbridge was a Poor Law Guardian in Ballinasloe union and had a 112-acre farm, under lease from Thomas J. Tully, at Shralee, two miles outside the town of Ballinasloe.[12] He served as vice-president between 1876 and 1878 and as president from 1878 to 1880 and was to the forefront of all the association's public demonstrations. He was also a committee member and senior judge of the Ballinasloe Agricultural Society. Among the other prominent members of the association's council were Patrick Madden of Dunloe St, Ballinasloe; John J. Madden, Poor Law Guardian; William Kilroe, Shannonbridge; and William Ivers and John Callanan of the *Western News*. While Kilmartin saw himself as the driving force and instigator of the organisation when it was established and stated so on a number of occasions but it was the work and involvement of O'Sullivan and Harris which gave the movement its appeal and impetus. Kilmartin said he was a man of the people and an agitator, 'because I go to these meetings, and I have been the cause of getting up those land meetings in our districts', but his statements over the years of the association's existence indicate he was full of his own importance.[13]

What made the Ballinasloe TDA different from other such associations was the involvement of Fenians, large farmers, graziers, small farmers and townspeople. Bew maintains that Harris and O'Sullivan were close to traditional Fenianism, but they were aware of the importance of uniting the agrarian and national questions.[14] Throughout the early 1870s the Fenian movement in Connacht recruited the small tenant classes and saw the agrarian question as the issue to unite all sections of the community.[15] Much of the credit for the organisation and expansion of the Fenian movement in the east Galway-south Roscommon region in this period must be attributed to Matthew Harris. Harris had been actively involved with the revolutionary movement since the late 1860s and was campaign manager for Ballinasloe-born Fenian, John O'Connor Power, during his successful parliamentary campaign in Mayo at the 1874 general election.[16] Harris's organisational capabilities played a major role in bringing together the various groupings in the Ballinasloe region. While Clark points out that two of the principal members of the Ballinasloe TDA were townspeople, Harris did come from an agricultural background.[17] Strong economic connections also existed between the urban and rural communities, and a decline in agricultural fortunes impacted on those living in the towns.[18] As John Walsh, a small trader in Ballinasloe, stated in October 1879, the town suffered as a result of clearances and the decision by some sections of the farming community to purchase their goods elsewhere, as it was more fashionable than trading in Ballinasloe.[19]

While Fenian involvement was important for the origins and advancement of the association, the participation of James Kilmartin, Edward Duffy and the other elected representatives was significant in earning the association credibility among the wider community. In the early stages Kilmartin and Duffy were the main spokesmen and public figures within the association, with organisational matters left to Harris.

An important feature of the Ballinasloe TDA was that it was under lay leadership, unlike the agrarian organisations of the 1850s and the other tenant defence associations then in existence. While clerics such as Revd Malony, Ballinasloe, Revd J. Kirwin, Ballinasloe and Revd O'Reilly of Shannonbridge were council members they never became officers. As a result of the lay leadership, the Ballinasloe TDA was more radical in its approach and aims than other such organisations. The rift between the leadership and the local clergy in the early stages can be seen in the failure of the priests to attend the meeting organised by the association on 1 December 1876 during which the two county Galway MPs, Captain John Philip Nolan and Mitchell Henry addressed their constituents in Ballinasloe as to their parliamentary actions.[20] It was maintained that the Ballinasloe TDA had not consulted the local clergy about the demonstration and as a result they stayed away, although a letter was read from Dr Patrick Duggan, Bishop of Clonfert, praising the two representatives' parliamentary activities. While the clergy had no leadership role in the organisation they did chair demonstrations in places like Creagh and Shannonbridge. However, the association realised that clerical support was vital for its advancement and in October 1877 Bishop Patrick Duggan of Clonfert and Archbishop John MacHale of Tuam were invited to become members.[21] Their public support and endorsement gave the association a major boost as it meant the laity would largely follow the lead of their ecclesiastical leaders. In a further attempt to strengthen the movement's support base it was decided on 8 January 1878 to write to clergymen of all persuasions, Poor Law Guardians, town commissioners and jurors, within a twenty-mile radius of the town, inviting them to join the association and publicly show their support.[22]

One of the advantages which the association enjoyed was its geographical location. Its first major public demonstration was held at Shannonbridge on 25 May 1876, where Connacht meets Leinster. The strategic location was picked to give the appearance of a wide geographical influence. Its impact in the late 1870s was not just confined to the immediate Ballinasloe area, but straddled three counties – Galway, Roscommon and King's County – so that its significance, and in particular its political influence, had a wider appeal. From its inception in May 1876 to the end of 1878 the association held approximately twenty public meetings, at none of which was the main landed proprietor in the Ballinasloe district, the Earl of Clancarty, denounced. This estate was well managed and the Earl was considered a good landlord, as highlighted by the fact that at no stage was he publicly criticised by any of the association's leaders. Instead, the association focused its attention on the overall issues of land ownership and land laws and acted as the watchdog for the tenants' interests in the region. Local proprietors who adopted a harsh approach towards their tenants were publicly condemned and censured. On 25 March 1877 the Ballinasloe TDA organised a major demonstration at Taughmaconnell in response to notices-to-quit that had been served on eleven tenants by Mrs Denis O'Brien of Ballinasloe. The meeting was chaired by the local parish priest, Revd Walsh. The harsh treatment of tenants was highlighted in the case of Matty Kinnane of Togher, who had taken over his farm in 1863 and had his rent increased from £23 10s to £43, although the government valuation was only £13 10s. Michael M. O'Sullivan told the demonstration that while Home Rule and education were major issues, 'the employment of the multitude depends upon the land question'.[23] The association was also prepared to publicise the grievances of individual tenants who were in dispute with their landlords. In February 1879, tenants on the Pakenham Mahon estate at Strokestown, county Roscommon, forwarded information on rent increases that had been put in place on the property to James Kilmartin, who had them published in the *Western News*.[24] In January 1878 the association was asked to arbitrate in a dispute between Mitchell Henry, MP for Galway, and his tenants at Kylemore.[25] The association succeeded in curtailing landlord excesses in the region and at a demonstration in Ballinasloe on 3 November 1878, John O'Connor Power MP stated that one of the main achievements of the local defence association was its success in preventing the eviction of men who otherwise would have been turned out of their homes.[26]

In its early stages the Ballinasloe TDA focused its attention on securing support for Butt's land bill and denouncing local parliamentary representatives who opposed it. Throughout the summer of 1876 the association pushed for support for Butt's bill through a series of demonstrations in the east Galway-south Roscommon region, in places such as Moore, Creagh, Taughmaconnell and Shannonbridge, with the *raison d'être* for these meetings was to condemn the parliamentary actions of The O'Conor Don and Charles French. At the meeting in Creagh churchyard on 31 July the following resolution was passed:

> That we the electors and people of the barony of Moycarn, and adjacent parishes, in public meeting assembled, do hereby empathically condemn the action of our representatives, The O'Conor Don and the Hon. Charles French, in voting against the Butt Land Bill.

Matthew Harris told the assembly that if the people wanted to be properly represented in parliament they needed 'to become properly organised'.[27] Similar sentiments were expressed by Fr Walsh, who chaired the Taughmaconnell demonstration in early July, days after the bill's defeat in the House of Commons. Walsh informed the crowd that they were watching their representatives' every action and added, 'I have every reason to hope that in any future elections no member will ever be elected who will not adopt our principles…'[28] The condemnations continued well into September and at a council meeting on 26 September 1876 a resolution was passed repudiating 'the sentiments of The O'Conor Don, as contained in his speech on the debate of Mr Butt's land Bill'.[29]

The leadership of the Ballinasloe TDA used every opportunity to condemn the parliamentary actions of the Roscommon representatives. Besides resolutions at demonstrations and letters to newspapers condemning their record, delegations from the association were sent to meetings which were addressed by The O'Conor Don and French. A hastily arranged meeting was convened on 27 September 1876 at Roscommon Courthouse where both Roscommon MPs attempted to justify their actions during Butt's land bill. A delegation from the Ballinasloe association attended, led by James Kilmartin, Edward Duffy and Mr O'Connor, and the meeting quickly descended into chaos and disorder as supporters from both sides attacked each other. Kilmartin condemned The O'Conor Don's voting record on Irish measures and newspaper reports indicate that both sides were evenly divided in relation to their opinions on the Roscommon MPs.[30] Over the next four years the association mounted a relentless attack on The O'Connor Don and French, and were severely critical of the representatives for King's County, Sir Patrick O'Brien and Sergeant Sherlock.

It was not until May 1877 that the Ballinasloe TDA issued its address to the people of the west as to its aims: to advocate through the public press and from public platforms the undeniable right of the Irish people to occupy, to till and enjoy the soil of Ireland; to protect the people from the harshness and capriciousness of bad landlordism by every means at their disposal; and to secure the support of public opinion which had for too long lain dormant. The address proclaimed to both the political establishment at home and in Britain the Irish people's determination not 'to take their rule or their customs from Britain'. It also stated they were opposed to those landlords who rack rented and evicted their tenants. It said its motto was: 'Fixity of Tenure, Fair Rents and Free Sale. Our doctrine is, that the land was made for the people, and the people for the land; and we strongly deny the right of absolute ownership of the soil.'[31]

The radical approach to agrarian and political issues resulted in the association having a major influence outside its regional base. Support from local and regional newspapers was important for the advancement of the organisation so that its aims, objectives and development could be publicised to a wider audience. The 1860s and '70s had seen a major expansion of local newspapers in the west of Ireland and these tended to be sympathetic to nationalist and agrarian issues.[32] Most of the influential newspapers in Mayo and Galway were sympathetic to the Ballinasloe TDA from its inception, with the *Tuam Herald*, the *Western News* and in particular the *Connaught Telegraph*, giving widespread coverage to its activities. The editors of these newspapers attended and spoke at the demonstrations and Alfred O'Hea, joint editor and proprietor of the *Connaught Telegraph*, and John Callanan, editor of the *Western News*, became members of the council of the association.[33] The activities and vibrancy of the Ballinasloe TDA were seen as an indication that Connacht farmers were no longer content to be docile and that the agrarian classes could be mobilised. The *Connaught Telegraph* published details of the group's activities and urged its readers to join the movement. An editorial on 1 July 1876 stated, 'It is the duty of the tenant farmers of the five counties of Connacht to give their warmest support to the Ballinasloe association'.[34] The leadership of the Ballinasloe association continued to use the *Connaught Telegraph* as its principal medium for correspondence. It was used to generate support and highlight difficulties, such as in December 1877 when Michael M. O'Sullivan complained of the general apathy among the tenant body adding, 'What good will the energetic action of a few accomplish, if unaccompanied by the united and hearty voice of the people?'[35]

One of the consequences of the Ballinasloe TDA's public activities was the encouragement it gave to calls for similar organisations to be established throughout the west of Ireland. In a speech in Ballinasloe on 15 August 1876, John McPhilpin, editor of the *Tuam Herald*, called for other such organisations to be established in Mayo and Roscommon so the region would have a major input at national conferences on the land question, while in November 1876 the *Connaught Telegraph* reported that a tenants' defence association was to be established in Mayo modelled on the Ballinasloe movement, but this failed to materialise.[36]

The activities and influence of the Ballinasloe TDA resulted in other such organisations being established in Connacht. However, these were more a response to local landlord excesses than to general concern about the land laws and the overall position of tenants. The Headford TDA was established on 1 February 1877 to protest against exorbitant rent increases introduced by local landlords, while the Connemara TDA was formed in Clifden in late January 1879 to protect the people of the region from 'unjust landlords and worse agents'.[37] Apart from the demonstrations which set up these organisations no other public meetings were held, indicating that once the excesses of local landlords had dissipated there was little to motivate the tenantry to agitate. The Ballinasloe TDA was represented at both demonstrations, with James Kilmartin proposing the first resolution and delivering a speech at the Headford meeting. The influence of the Ballinasloe organisation was also evident when the Mayo TDA was eventually established in Castlebar in October 1878 by James Daly, John O'Connor Power and others, with similar aims to the Galway organisation. Daly had spent over two years trying to get his organisation established and modelled it on the Ballinasloe TDA.[38]

The Ballinasloe TDA was involved with the national agrarian campaign, sending representatives to the national land conferences at the Rotundo in Dublin in 1876 and 1877, but major differences were evident between the Ballinasloe TDA and the other local organisations. While most of the farmers' clubs established in the 1860s and '70s catered for large farmers, from the outset the Ballinasloe association attempted to unite both large and small farmers, and a special appeal was made to the smaller farmers to join the movement at its inaugural meetings in May 1876.[39] It also denounced the graziers for the injuries they inflicted on their smaller colleagues as highlighted by a speech that Harris delivered on 15 June 1876 in Corbett's Hotel, Ballinasloe, in which he stated: '...the typical grazier cares little for his country; he is as remarkable for his want of public spirit as he is for the absence of every quality that fits men for social intercourse or the amenities of civil life.'[40] Harris had little time for graziers, maintaining that they were injuring the agricultural interests of the country and prepared to intrigue with bailiffs and agents to secure the holdings of poorer tenants. This affected both the urban and rural communities as 'the small towns fall into decay as soon as grazing becomes prevalent in the district around'.[41] In his evidence to the Bessborough Commission in October 1880, James Kilmartin reiterated this point stating, 'I look on the graziers as the curse of the country'.[42]

Given the composition of the Ballinasloe association it was inevitable that the radical approach of Harris and O'Sullivan would create tensions with more moderate members. This became apparent at the association's annual general meeting on 26 April 1877, when the more radical members within the group condemned The O'Donoghue, MP for Tralee, for his past parliamentary activities even though he was an advocate of tenants' rights. The moderates, led by Kilmartin and William Kilroe, argued that the land question was more important than personalities and that support should be given to individuals who advanced the tenants' cause. The meeting highlighted the fact that radicals like Harris and O'Sullivan were taking a more advanced position on the agrarian question and were prepared to condemn any public representatives whose loyalty and past actions were questionable.[43] The divisions became more apparent at a council meeting on 13 September 1877 when Harris attacked Butt's parliamentary tactics which he maintained would lead to the break-up of the Home Rule Party and would be disastrous for the national cause.[44]

In early 1878 it was becoming increasingly obvious that the Ballinasloe TDA, and in particular the neo-Fenian group, was drifting away from the mainstream aims and objectives of the general tenant body over the issue of which group of tenants should be given security of tenure. On 14 May 1878 Harris proposed a resolution which would exclude security of tenure to tenants with holdings over sixty acres as it 'would be injurious to the general interests of the country, as tending to create a class of middlemen, and exclude small farmers from ever again occupying the lands from which they have been driven'.[45] This was in line with his attitude towards graziers who were largely shopkeepers and merchants with little background in agriculture, but who took on land to maximise their profits. The resolution was amended and farms over £50 Griffith's Valuation would be excluded. There was strong opposition to the resolution within the committee, with James Kilmartin arguing it was divisive and that the tenant body should adopt a united front.[46] In his evidence to the Bessborough Commission in October 1880 Kilmartin stated that large farmers had experienced serious difficulties over the previous years, largely as a result of declining agricultural prices and American competition.[47] Harris's proposal was also attacked by Thomas F. Joyce from Mounterone House, Joyce Country, a member of the Ballinasloe TDA, who agreed with Kilmartin that unity was the most important consideration and that the proposal would divide the tenantry and delay the securing of peasant proprietorship. This approach was agreed upon by the *Connaught Telegraph*, the association's main newspaper supporter in the west.[48] Kilmartin continued his attacks on Harris and those who advocated placing restrictions on security of tenure for large farmers, and as late as March 1879 was condemning the proposal, stating that if it became law it would turn the small farmers against the graziers.[49] The controversy highlights the different factions within the association and while the Ballinasloe TDA had shown unity up to this point, the divisions between graziers and small farmers were never far from the surface. Harris's proposal also led to disagreement within the general tenant body in the country and a series of letters between him and Thomas Robinson of Narraghmore, Athy, county Kildare (one of the leading personalities in the Central Tenants' Defence Association), published in the *Connaught Telegraph*, indicate the fundamental divisions. Robinson argued that the resolution would result in divisions within the tenant movement and that all farmers, regardless of the size of their holdings, should have security of tenure. In his replies, Harris maintained that graziers were more severe on the small tenant farmers than landlords and connived in their displacement by supporting the changeover from tillage to pasture, adding, 'We blame the landlords for exterminating the people – the occupiers of large farms for introducing the bullocks and sheep.'[50] The controversy indicates the fragmented state of the tenant body and the problems in pursuing a united front between the smaller holders of the west of Ireland and the graziers of Leinster and Munster. It was the prelude to the divisions that would surface in the Land League in the spring of 1880 between the graziers of the south and east and the small tenant farmers of the west.[51]

A radical approach was also evident in relation to politics as members adopted a more advanced attitude towards the Home Rule Party and its parliamentary tactics. Divisions were becoming apparent within the Home

Rule Party over Isaac Butt's approach in the House of Commons, with a group led by Charles Stewart Parnell, Joseph Biggar and John O'Connor Power pursuing a policy of parliamentary obstruction. The Central Tenants' Defence Association and most of the local farmers' associations continued to support Butt but members of the Ballinasloe TDA were becoming increasingly frustrated with the leader's approach, feeling it was unlikely to result in beneficial legislation for Ireland, particularly with regard to the land question. Criticism of Butt and the conservative wing of the party first became apparent in September 1877 when Harris delivered a speech at a council meeting advocating support for parliamentary obstruction 'when it is known that a government is determined to do nothing for this country...' In advocating obstruction he maintained that Butt's followers were 'men of doubtful antecedents, and of doubtful honesty as politicians'.[52] Representatives whom the association had previously supported and who had attended the association's demonstrations, such as Mitchell Henry and Captain Nolan, were now criticised for their failure to support Parnell's parliamentary tactics. At a demonstration in Ballinasloe on 3 November 1878 both Michael M. O'Sullivan and James Kilmartin called on the people to elect representatives of the calibre of Parnell and O'Connor Power.[53] Animosity towards the county Galway MPs was evident at a council meeting in Shannonbridge on 1 February 1879, when Harris attacked both Nolan and Henry, stating that neither had ever given a subscription to the Ballinasloe TDA and that if they were in favour of the tenants' cause they should have helped establish similar associations in every part of the county.[54]

The language used at the association's meetings was becoming increasingly radical. Individuals such as Michael M. O'Sullivan were prepared to advocate the use of physical force when appropriate and as early as the Shannonbridge demonstration on 25 May 1876, O'Sullivan stated that while it was rash to attempt to overthrow the British government under the existing circumstances, he suggested it should not be completely ignored.[55] Harris and O'Sullivan were becoming increasingly frustrated with the lack of progress in securing the demands of the association, and the realisation that the Central Tenants' Defence Association was not promoting small farmers' grievances. At the Ballinasloe demonstration on 3 November 1878, which was addressed by Parnell, O'Connor Power and James Daly, Harris stated there was no difference between 'good' and 'bad' landlords and that this argument only weakened the agrarian campaign and 'enfeebled all your efforts'.[56] The more radical rhetoric at the meetings resulted in the authorities taking a greater interest in the association's activities, including a raid on the homes of Harris and O'Sullivan during the summer of 1878 on the pretext of searching for arms. Harris maintained that the real motive was to go through his personal papers and correspondence.[57]

The moderates within the organisation were becoming increasingly unhappy with the radicalism of Harris and O'Sullivan and in late 1878 and early 1879 it was claimed that the organisation was becoming too politicised. In an attempt to win back members, a resolution was proposed in June 1879 by Walter Duffy that in future the association would not discuss political issues, but should concentrate on agrarian questions exclusively. Harris and O'Sullivan, who had been absent from the council meetings for a number of weeks because of their involvement with the Land League agitation, attended the 11 June council meeting when the motion was being discussed and were instrumental in having it defeated.[58]

There were periods when the association's activities appear to have stagnated as their proceedings were not reported in the local newspapers, in particular the *Connaught Telegraph* and the *Western News*. This was certainly the case between June and November 1878. This confirms James Kilmartin's view in a letter to the *Western News* in April 1879 in which he stated:

A noticeable feature in the Irish Land Agitation is that it is always intermittent. At one time it blazes out fiercely, and from end to end of the island the cry of the tenants and their friends for redress of grievances is heard in every town and village… It is at one time like a blazing conflagration, and at another time like a smouldering fire.

He said the land agitation in Ireland was then at its lowest point and called on the people to organise and agitate.[59] This was just a few weeks before the historic Irishtown demonstration and suggests Kilmartin was not being informed of developments by Harris and O'Sullivan. It was also only a few months after the major demonstration in Ballinasloe on 3 November 1878 which received widespread local and national coverage because of Parnell's involvement. This meeting is often regarded as the first occasion on which Parnell addressed a meeting in Ireland on the land question and while it is sometimes suggested that it formed the basis of his future agrarian policy, it is more likely that he was testing the waters before deciding on what direction to take.[60] At this demonstration the slogan 'The Land of Ireland for the People of Ireland' was first used by John O'Connor Power and it became the motto of the Land League. In his contribution, Harris began by calling on all present to 'Save the People' and launched a bitter attack on those parliamentary representatives who voted against measures that would benefit Ireland, including The O'Conor Don, Charles French and Sir Patrick O'Brien. Calling for Irishmen to join associations, he stated that even if they were opposed to the Ballinasloe TDA they should still join a movement that would suit their needs, 'As Irishmen, you dare not forget these crimes against your country even if you would, but it is not enough that you do not forget them, you should strive to end them'.[61]

The demonstration failed to motivate the tenantry into agitation and the Ballinasloe organisation remained stagnant with membership on the decline, although regular council meetings were held. There are two possible reasons for this: first, a feeling that the organisation had become irrelevant, which may have stemmed from the failure of existing members to renew their subscriptions. During its existence the association does not appear to have been well organised as no minutes were taken of the resolutions passed or of the proceedings.[62] Secondly, the neo-Fenian section of the association was becoming more aligned to the new approach being contemplated by Michael Davitt. This was evident in the roles that Harris and O'Sullivan adopted towards the existing system and O'Sullivan, in a letter in December 1878, hinted that if parliament was not prepared to legislate for Irish grievances other methods should be considered: 'If she does not obey the voice of reason and of wisdom we must have recourse to other means to break up reason and argument. We must not abandon the struggle for our country's freedom as long as any other means remain untried.'[63]

From November 1878 the foundations were being laid for the New Departure which saw constitutional nationalists, Fenians and John Devoy's

Clan na Gael organisation in the United States join forces to promote a new land agitation.[64] Given his involvement with the Ballinasloe TDA and his position as a member of the Supreme Council of IRB, it was not surprising that Harris was a committed supporter of the second New Departure when it was first proposed by Davitt, Parnell and Devoy in January 1879. This was despite the outright opposition from the Fenian leadership within Ireland. It was Harris's opinion that the policies of James Stephens and the other Fenian leaders were self-defeating and incompatible with the spirit of the age. In a letter to the *Irishman* in January 1879 Harris stated that national independence would never be won by peaceful means alone, and attached more importance to secret organisation than parliamentary action. However, as long as Ireland's connection with England was in place, it was in the best interests of nationalists to use parliament for all it was worth.[65] Other Fenians held similar views to Harris and saw what was being achieved in Ballinasloe. One of these was Michael Davitt who during his period in prison had come to the conclusion that the land question was the issue which would revolutionize the national question. One of the first people Davitt made contact with when he returned to the west of Ireland in February 1878 was Harris and he witnessed at first-hand how the different sections of society could be mobilised into an effective agitation.[66] Thus, the groundwork for the second New Departure had already been prepared by Harris in Ballinasloe and this was one of the reasons why Davitt visited Ballinasloe in the spring of 1878. As a result, Harris was beginning to play a leading role in the new agitation that came into existence during the spring of 1879 and it was during this period that the Ballinasloe TDA began to go into decline.

While the 'Low Rent' agitation and subsequent demonstrations in the spring of 1879 helped awaken the local tenant defence associations from their inertia, with public meetings being held by the Edenderry, Mallow, Tipperary and Limerick Farmers' Clubs, it did not have the same impact on the Ballinasloe TDA. The association's activities were in decline and apart from the monthly council meetings there were no public demonstrations except for the 23 November meeting in Ballinasloe. This is surprising given the number of demonstrations that were organised in north and east Galway in places like Milltown, Athenry and Tuam during the summer of 1879.

The decline in activities coincided with the departure of Michael M. O'Sullivan from Ballinasloe, and Harris devoting an increasing amount of his time to the new land agitation as noted in his attendance at approximately twenty demonstrations in the Mayo-Roscommon-Galway region between April and December 1879. The strained relations between the moderates in the Ballinasloe TDA and the new agitation can be seen in a statement James Kilmartin made to the Ballinasloe Board of Guardians meeting on 18 June 1879. He stated that the association did not countenance the land meetings that were taking place, 'but it was open to any of its members in their private capacity to attend them, but not in the name of the association'.[67] He was referring to Harris and O'Sullivan who had attended and addressed the first three meetings of the new agitation at Irishtown, Westport and Milltown.

As the Land League progressed from a local to a more regional base in the autumn of 1879 it was clear the moderate section of the Ballinasloe TDA were not actively involved in the new movement. Kilmartin and Edward Duffy were confining their activities to dealing with the agrarian issue at a local level, with Kilmartin writing regularly to the newspapers on issues such as the problems facing the industrial and urban classes and the restoration of wastelands. Kilmartin stated '...we should agitate to right the wrongs of all classes' and he called for the compulsory building of labourers' cottages and an end to the distinction between town and country.[68] He also proposed motions to the Ballinasloe Board of Guardians calling on the government to come to the aid of the farming community. This was not met with unanimous approval, as some guardians highlighted the revolutionary language being used by speakers at Land League meetings and attributed the radicalism in the Ballinasloe area to the local tenants' defence association.[69] This was no doubt a reference to O'Sullivan's contributions at Irishtown and Milltown. At the Westport demonstration he had told the audience:

> All I have to say is that you may continue the demand for Home Rule, for you will never get it peaceably, and keep your eye steadily on the other. Moral force is truly a great power; but it becomes a greater power when backed up by physical force by the power of the sword. Do not expect autonomy from your hereditary enemies by peaceful means.[70]

At the same time, Kilmartin's only direct involvement with the Land League in this period was confined to the Ballinasloe demonstration on 23 November 1879 which he helped organise and which was addressed by Mitchell Henry, Captain Nolan, Michael Davitt and Matthew Harris.

While the Ballinasloe TDA was advocating the same demands as the new land agitation, its approach was fundamentally different. At the annual general meeting of the association on 22 May a resolution was passed calling for general rent reductions due to the depressed economic conditions.[71] The resolution resembled what was being advocated at the Land League demonstrations such as the historic meetings at Irishtown and elsewhere. While the new agitation was pushing its demands through mass demonstrations and the mobilisation of the agricultural classes, the Ballinasloe association confined its activities to resolutions at council meetings and in the local elected assemblies, but with little general overall impact. By late 1879 it was clear that the organisation was making no advances and in February 1880 it was proposed that the Ballinasloe TDA affiliate with the Land League.[72] When the merger took place former leaders such as James Kilmartin lost their influence and authority, although he was a member of the local Land League branch council.[73]

Conclusion

The importance of the Ballinasloe TDA is apparent in the role model it created for the advancement and development of the Land League. It laid the ground work for the agrarian agitation that swept the country between 1879 and 1880 and resulted in a radical change in landlord-tenant relations. It provided Michael Davitt and others with the model on which to base the new agrarian agitation. The Ballinasloe association showed how ordinary people could be mobilised and how to unite the various social groups and political traditions in rural society. The practice of bringing farmers, Fenians and urban groups together with the aim of improving the welfare of the community was replicated in many parts of the country in the summer of 1879. While the association's achievements were few, its influence and impact must be viewed in a wider context. The association succeeded in concentrating the minds of the public in the east Galway-south Roscommon region on the agrarian question at a time when the issue was losing support nationally. Through demonstrations, and use of the press to highlight the farmers' grievances and defend tenants against the landlord excesses, the association kept the land question to the forefront of the public mind. Their actions also drew attention to the role and activities of public representatives in the region and their obligations to serve the interests of their constituents. Representatives like The O'Conor Don and the Hon. Charles French could no longer ignore the grievances of the agrarian classes and were becoming increasingly accountable to their constituents. The radical section of the Ballinasloe TDA was later to play a major role in the national agrarian campaigns of the Land League and the Plan of Campaign. The influence can also be noted in that two of its leading personalities, Harris and O'Sullivan, played important roles in the development and advancement of the Land League, occupying positions of authority within the movement. From December 1879, Michael M. O'Sullivan was employed as a full-time salaried secretary or chief clerk at the League's head office, while Harris became the movement's paid organiser in the Ballinasloe region.[74] Harris became the conscience of the new organisation, constantly reminding it of its roots and of its failure to look after the interests of its original support base, the small farmers of the west of Ireland. What was even more significant was the legacy of radicalism the movement left in the east Galway region. Throughout the 1880s the area was noted for the strength of its opposition to landlord authority and agrarian radicalism as seen in the high levels of agrarian crime. The framework for this radicalism had been put in place by the Ballinasloe TDA.

5

PROTESTANT TENANT FARMERS AND THE LAND LEAGUE IN NORTH CONNACHT

Miriam Moffitt

THE COMMENCEMENT of populist land agitation in the late nineteenth century created a dilemma for Protestant tenant farmers. Was it in their best interest to support their Catholic neighbours, showing solidarity within their social class, or were they better served by aligning themselves with landlords, thereby demonstrating a religious cohesion? As the religious and social attitudes of Protestant tenant farmers to land reform were further complicated by the contemporaneous demands for Home Rule, it is difficult to isolate Protestants' reaction to land agitation from their response to a proposed Irish parliament.

Populist movements to reform land ownership were extremely powerful forces in rural Ireland in the late nineteenth and early twentieth centuries. They can be described as occurring in two phases, both of which had their beginnings in county Mayo. The first phase, the Land League, followed by the National League, was active in the 1880s and '90s and targeted its activities against the landlord class, seeking to bring about the division of large estates. The second phase, the United Irish League (UIL), was active to varying degrees from its foundation in 1898 to the outbreak of the First World War. The aim of UIL was to bring an end to the large grazing farms, thereby providing further parcels of land for distribution among the large number of persons clammering for access to and ownership of land.

The religious composition and land-holding pattern of Connacht in the second half of the nineteenth century reflected the redistribution of land that had taken place 300 years earlier. Portions of north Leitrim were planted in the early seventeenth century; the remainder of county Leitrim, together with county Sligo and the Tyrawley barony of county Mayo was granted to Cromwellian soldiers.[1] These plantations resulted in an influx of Protestant settlers who introduced a new community of tenants and workers. This formed the nucleus of a Protestant population that spanned the social spectrum and gave rise to a community of Protestant farmers, agricultural labourers and tradesmen. As the remainder of the province was not planted, this social composition was not found elsewhere in Connacht. In Counties Galway, Roscommon and in the remainder of county Mayo, the Protestant population was comprised of the landed classes, augmented by estate employees and Protestant servants of the state (for example, coastguards or members of the military forces). Therefore the number of Protestant tenant farmers was significantly higher in Counties Sligo and Leitrim than in Counties Galway, Mayo and Roscommon. For instance, 1,415 Protestants in Leitrim identified themselves as farmers, farmer's sons or agricultural labourers in the census of 1881; the corresponding figure for the adjoining 'unplanted' county of Roscommon (with a population almost 50 per cent greater than Leitrim) was 330 persons.[2]

While Protestant farmers of Sligo and Leitrim were certainly not rich and could never be identified with the landlord class, their farms were generally larger and their houses more substantial than those of their Catholic neighbours. An analysis of the 1901 census of Protestant farms in county Sligo and the 'planted' section of county Mayo returns confirms that houses of Protestant farmers were more likely to be of the 'class two' variety than 'class three'; they contained more rooms, more windows and a higher percentage of permanent roofs than those owned by nearby Catholic farmers. Valuation Office records also show that Protestant farmers possessed larger farms and a greater number of outbuildings.[3] This is mirrored in the findings of the 1926 census, the first to analyse land ownership by religion. It must be recognised that a considerable number of farming Protestants left north Connacht in the interim.[4] Protestants owned just under 7 per cent of farms in Leitrim in 1926 (711 farms). Most farms in the county were less than thirty acres in size (7,479 or 73 per cent of total farms), Protestant ownership of farms of this size only amounted to 216 or 3.93 per cent. They owned a greater proportion of farms of between 30 and 100 acres, 349 out of a total of 2,556 or 13.65 per cent of farms at this size range.[5] There were only 230 farms of over 100 acres in the county, sixty-eight of which were owned by Protestants. This confirms that, in comparison to their Catholic neighbours, Leitrim's Protestant farmers were less likely to hold farms of under thirty acres, and more likely to farm holdings of between 30 and 100 acres. The 1926 statistics for county Sligo are almost identical, whereas those for counties Galway, Mayo and Roscommon confirm the absence of significant numbers of Protestant farms across all size ranges.

In order to understand the Protestant reaction to the proposed political and land reforms of the late nineteenth and early twentieth centuries, it is essential to appreciate their perception of the direction in which Ireland was moving at that time. From a Protestant/unionist perspective, the years 1870 to 1912 presented a series of humiliations as the Church of Ireland, the dominant Protestant Church, was deprived of her established status with the passage of the Irish Church Disestablishment Act (1869). This was followed by a number of concessions to the majority population relating to tenant right, the exercise of franchise and the administration of local government. A Protestant of the late nineteenth and early twentieth century could be forgiven for bemoaning the British policy of killing Home Rule with kindness, as the government's attempts at benevolent reform, while not essentially sectarian in character, diminished the privileges long associated with Protestantism.

Protestant tenant farmers, conditioned by their education, upbringing and associational culture, were less likely to be drawn to the reform agendas of the nationalist movement. In distancing themselves from nationalist movements, they operated in line with accepted mores of their social and religious communities, and in some instances were bolstered in their actions by a strong associational culture within Protestantism. The Orange Order considered that the Land League operated purely for the purpose of 'uprooting and extinguishing Protestantism' from Ireland, a fact that was hidden from the mass of gullible Roman Catholics by large helpings of 'craft and cunning'.[6] With leading figures in their community imparting such a malevolent interpretation of the land reform movement, Protestant tenant farmers were less likely to participate in agrarian organisations, a fact acknowledged by Arthur Balfour.[7] Some landlords specifically favoured tenants 'who have never been, and are not ever likely to be, connected with such organisations as the National League and Plan of Campaign', a criterion more likely to be fulfilled by persons of the Protestant faith.[8]

From the Catholic/nationalist perspective, reforms regarding the ownership of land were long overdue and were hard won through the strength of communal agitation and, in the case of tenant right and access to judicial rents, these reforms were extended to Protestant farmers as well as Catholics. For Catholic farmers, the common foe was the unjust system of land ownership and nationalist leaders sought (often successfully) to include Protestant farmers in land agitation movements. In associating with nationalist land agitation to overthrow the landlord system, Catholic farmers had the tacit, if not overt, support of most of their clergy whose political aspirations leaned in favour of land reform and a reduction of British involvement in Irish administration.

The situation for Protestant farmers was entirely different as Protestant clergy had no desire to promote the division of estates or the departure of landlords. The Church of Ireland had become largely dependent on the landed class since the removal of state support at disestablishment. The *Irish Ecclesiastical Gazette* of 6 July 1894 explained that following the division of estates, landlords would retain sufficient funds to maintain their families, but not enough to provide for their church. As well as ensuring the maintenance of Church finances, Protestant anxieties were heightened by the two-pronged attack of land reform and Home Rule and many considered that concessions on either front would be disastrous for the maintenance of their way of life. Reared and educated in a largely pro-imperial environment, Protestants were less likely to embrace the radicalism of the agrarian or Home Rule movements and more likely to defy the law of the League. In 1908 Alfred Elliott, Bishop of Kilmore, Elphin and Ardagh, revealed the manner in which Protestants felt threatened by the concessions granted to the majority population:

In the Middle Ages there was a punishment in use to which in spirit we have been subjected. A prisoner was placed in rooms large enough for exercise. For a while he was comfortable, if not happy. One morning it seemed to him that the room seemed smaller than usual. He dismissed the thought, but in a few days it returned with greater force, the room was certainly becoming smaller, and the contracting process went on day by day until he was crushed to death by the embracing walls. This is the fate with which we are threatened. Our privileges have been taken away, our influences weakened, our numbers reduced, our friends impoverished, our opinions disregarded and our voices overborne by the shout of the multitude, because we are locally, but only locally, a minority. If all this was part of a readjustment intended to bring about an even balance of rights and privileges in every part of the community, complaint would be unreasonable. But the even balance is long since passed and, if things proceed in the same direction, Protestant Unionists will find no place in rural Ireland.[9]

The power of land reform movements lay in their ability to persuade or coerce a large portion of the population into obeying their demands, namely that land from which another was evicted should be left idle. The tactics of the Land League, which were continued by the National League and the United Irish League, were outlined in 1880 – 'to refuse to pay all unjust rent, to take no farm from which a tenant has been evicted, to buy no cattle, crops or other property seized for rent...'[10] This treatment was extended to 'land-grabbers' who took possession of evicted farms and by the early twentieth century these were regularly equated with blackleg labour.

In the west of Ireland, 'obnoxious' persons who defied the 'law of the League' which insisted that evicted land should lie unoccupied could expect to incur intense boycotting, intimidation and – on occasion – attacks on their property or person. Those subjected to a rigid boycott were unable to obtain labour as employees refused to work for them; they found it impossible to get the services of a blacksmith, a thresher, or any form of tradesman; they were unable to get animals to sire their mares or cows. They could not sell their produce and were shunned at fairs; they were unable to obtain provisions and were refused in shops. There were even instances of women dying in childbirth because a midwife could not be procured.[11] Persons who assisted boycotted grabbers were likely to be themselves boycotted but this was generally less stringently applied. Police records differentiate between rigid and partial boycotting and suggest that boycotting was intermittently applied where there was a degree of understanding between the parties. However, in the absence of such an understanding, a rigidly boycotted farmer had to rely on his family to sow and harvest his crops and to tend his livestock, and was forced to sell animals and produce to sympathetic or opportunistic purchasers at whatever price they were willing to offer.

Although the Land League and the United Irish League were criticised by the Catholic hierarchy, they commanded the support of a very large portion of clergy at parish level, especially among the younger curates. The enthusiastic support of many Catholic priests for the United Irish League was outlined in the unionist publication, *Notes from Ireland*, which published monthly lists of Catholic clergy who sat on public platforms at UIL meetings. Through the public support of Catholic clergy, and the holding of League meetings outside the church premises after Sunday mass, the Leagues (Land League, National League and United Irish League) commanded the support of most of the Catholic population in rural Ireland.

Strenuous efforts were made by the Protestant establishment from the outset to ensure that Protestant farmers distanced themselves from campaigns for land reform. The foundation of the Land League in 1879 resulted in the revival of dormant Orange Lodges and the establishment of lodges in new locations. When four lodges were established in King's County with the specific purpose of frustrating agrarianism, the Order delighted in reporting the sense of cohesiveness engendered therein, 'It is gratifying to be able to inform you that in many of these… the peer and the peasant sit side by side as brethren; and where they so meet in Lodge, there is no danger of their differing outside.'[12]

Dormant Orange Lodges were revived and new lodges established throughout Sligo and Leitrim during the Land War to provide a sense of solidarity to Protestant farmers who wished to resist the orders of the Land League; they also acted as a deterrent to prevent Protestant compliance with League demands.[13] In some districts, pressure to join the Order was increased by the involvement of parish clergy.[14] Two members, suspended by the County Sligo Grand Orange Lodge in 1881 for engaging in League activity, appealed to the Grand Orange Lodge of Ireland who, while recording its 'utter detestation of the Land League, and our condemnation of any complicity whatever with it', reduced the suspensions to one year for Bro. Lougheed and nine months for Bro. Mullins.[15] The following year, three Sligo-men were expelled from the Order for 'violating the laws of the institution', and another was expelled four years later.[16]

An Orange Emergency Committee was established in 1880 to undertake the duty of protecting loyalists scattered in the south and west of Ireland; this was revived in 1909 to safeguard Protestants whose lives were 'beset with outrage, crime and barbarism of an illegal character' inflicted by the 'merciless tyranny' of the United Irish League.[17] The County Sligo Grand Orange Lodge passed a vote of gratitude for its efforts on behalf of the 'oppressed and down-trodden loyalists of the South and West of Ireland' and promised that district and private lodges would meet to undertake this work in the county.[18] However, many of the lodges opened in the 1880s had closed by this time.

Evidence suggests that boycotted Protestants in areas outside Connacht relied heavily on communal solidarity and police protection to withstand League pressure. When it was enquired why Queen's County Protestants were helpless in defending themselves in the face of popular agitation between 1920 and 1923 as they had resisted similar agitation during the Land War era, a local clergyman explained that Protestant farmers had formerly 'banded together' and went from farm to farm in large parties 'sometimes with the protection of the RIC', while in the more recent episodes, the Protestant farmers were disarmed and the RIC had been withdrawn.[19]

Not all Connacht Protestants approved of the tactics of the Orange Order. In Ballymote, county Sligo, most distanced themselves from the efforts of a recently reconstituted local Orange Lodge to persuade landlords to preferentially grant farms to Protestants 'upon whom reliance can safely be placed in these times of pending danger to life, property, and the union of Ireland with the British Throne'.[20] A resolution passed by Ballymote's Orange Lodge in 1884, termed the 'Plantation Circular', contained a list of

five clergymen who offered to act as a conduit between landlords and prospective Protestant tenants, one clergyman immediately dissociated himself
from the venture.[21] At a local protest meeting, Canon John McDermott,
parish priest of Ballymote, asserted that if these 'parsons' wished landlords to grant farms to their 'religious slaves', they would be 'walked out
of the country', another speaker assured the assembled crowd that most of
Ballymote's Protestants would not 'sully their character' by associating with
the Lodge.[22] When two brothers, both lodge-members, fired shots into the
crowd at the above meeting, the family coach-building firm was boycotted
and went into severe decline. Although one brother, Jammet Murray, was
expelled from the Order five years later for 'endangering the honour and
dignity of the institution',[23] the family maintained close connections with
the Order. The rector of Ballymote remarked forty years later that these
men 'were out and out Orangemen and were hated for being so and marked
men accordingly…'[24]

Although there is evidence that some, but certainly not all Protestants fell
foul of reform organisations, it appears that the majority of Protestants in
north Connacht abided by these populist movements, especially during the
era of the United Irish League. While little direct evidence of Protestant
support for land agitation can be found, Protestant participation may be
inferred from the almost total adherence to the demands of the Leagues,
as police reports regularly told of rents being universally withheld, even in
areas with considerable numbers of Protestant farmers.[25]

Under the terms of the 1881 Land Act, the rights of permanent tenants
were greatly increased as fair or judicial rents could be decided by the
newly-established land courts. To circumvent this situation, many landlords
opted to rent large tracts of grazing land on short-term leases, termed the
'eleven-month system'. Much of the UIL's energies were spent on forcing
large graziers to surrender these 'eleven-month' farms.[26] Scarcity of land
in north Connacht fostered intense resentment at the fact that much of
the best land was 'in the hands of the landlord and the grazier or someone
connected with them',[27] and was now used 'for the propagation of sheep
and bullocks'.[28]

The return of William O'Brien to the UIL in 1908 sparked a renewed
campaign of intimidation and violence against farmers who were perceived

as transgressing the rules of the League. This campaign was particularly directed at those who held land from which others had been evicted, those who took land on the eleven-month system and those who held large grazing farms. Although Catholics and Protestants alike were engaged in practices considered 'obnoxious' by the UIL, and although grazing farms were held by both Catholics and Protestants, the Protestant community suffered disproportionately, not on account of their religion, but because they were more likely to hold larger farms. It must be recognised that while Protestant graziers were not victimised because of their religious allegiance, the political and cultural environment into which they were born rendered them less sympathetic to the aims of the League and less susceptible to its control. As was later stated, Irish Protestants were 'baptised, not only into a religious faith, but into a political camp'.[29] It can be argued that this was also the case for Irish Catholics.

The evidence from north Connacht confirms that the majority of Protestant farmers, both tenant farmers and owner-occupiers, obeyed the law of the UIL with some taking an active part in its organisation. Church of Ireland farmers were members of a tenant committee established to organise the subdivision of the Hillas estate at Dromore West in county Sligo in 1904, suggesting their participation in League activities.[30] The Inspector General of the RIC recorded in September 1901 that rents were universally unpaid on some Leitrim estates situated in areas with considerable numbers of Protestant tenant farmers.[31] Similarly, he reported in January 1904 that rents were withheld on the Johnston estate at Manorhamilton because the owner refused a reduction; he noted that only one tenant had remitted his rent 'and he by post letter'.[32] Alfred Elliott, Church of Ireland Bishop of Kilmore, Elphin and Ardagh, whose large diocese included all of county Leitrim and parts of Counties Sligo, Roscommon, Galway, Longford, Fermanagh and Cavan, conceded that some of his flock had allied themselves with the League, bemoaning the fact that they would have resisted any curtailment of their religious or civil liberties but were won over when approached 'through the pocket'. He admitted knowing Protestants who were 'leaders amongst the local agitators', while others contributed to the League and sympathised with its aims. He also told of Protestants being intimidated into withholding rent, and of others who gave him money to remit on their behalf.[33] In spite of the fact that many Protestants abided by the demands of the League, the public manner in which its orders were defied by a small number of their co-religionists may have sown seeds of bitterness in the minds of some Catholic nationalists, reinforcing the unfounded belief that all Protestants wished to frustrate the progress of land reform.

The enormous gulf that existed between those who supported the efforts of the UIL and those who were horrified by what was seen as the breakdown of law and order occasioned by its activities reveals the absolute divergence of sympathies. Not only was each party vehemently convinced that right was on their side, each saw themselves as being victimised by the other. Writing about the activities of the UIL in south Leitrim, the ultra-conservative *Notes from Ireland* told how 'opprobrious' terms such as 'grabber' and 'emergency men' were applied to 'ordinary law abiding people who refuse to be guided by the rules, or obey the particular behests of the League' and described how the UIL was 'leaving no stone unturned to mete out starvation, pure and simple, to the unfortunate people who have become their victims'.[34] In contrast, the UIL argued that shopkeepers who supplied grabbers or emergency men were 'the deadly enemies of the tenant farmers of the country, and also the aider, the abettor and supporter of the few remaining heartless landlords who still endeavour to keep their iron feet on the necks of the poor tenant farmers who still struggle to exist under them'.[35]

Bishop Elliott told the Elphin Diocesan Synod in 1908 that Ireland was going through a time of crisis which was 'bound to effect radical changes in the social, and possibly in the political constitution of the country'. He criticised the 'grandmotherly legislation' which aimed to parcel the land for a people who 'as a class, have neither capital, intelligence nor energy'. The government, he claimed, was clearly not on the side of law and order as it made excuses for the outrages perpetrated throughout the country. He explained that in times of previous unrest, Protestants could confidently expect that things would eventually settle down 'on the side of the Union' but he considered that such optimism was unwarranted at this impasse as clearly 'a down grade is winked at by our rulers' which gave an impetus to lawlessness and discontent. He told of Protestant farmers pressurised into subscribing to the UIL and spoke of Protestant shopkeepers forced to deny goods to boycotted persons lest they themselves be boycotted, and warned that soon Protestant Unionists would have no place in rural Ireland.[36] A few weeks later, Bishop Elliot railed against the danger to which his scattered flock was exposed, asking the Kilmore Synod:

> Can we do nothing to protect and encourage our few and scattered brethren against becoming prey to the terror, or still worse, the wiles of this disloyal combination? Can nothing be done to sustain and advise those of our people who suffer at its hands?[37]

Bishop Elliott was probably correct in stating that some Protestants reluctantly abided by the orders of the UIL. At a meeting of the UIL in county Sligo in August 1906, Thomas Rolston, a Church of Ireland farmer from Dromore West, promised to abide by the its demands since 'he might as well be dead as under the censure of public opinion any longer',[38] and shopkeepers in Ballinamore, county Leitrim were severely rebuked for supplying provisions to emergency men, 'crawling reptiles, who are the henchmen of the plunderers of our race…'[39] The South Leitrim Executive of the UIL passed a resolution that members should not allow their animals to sire cows or mares belonging to 'grabbers, emergency-men, planters and particularly their supporters, as the hypocrites who aid or correspond with emergency-men, grabbers &c. either directly or indirectly are most dangerous members of society and should be watched'.[40]

Two case studies will explore the role played by religion in the attitudes and behaviour of the Catholic and Protestant farming communities. In the first study, boycotting of Protestant 'grabbers' resulted in the sectarian polarisation of neighbouring towns while Protestants living closer to the episode appear to have withheld support from their co-religionists (Aughavas, county Leitrim). The second study examines two episodes in adjacent districts of county Sligo, one where Protestant farmers were victimised for not joining the UIL (Riverstown, county Sligo) and another where a Protestant family enlisted the support of the UIL in an effort to settle a family dispute over ownership of land (Roscrib, county Sligo).

The McNeills of Aughavas

In 1889, the Church of Ireland brothers, John and Robert McNeill, took possession of two farms in Aughavas near Carrigallen, county Leitrim. Dominic Maguire, the former tenant, had been evicted from one of these farms seven years previously; the name of the second tenant is unknown but may have been Smith.[41] As happened on the Clanricarde estate in east Galway, the evicted Maguire family remained in the district in a Land League hut, but later emigrated to the United States.

The McNeills (John, Robert, with David from the next generation) retained possession of these farms and by 1902, four persons in this area were in receipt of police protection for employing labourers from the Property Defence Association (PDA), an organisation which aided those victimised by the activities of the League. It is likely that the protected included members of the extended McNeill family as police reports tell that Francis Cooke, father-in-law of David McNeill, was boycotted for assisting 'obnoxious' persons and for employing PDA labourers.[42] Things appear to have settled down as the McNeills and Cookes are not found among the list of boycotted persons in Leitrim during the following years, but when a member of the Maguire family returned from America in 1907 and sought readmission to his family's former holding, the UIL renewed its agitation against the McNeills.

In November 1907, nine persons were arrested at a turbulent UIL meeting held at Carrigallen when a rigid boycott of the McNeills was announced. A crowd of over 4,000 persons, together with the Killeshandra AOH band, celebrated the release of these prisoners from Armagh Jail two months later. Thomas Smyth, Irish Party MP, addressed the assembled crowd and expressed the hope that 'planters' might soon be as rare in Ireland 'as the reptiles banished by Saint Patrick'.[43]

By this time police protection had been granted to the McNeills, who were rigidly boycotted.[44] Police reports confirm that they could secure provisions from the considerable number of Protestant shops nearby, and especially in nearby county Cavan.[45] Local Protestant traders initially paid no heed to advice from the League to refuse the McNeills; Eliza Jane Matthews, a Protestant grocer in Carrigallen, ignored the warnings of Dominic Maguire, son of the evicted tenant, and reported his visit to the police.[46] As the McNeills were later forced to journey under police escort to the Cavan towns of Arva and Killeshandra for provisions, the League must have persuaded Miss Matthews to change her mind.[47]

Few families persisted in their occupation of evicted farms in the face of such concerted opposition; police reports identify individuals condemned on one or two occasions at UIL meetings and who eventually came to comply with the regulations of the League. Only two Leitrim families defied the power of the League over a long period; both were Protestant: the McNeills of Aughavas and the McCordicks of Stroke.[48] Boycotting in Aughavas appears to have been extended to the wider McNeill family. Notices were posted at Aughavas chapel on the night of 25 July 1908 forbidding labourers from working for John Abbott JP, who had assisted his cousin, Robert McNeill; two weeks earlier a local blacksmith was rebuked for carrying out work for Francis Cooke, David McNeill's father-in-law.[49] By August 1908, seven families were boycotted to varying degrees; two for holding farms and five for assisting them.[50] By February 1910, the number of boycotted families had risen to ten.[51]

Intimidation and boycotting was intensified in the years 1908 to 1910, often resulting in physical violence. Dominic Maguire was fined for assaulting David McNeill at Arva fair in May 1908.[52] Boycotting resolutions were published in the *Leitrim Leader* and the *Roscommon Herald*, and the south Leitrim executive of the UIL passed a resolution at a meeting in Fenagh in December 1909 ordering the McNeill brothers to surrender the evicted farms.[53] Members of the UIL shadowed the McNeills round the shops of Killeshandra on 19 January 1910, warning traders not to supply them; this was repeated at Arva two days later and again at Arva fair on 28 January when extra police were drafted in to maintain order. Additional police were also required at the McNeill farms, where crowds regularly converged and where 'vicious and criminal' language was used by Thomas Smyth MP. Police reports recorded that such language 'used to a semi-educated and semi-civilised people had the most disastrous effect', resulting in damage to livestock and property belonging to the McNeills and causing the boycott of two additional families.[54]

In January 1910, John Abbott testified that local shopkeepers were afraid to serve him and that his labourers had left him. This courtroom evidence was given when his son, Thomas Abbott, claimed compensation for the loss of hay, a hayshed, a mowing machine and farming implements damaged by fire. Thomas told the court that he could not get his horse shod in the district and that he had been 'treated disrespectfully' since 1908, and that his father had received a letter from 'A Staunch Aughavas Boy' warning him that the family would be harmed if they continued to assist the McNeills.[55]

Intimidation intensified against traders in Arva and Killeshandra who supplied the McNeills.[56] However, unlike the situation in Carrigallen, these towns had sufficient Protestant populations to withstand a nationalist boycott. Trading in Arva became polarised along sectarian lines as Catholics refused to deal in shops such as Robert Keith's, but 'as the Orange party is strong in that neighbourhood, and is backing up Keith, his trade has really increased'. The result was a contest in boycotting. What had begun as an agrarian dispute spiralled into a 'party and religious matter' and boycotting took the form of 'a mutual transference of trade on the part of Roman Catholics and Protestants'.[57] Tensions heightened as the months passed and shots were fired at Robert McNeill as he travelled home from a shopping trip in March 1910.[58] Events at Aughavas were raised in the House of Commons in March 1910 and in the House of Lords four months later.[59]

Sectarian trading in Killeshandra and Arva continued until the autumn of 1910 when Robert McNeill accepted a farm in county Tyrone and agreed to surrender his evicted farm. Most of the trouble appears to have temporarily ceased at this point – but would resume ten years later. Boycotting came to an end and police protection was withdrawn.[60] The police report for January 1911 recorded that only one family held an evicted farm in the county; it did not specify whether or not this was David McNeill. Animosity against this man continued to some degree; in September 1912 he was assaulted in the town of Mohill.[61]

While this episode might appear to centre on a clear-cut agrarian episode, namely the occupation of evicted farms and the victimisation of 'land-grabbers', events at Aughavas cannot be so easily explained. The fact that the new occupiers were Protestant and the evicted tenants Catholic imbues the story with a sectarian hue. This intermix of sectarianism and agrarianism occurred elsewhere in Leitrim at the same time. The RIC County Inspector's report for May 1908 reported that Catholic tenants on an unidentified estate in the Newtowngore district refused to sign an agreement for its sale to the Estates Commissioners until previously evicted tenants were restored, explaining that 'The holders of these farms are Protestants who will not yield and hence the struggle has assumed to some extent a sectarian character.'

It appears that the McNeills and most, if not all, of those boycotted at Aughavas were members of the Church of Ireland, such as Thomas Patterson of Carrigallen who was singled out because he gave McNeill the use of his bull.[62] John and Thomas Abbott, cousins of the McNeills, were also Church of Ireland, as was the shopkeeper, Miss Matthews and also, Robert Navan, a neighbouring farmer, who was boycotted for associating with 'the grabber Robert McNeill'.[63] This should not suggest that all Protestant families in the region drew the ire of the UIL; in fact the number of Protestants who were boycotted amounts to only a small proportion of the total. There were over ninety Protestant houses in the combined district electoral divisions of Aughavas, Carrigallen East and Carrigallen West in the 1901 census, the vast majority of whom were not in any way involved with the McNeills. The fact that only ten families from the entire district were boycotted suggests an agrarian motivation for the episode but the religious difference and the anti-Catholic sentiments expressed by members of the extended McNeill family cannot be ignored. It was reported that a favourite occupation of the McNeills was to publicly 'curse the pope' – for which they had been reprimanded by their police escorts, and a Carrigallen man gave evidence of hearing one of the McNeills shout 'Hurray for King William that freed us' and 'To hell with the Pope'.[64] The lack of support given to the McNeills by Carrigallen's Protestant community is all the more surprising when we consider that the parish rector from 1908 to 1911 was Grand Master of County Leitrim Grand Orange Lodge and that his successor was its Grand Chaplain.[65]

It is extremely likely that David McNeill was a member of the Orange Order; his father-in-law, Francis Cooke, was County Grand Master of Leitrim for four years and his brother-in-law, Edmund Cooke, was

Worshipful Master of Carrigallen Orange Lodge (LOL 679). Edmund Cooke stated, in an unsuccessful application to the Irish Grants Committee (IGC), that although his farm was held by his family for almost 300 years, they were still regarded locally as British. This application, which claimed that the Cookes and McNeills were persecuted on account of their loyalty to the Crown, makes no reference whatsoever to agrarian tensions. A letter from a former RIC man confirmed that Edmund Cooke's father was 'a prominent Unionist & took an active part on behalf of the Landlords and Government against his neighbours, was boycotted and under police protection on and off for about 30 years before his death'.[66]

It would appear that agrarian issues troubled the life of David McNeill as late as May 1920, when he received a threatening letter warning him to leave the locality and when notices were posted warning people to have nothing to do with him on account of 'Smith's farm' which he held at that time.[67] In contrast to the episode of a decade earlier, and possibly in consequence of the rising nationalist power, McNeill immediately yielded to pressure and surrendered said farm.[68] It would appear that old scores regarding land ownership were settled throughout Leitrim at this time as a Catholic farmer at Corduff, near Mohill, was ordered in June 1920 to surrender land 'grabbed' by his father to descendents of the former tenant.[69] This man must have had an easier time than the McNeills in former years, as police records do not record that he was boycotted or intimidated during the previous decades.

David McNeill, in his claim to the IGC, told how he was forced to flee the district in 1920 on account of his allegiance to the state, telling that he escaped an IRA raid and fled to Belfast where he lived under an assumed name. This was confirmed by a police report which told how 'disguised men' entered the house of David McNeill, a loyalist, with the object of murdering him.[70] McNeill was accommodated at the camp for 'distressed unionists' at Newtownards (probably Clandeboye), where he remained for four years. His wife and family joined him in Belfast at a later date; by then his wife's mental health had broken under the strain and his farm at Aghadruminshin, Aughavas, was sold for a fraction of its value. He attributed his treatment at the hands of the IRA to assistance he gave to the Crown forces and received compensation of £2,700. He made no mention of the fact that his family had endured years of animosity and had lived for long periods under police protection.[71]

The McNeills retained possession of a second farm in Aughavas until May 1922 when William McNeill was forced to surrender the Agharan farm to a former tenant. Writing from Liverpool, William sought compensation of £720 from the Free State government but does not appear to have been successful.[72] Mrs Eliza Abbott, widow of John Abbott, was also unsuccessful in her claim to the IGC. She told how her neighbours refused to work for her on account of a rigid boycott, which was in place owing to her son serving with the RIC. Following numerous raids on their property and assaults on her son, they were obliged to sell the farm at a loss and move to the safer district of Belturbet, county Cavan. Yet again, her application gave no inkling of a long-standing agrarian hostility.[73]

This study confirms that the violence experienced by the extended McNeill family of Aughavas was primarily agrarian in character. It also demonstrates that the boycott of this family did not extend to the wider Protestant community in the district, who complied with the orders of the United Irish League to completely dissociate from this family.

Riverstown and Roscrib

Tensions were running high in Riverstown, county Sligo in the summer of 1908, when the local branch of the UIL instituted a system of boycotting against thirteen Protestant farmers who refused, on principle, to subscribe to its funds. These people were, it was claimed in court, 'for the most part small farmers, they were not graziers, and they belonged to an old stock, and in no sense could be regarded as important in the country'.[74] The boycott persisted despite the efforts of the parish priest, Canon Maher, and local MPs, Patrick McHugh and John O'Dowd, who condemned it at a meeting in Ballymote.[75]

There was intense Catholic resentment that Protestants refused to subscribe to the UIL. From a nationalist perspective, Protestants as well as Catholics were seen to have benefited from the transfer of land-ownership to former tenants, a fact that was outlined to the Protestant owner-occupiers of

Riverstown.[76] Had these Protestants agreed to join the League, they would have been obliged to discontinue their letting of pasture on the eleven-month system. According to Stephen Gwynn, Protestant nationalist MP for Galway, this practice placed the Protestant farmers of Riverstown in the same position as blacklegs in a trade dispute:

> I infer that in this district the Protestant farmers have all elected either to be blacklegs or to support the blacklegs. They are boycotted not because they are Protestants, but because they are blacklegs. But they very naturally band themselves under the Protestant name to elicit religious sympathy.[77]

The Protestants of Riverstown did nothing to draw attention to their plight, they made no complaint to the police who learned of the boycott from independent sources and who admitted that Riverstown's Protestants were reluctant to divulge information.[78] According to police records, the ensuing court proceedings were initiated by the RIC, although the media reported that Riverstown's Protestants banded together to form the 'Protestant Mutual Defence Association', and brought a charge against the leadership of the UIL at Riverstown Petty Sessions. Catholic opinion asserted that this association was founded by the local Protestant postmaster to compel Protestants to transfer their custom from Catholic to Protestant businesses.[79] The police recorded that two bakeries, one in Sligo and one in Dromahair, refused to supply the Protestant traders as to do so would cause their bakeries to be boycotted. They also recorded that no violence was used or threatened.[80]

By the time the case came to court on 12 November 1908, hostilities in the locality had escalated to extreme levels, as a confrontation between the police and the UIL resulted in the shooting dead of a nineteen-year-old Catholic, John Stenson two weeks earlier. Head Constable Donovan of Ballymote was also seriously injured in the episode which occurred when the RIC tried to prevent the UIL from driving cattle from land owned by a Protestant grazier, Mr Phibbs.

Alexander Lyons of Sligo, solicitor for the plaintiffs, asserted his clients had been ceaselessly boycotted in recent months, and that local Catholics had made every effort to destroy their property.[81] James Craig, MP for East

Down, told the House of Commons that Riverstown's Protestants had been subjected to a reign of terror, intimidation and boycotting, which was contradicted by John Brownlee Lonsdale, MP for Mid-Armagh, who asserted that the district had been peaceful until the establishment of an aggressive Protestant organisation the previous summer.[82]

The case worked its way through the lower courts to the *Nisi Prius* Court in Dublin, where details of the intimidation and boycotting were outlined in May 1909.[83] James Johnston Snr, for example, who farmed eighteen acres at Drumfin, explained that his Catholic neighbour, William Tonry, used to carry milk from various farms to Riverstown creamery, a distance of two or three miles. When Johnston refused the demand of William King, a local blacksmith, that he donate a shilling for the League, Tonry ceased to carry milk for him and for all other Protestants who likewise refused. Thomas Morrison's experience was identical; his carter stopped collecting milk at the end of July 1908 and the blacksmith, William King, refused to shoe Morrison's horse lest his own milk be 'let down'. When the sale of Margaret Rowlette's twenty acres of meadow was boycotted she was informed that 'if you paid to the League you would have got your meadow sold' and Elizabeth Meredith's meadow was spiked, which caused damage to a mowing machine and her milk was not carried. Thomas Mulligan, a Catholic mason erecting a building on the lands of Mrs Meredith's brother, Thomas Bright, was ordered to stop work and to apologise at a meeting of the League.[84]

The degree of actual animosity between individuals is open to question. The nationalist *Sligo Champion* acknowledged that the boycott was reluctantly enforced. It asserted that the boycotted Thomas Middleton knew that his neighbour, Edward McDonagh, was willing to carry his milk but believed that the social cost was too high. Margaret Connor, a Protestant, said she was on the best of terms with her neighbours and if she needed help with anything it was to William Tonry, one of the accused, she would turn.[85] The Lord Chief Justice commented on the fact that the parties appeared to be on good terms with each other, that the boycotting and persecution was carried out under the coercion of the League. He acknowledged that those who refused to carry milk withheld their services out of fear as anyone who assisted a boycotted Protestant was likely to suffer, as the Catholic blacksmith, John Cannon, who shoed a horse for Thomas Harte (Protestant) found to his cost when his anvil was stolen.[86] The police even gave evidence that the persecutors were of good character and, as proof of good relations, it was claimed that when William Tonry was short of money, he turned to his Protestant neighbour, James Johnston, for assistance.

As it was clear that this boycott was reluctantly enforced, the jury was unable to reach a verdict and was discharged; the case was never retried.[87] Riverstown's Protestant Defence Association continued to function; in November 1909 Brian Cooper commended the association at a meeting in the Cooper Memorial Hall, Riverstown, and warned that their troubles were far from over.[88]

Although Riverstown Protestants were reluctant to associate with the United Irish League in 1908, some Protestant ladies who lived about ten kilometres away sought the League's protection in a family dispute four years later. Two elderly Protestants, Richard and Joseph Gillmor, who each owned large farms at Roscrib, Ballymote, died in January 1911 and September 1911 respectively, leaving an annuity to their sister, Margaret Gillmor, and bequeathing their farms to their nephews, Samuel Gillmor and Jackson James Gillmor. Margaret Gillmor lived on one of the farms with her niece, Rebecca Reid; a second niece (Harriet Reid) and a nephew (Richard Reid) subsequently moved in with their aunt. Possession of the farms was demanded in November 1911 when the Sligo legal firm of Fenton and Lyons provided Margaret with a copy of her brothers' wills. Margaret, although a Protestant, contacted the UIL. The League, taking up the cudgels for Margaret and Rebecca, described these actions as 'heartless and particularly cruel' as these ladies had devoted their lives to house-keeping for the deceased brothers.[89] A leading article in *Sligo Champion* described the ladies as 'destitute' and outlined how Jackson Gillmor, a banker in Clones, had instigated the eviction of these ladies from the house where they had 'toiled from dawn to dusk'.[90] The executor of the will challenged the 'destitute' tag, saying Margaret had received an annuity of £80.[91]

John O'Dowd, MP for Sligo, obviously relishing the fact that Protestants had turned to the UIL for protection, praised 'the noble and self-sacrificing efforts of our Protestant fellow-countrywomen in our long struggle for freedom' and promised that the League 'would show its gratitude for the services of their illustrious co-religionists in the past who willingly faced the scaffold and dungeon as a protest against British tyranny and the persecution of their Catholic fellow-countrymen'.[92] The League advised the ladies to remain in the house and removed the crops and livestock, including thirteen horses, to prevent their sale. In doing so, it was claimed that the League sought to deprive the deceased owners of the land of their right to dispose of it as they wished. This was ultimately the opinion of the court which sided with the nephews, who were granted possession.[93]

Although relations between the communities in the Riverstown district appear to have been reasonably cordial, a distinctly Protestant ethos was maintained in the district. An Orange Lodge (LOL 1733) functioned in Riverstown since the commencement of land agitation, with services and social functions held in the Cooper Memorial Hall each July and Christmas.[94] Charles Kean O'Hara of Annaghmore chaired a unionist meeting in this building on 12 May 1914, at which Revd Thomas Allan, rector and Miss ffoliott of Boyle addressed the audience and this was followed six weeks later by the annual Orange Service.[95] It is unclear when Riverstown LOL ceased to function, the nearby lodge at Ballymote (LOL 794) folded in 1913;[96] and by 1921 members of the former Riverstown LOL were associated with the lodge in Sligo town (LOL 464), with a Riverstown Orangeman acting as Grand Marshall for county Sligo. It appears all Orange activity in the county ceased with the establishment of the Free State.

While it is clear that reasonably good relations existed between the Catholic and Protestant communities of Riverstown, and although it was acknowledged that this campaign of intimidation caused little animosity between individuals, the episode added to the armoury of politicians and propagandists. A few years later, as the threat of Home Rule grew, Brian Cooper was greeted with loud applause when he reminded Monaghan Orangemen that Riverstown's Protestants 'did nothing beyond refusing to subscribe to the United Irish League and yet they were subjected to this tyranny'. 'But', he added, 'there was an Orange Lodge there, and they fought, and in the end they won'.[97] The UIL was equally adept at utilising such episodes to promote its objectives, despite relatively good relations between the communities. In spite of the fact that the Roscrib episode did not involve the ownership of large tracts of land, the League's efforts in support of the Gillmor ladies were depicted as a struggle against the 'decaying members of a tyrannical garrison who have been the curse of our land for centuries'.[98]

Conclusion

It is clear from the above studies that no simple verdict can be delivered regarding the participation of Protestants in land agitation, although they were less likely to be drawn to the reform movements by virtue of their educational and associational background. As was later explained, 'For all practical purposes, the frontiers of Church and Party are coterminous'.[99] While this may indeed have been the case for the era of the Land League and National League, evidence from north Connacht suggests that Protestant farmers tended to abide by the demands of the UIL to the dismay of their clerical leaders, as acknowledged by Bishop Elliott of Kilmore, Elphin and Ardagh who regretted that many of his flock willingly embraced the movement, but added that others were intimidated into granting support.[100]

Regardless of the 'spontaneity' of Protestant support for the UIL, it cannot be denied that few Protestant farmers in north Connacht dared to defy its demands. The universal withholding of rents in areas where around 10 per cent of farms were held by Protestants suggests a strong level of support for the UIL among the Protestant farmers of Leitrim. Only ten Protestant households (out of at least ninety) in Aughavas braved the boycotting and intimidation meted out to those who disobeyed the law of the League – and at least five of these households belonged to the extended McNeill family. The remainder of Aughavas's Protestants not only distanced themselves from the 'obnoxious' persons, they did so in defiance of the parish rector, an active Orangeman. Their distancing from the 'obnoxious' McNeills may have stemmed from fear and many, like the grocer Eliza Matthews, may have needed a little persuasion. Protestant traders in county Cavan, by virtue of a stronger Protestant population, were in a better position to withstand UIL pressure so that a pattern of sectarian trading stemmed out of this agrarian dispute. The polarisation of shopping in Arva and Killeshandra may have brought members of the wider community (both Protestant and Catholic) into the ambit of agrarian agitation, persons who might otherwise have been undisturbed by the workings of the League.

Protestant farmers were not specifically targeted by the UIL because of their religion, but rather because they were more likely to hold larger tracts of land, and because some were more likely to refuse to take part in popular agitation, on a point of principle. When the Protestants of Riverstown refused to join the UIL for this reason, the Catholic population was pressurised into implementing a boycott. Evidence confirms that both communities remained on good terms and that the withholding of services from Riverstown's Protestants was reluctantly undertaken. It appears this did not undermine the genuine trust and friendship between the communities as Riverstown's Protestants realised that their Catholic neighbours withheld their services out of fear.

Certainly the presence of ultra-Protestant organisations such as the Orange Order encouraged Protestant farmers to resist the pressures of the League; in fact, organizations of this nature were specifically established to frustrate the efforts towards the reform of land ownership. This may have offered some degree of support to the Protestants of Riverstown but does not appear to have influenced those of Aughavas. Despite the fact that Orange Lodges operated throughout Leitrim in the early years of the twentieth century, Protestant farmers were more likely to disobey the commands of the Lodge than those of the League.[101] It must be repeatedly stressed that in doing so, they defied the leaders of their society and ran counter to the influences of their education and culture.

Those who persisted in their defiance of the UIL, such as the McNeills of Aughavas, were dependent on the protection of the state, but once this was withdrawn in 1920, their vulnerability was evident. The unsettled conditions of the revolutionary years provided conditions where longstanding agrarian resentments were settled, but many dispossessed at this time claimed compensation on the basis of their loyalty to the Crown, making no mention of decades of hostility.

The agrarian movement in rural Ireland was not essentially sectarian in nature but was more likely to be resisted by members of the Protestant faith.

In Aughavas, where most Protestants embraced the UIL, and in Riverstown, where most refused to join, little inter-faith animosity was engendered between Catholics and Protestants, while at Roscrib, two Protestant ladies approached the UIL for assistance. When the League encountered entrenched opposition from Protestant farmers as happened at Riverstown and Roscrib, the episodes were exploited by both Catholic and Protestant politicians to depict a cleavage of rural society along a religious fault-line. In spite of evidence of accommodation between the communities, political leaders on both sides imbued agrarian hostilities with sectarian influences and portrayed them to a wider audience in a manner that did not accurately reflect the more accommodating situation on the ground.

6

MEDICAL RELIEF AND WORKHOUSE INFIRMARIES IN THE LATE NINETEENTH CENTURY

A Case Study of the Westport Poor Law Union

Donnacha Seán Lucey

T RADITIONALLY THE Poor Law system in Ireland has evoked highly negative connotations and is largely associated with the Great Famine when Irish workhouses were scenes of widespread disease and death. Within Irish nationalist opinion the Irish Poor Law has also been regarded as a colonial imposition and a symbol of English domination.[1] Notwithstanding such long-standing opinions towards the Poor Law in Ireland, recent historiographical developments have provided a more nuanced interpretation of the system. Increasingly workhouses and poor relief have been placed within the context of issues relating to respectability, class and nationalism while an increased attempt to understand the social composition and characteristics of the large numbers in receipt of such relief has emerged.[2] Specific regional trends in poor relief distribution have also been identified. In relation to the west of Ireland, the Poor Law developed significantly differently than other regions in the country. Marked by poor agricultural land, much of the west, particularly along the seaboard, had high levels of poverty and was subject to a series of crippling economic crises throughout the latter half of the nineteenth century. In turn, the government introduced a number of emergency measures, often through the Poor Law system, to relieve the distress of large numbers of agricultural labourers and small farmers.[3] Developing on from this emerging historiography, this chapter concentrates on the emergence of workhouse infirmaries as general hospitals for the poor in the post-famine period. With 158 workhouses located countrywide, the Poor Law provided the most extensive form of institutional medical relief in Ireland. This chapter explores attempts by the central authority of the system, the Poor Law Commission, which after 1872 became the Local Government Board (LGB), to establish workhouse infirmaries as general hospitals for the poor and not just the destitute classes. In particular, it provides a case study of the Westport workhouse infirmary. Located on the western seaboard of county Mayo, Westport was a typical impoverished region in the west of Ireland. In examining the place of the workhouse within this overall delivery of medical relief in Westport, the chapter highlights how standards in institutional medical relief grew at a disproportionally slower rate than national trends due to the region's financial instability. Similar to much of the west, the general poverty of the region meant that local Poor Law Guardians were unable or unwilling to provide significant financial investment in such medical provision. Central government attempts to enforce a range of medical reforms in relation to conditions in workhouses and the controversial issue of 'pauper' nursing led to extensive debate and diverging opinions concerning the role of the state in healthcare provision, responsibilities of central and local government, and the place of the workhouse in providing medical relief.

In nineteenth-century Ireland hospitals were largely divided into voluntary hospitals, county infirmaries, workhouse infirmaries and fever hospitals. General voluntary hospitals were established in most cities such as Dr Steeven's Hospital in Dublin (1733) and the Cork North and South Charitable Infirmaries (1798). Many of the eighteenth-century institutions were established and managed by Protestant upper- and middle-class philanthropists while during the nineteenth century the rise of Catholic religious orders led to the establishment of Catholic-orientated voluntary hospitals, such as the Mercy Hospital in Cork

(1857) and the Mater Misericordiae (1861) in Dublin. Voluntary hospitals were independent from the state and were traditionally reliant on financing through charitable subscriptions, fees from trainee medical students and contributions from patients.[4] Although these institutions were established for the 'sick poor', certain restrictions were often in place which limited access. Voluntary hospitals in general subscribed to notions relating to respectability when granting medical assistance, and patients were regularly interviewed by hospital authorities to determine if they were appropriate candidates or 'deserving' recipients of charity.[5] These institutions, particularly the voluntary hospital network in Dublin, were prestigious, often closely associated with the medical profession and provided clinical training for medical students.[6] However, they were largely confined to urban areas and the province of Connacht did not witness the establishment of any voluntary hospitals. The west was omitted from this network and the region remained on the periphery of the leading developments in Irish hospital provision.

With no major voluntary hospitals in the west, county infirmaries were the only hospitals available for the general sick poor who wished to avoid the stigmatising Poor Law system. County infirmaries were funded out of a combination of philanthropy through subscriptions from the leading figures in local society and local taxation from the county cess and Grand Jury system. With its origins in the eighteenth century, by the mid-1800s thirty-nine infirmaries were in existence in Ireland, each one staffed by a surgeon and governed by a committee which was made up of the leading subscribers who also had a right to nominate poor persons for admission. The county surgeon was a prestigious local position that was keenly sought after and was accompanied by a large private practice ensuring a high calibre of physician.[7] Although those that could afford to pay for their own physicians generally received medical attention in their homes and hospitals were places to be avoided by the wealthier classes, the county infirmaries had a good reputation. In Connacht county infirmaries existed in the provincial towns of Castlebar, Roscommon, Carrick-on-Shannon and Sligo.[8] By the second half of the nineteenth century the Galway County Infirmary provided clinical training for medical students in Queen's College.[9]

Regardless of the good standing of county infirmaries in many communities, the system remained limited. The constraints of the system were highlighted during the 1861 parliamentary inquiry into the Irish Poor Laws. The chief commissioner of the Irish Poor Law, Alfred Power, informed the inquiry that the existing system of county infirmaries, which were mostly located in the leading town of each county, prohibited larger numbers from receiving assistance. He complained that at times 'sick persons... have to travel perhaps sixty or seventy miles to reach them,' and highlighted counties Mayo and Kerry, both with extensive western seaboards, as the worst cases.[10] Power was of the opinion that in many counties 'very nearly three-fourths of the area [of such counties] was almost deprived of the benefit of the county infirmaries, the remaining one-fourth having nearly the exclusive use of it'.[11] The Poor Law Commissioners also criticised the county infirmaries for the lack of any overall central control or uniformity in management.[12] Furthermore, access for patients to county infirmaries was limited and many had to receive support from the infirmaries' subscribers. Much like the prevailing culture of moral entitlement in voluntary hospitals, access was frequently restricted on grounds of respectability and medical relief was often confined to the 'deserving' poor.[13]

The overall focus of the inquiry concentrated on the opening up of workhouse hospitals to the general poor and the religious registration of abandoned children in workhouses.[14] A degree of state healthcare had already been introduced for the general poor with the introduction of the dispensary system in 1851 under the Medical Charities Act.[15] This represented a form of medical relief through a system of dispensary doctors who either saw patients in their homes or in dispensary houses. Although the dispensary system was administered by committees which were subsidiaries of Poor Law Boards, the system was not as stigmatising as the workhouse.[16] However, hospital relief for the ordinary poor was limited to the county infirmaries and voluntary hospitals. While all Irish workhouses had infirmary wards, these were originally only devised for the destitute classes. Those who entered the workhouse seeking medical relief were subject to what was referred to as the 'workhouse test'. Conditions in workhouses were intentionally harsh in order to deter all but the truly desperate and destitute from seeking relief. The workhouse diet was notoriously limited and inmates were subjected to regimented and disciplined regimes. Family groups were broken up on entry into various wards based on sex, age and health. Willingness to endure such conditions was seen as proof of need and in turn termed 'the workhouse test'.[17]

During the inquiry the Poor Law Commissioners argued that workhouse infirmaries should provide non-stigmatising medical relief to the wider poor and not just the destitute. The chief commissioner of the Irish Poor Law, Alfred Power, informed the 1861 inquiry that his 'object was to bring hospital accommodation within the reach of the sick in every portion of Ireland'.[18] The Poor Law Commissioners acknowledged the reluctance of land holders and able-bodied labourers to enter workhouses. Notwithstanding this, the commissioners believed 'that it is scarcely accountable that the other classes of infirm and destitute persons should hesitate to avail themselves of it'. They highlighted that while during the Great Famine workhouses were 'open to animadversion' they maintained that the experience of latter years 'should show intelligent men the great difference in management at the present day'.[19] Although workhouses no longer suffered from the overcrowding and high mortality rates witnessed during the Great Famine years, the commissioners recognised that the Poor Law remained highly unpopular but argued that this should not be so.

In the course of the 1861 inquiry, Power's objective of establishing workhouse infirmaries as general hospitals for the poor was the focus of much criticism. Concerns focused on the moral character of workhouse paupers and the potential degrading influences such inmates would bestow on the 'respectable poor' seeking medical relief. In giving evidence to the inquiry the Archbishop of Dublin, Dr Paul Cullen, complained of the failure to classify and divide inmates into moral categories on entry to workhouses. He believed that this led to the intermingling of paupers 'who are brought to poverty by drunkenness, or dissipation, or the practice of the worst vices' with others whose destitution was created by 'some misfortune, without any vice or crime of their own'. With the opening up of workhouse infirmaries as general hospitals for the poor, Cullen argued that such 'wicked persons' would 'corrupt others... and have a very bad influence upon morality'.[20] In essence, Cullen was alarmed about opening up workhouses to the 'deserving' poor who would be relieved side by side with inmates who were believed to be 'undeserving'.

Extensive concern was also expressed regarding the issue of nursing. Invariably the number of fully trained nurses was low, particularly in the smaller country workhouses where resources were limited. Able-bodied female paupers were often put into nursing positions in workhouse infirmary wards and received benefits such as extra rations in lieu of money. The role of these 'pauper' nurses in workhouse infirmaries was controversial, especially considering many of these female paupers were unmarried mothers and women who were seen as highly 'immoral'. Cardinal Cullen argued that such paupers were 'generally the most unfit persons in the world for their duties' who besides having no training for nursing the sick 'are often times people of low character... very commonly women who have had illegitimate children'.[21] He stated that it was 'a great degradation for respectable poor women to have nurses of that description put by their side' claiming that was 'one reason why poor people do not wish to go into the poorhouse hospitals... [and that] no respectable person will go in'.[22]

Cullen's criticisms, which extended to the whole Poor Law system, can be contextualised within the wider religious tensions of the 1860s and the antagonism of the Catholic hierarchy towards what they viewed as another tenet of the Protestant state.[23] However, concern about the issue of female paupers nursing 'respectable women' was also expressed by other figures during the inquiry. The members of the inquiry questioned Alfred Power as to whether it would be a 'great evil' to induce respectable married women into workhouses who would come into contact with unmarried 'immoral' mothers.[24] The nursing of the sick poor was the first profession which middle- and upper-class women entered in large numbers.[25] Such women were viewed as the feminine ideal and through good example 'a nurse of better moral character could be a transmitter of upper-class values of order and good living'.[26] The prospect of female workhouse paupers treating the general 'respectable poor' greatly undermined such notions of nursing which concentrated on professionalisation and the moral education of the poor. Much of the questioning challenged Power's perception that workhouse infirmaries would be readily accepted by the general poor.[27] Extensive concern was expressed of the potential intermingling of the 'respectable' and 'unrespectable' and the 'moral' and 'immoral' within workhouses. Such attitudes reflected wider mid to late Victorian attitudes towards poverty, class and gender.

While the debate on the issue highlighted a range of attitudes towards the poor, poverty and the role of the state; the Poor Law Commissioners succeeded in enacting legislation to extend workhouse infirmaries for the medical relief of the general poor under the 1862 Poor Law (Ireland) Amendment Act.[28] Other clauses allowed local Boards of Guardians to send patients to extern hospitals if the workhouse medical official did not have the necessary skills required for treatment.[29] Central government also assumed more financial responsibility for such medical relief and in 1867 an annual grant was introduced which met half the costs of the salaries of the workhouse medical official and the medicines dispensed by him.[30] This contrasted to the provision of ordinary relief either in the workhouse or in the form of outdoor relief where all costs of officials and provisions had to be fully met by the local Poor Law rates.

The introduction of medical relief, for not just the destitute, but the ordinary poor represented an important development in the ideology underpinning the Poor Law and the role of workhouses in welfare provision. It challenged the principles of *laissez faire* which were behind the initial introduction of the Poor Law. The principle of less eligibility, which was a central tenet of the English Poor Law and deemed that public relief should be a last resort – 'less eligible' to the recipient than the minimum subsistence they could obtain without – was never applied in Ireland.[31] Although it was recognised that it would be impossible to make conditions in Irish workhouses worse than those in the homes of the ordinary poor without serious risk to the health of inmates, workhouses remained punitive in an attempt to deter only the truly destitute from seeking relief.[32] The opening up of workhouse infirmaries to the wider poor in need of medical relief signalled the expansion of state welfare from providing deterrence and stigmatising provision to relieve destitution into a more comprehensive measure. This was driven out of late-Victorian beliefs that more efficient

treatment of the sick poor would return the labouring classes to produc-
tivity and thus relieve the rate burden.[33] However, the system remained
integrated with the Poor Law and closely associated with the relief of the
destitute. The indiscernible nature of ordinary and medical relief was demonstrated in the annual parliamentary returns of admissions to workhouses
and expenditure of Poor Law Unions which did not distinguish between
such provisions.

Case study of Westport Workhouse Infirmary

This remainder of the chapter concentrates on a case study of the Westport
workhouse and the development of its infirmary. Located in county Mayo,
Westport was a typical western Poor Law union. Established initially in
1840, the union covered a district of 175,508 acres, making it one of the
larger unions in the country (out of 158 unions in the country Westport
was the twenty-fifth largest). In 1871 the union had a population of
24,766.[34] A predominately rural region, the local agricultural economy
was marked by low output as a result of poor land and the multiplicty
small holdings, while the pre-famine characteristics of potato reliance and
subsistence living predominated. This small farm economy was maintained
by a number of other secondary economic activities, including seasonal
migratory labour to Britain, kelp making, sale of turf, remittances from
America, and credit from various sources such as shopkeepers.[35] The
subsistence nature of the agrarian economy, not only in Westport but
throughout the western seaboard, ensured that the region suffered extreme
distress throughout much of the late nineteenth century.[36] At a local level
the Poor Law was run by Boards of Guardians which were composed
of local landlords and the Catholic middle classes. During the Land War
period (1879-82) many of these boards, including Westport, came under
the control of local nationalists. The widespread economic distress of the
Land War years, the subsequent reaction of the government authorities and
the place of the Poor Law in providing relief, along with the politicisation
of the local Boards of Guardians, has been the focus of a degree of attention
by historians and will not form the basis of this article.[37]

After the introduction of the 1862 Act, the emergence of Westport infirmary as a general hospital acceptable to the poor appears to have been somewhat successful in the region. In 1865 an examination of the Westport workhouse infirmary by a committee of local Poor Law Guardians reported that the 'hospital [was] in excellent order'. Despite the Catholic hierarchy's opposition to the Poor Law demonstrated in the attitudes of Cardinal Cullen, the Roman Catholic clerics in Westport endorsed the hospital. The chaplain of the workhouse, Revd Patrick Cavanagh, informed the Board of Guardians that he, along with Archdeacon Browne, visited the sick poor in the infirmary. The chaplain reported that 'the poor were very clean and orderly and edified us by their piety and devotion in approaching the sacrament. The beds of the patients in the hospital were very neat and clean.'[38] Conditions in the infirmaries were generally better than in other wards of workhouses.

In the Westport workhouse complaints frequently arose from the nurse and medical officials about the conditions of inmates entering the infirmary from other wards in the workhouse. For example, in May 1890 the nurse in the hospital complained that an inmate was sent from the infirm ward 'in an awful state of dirt covered' and stated that 'all the men sent from the infirm ward to hospital were in the same state of filth'.[39] While conditions for those in receipt of ordinary indoor relief were intended to be punitive in accordance with the principles of deterrence which underpinned the Poor Law ideology, conditions within infirmaries had to be of a higher standard in order to provide medical relief for the general poor.

A system of payment by patients that could afford to pay for their maintenance was established. In turn, patients from a broader spectrum of rural society than previously turned to workhouses seeking medical assistance while contributing to their maintenance. During 1866 a seaman on a vessel docked in Westport was admitted to the workhouse hospital as a paying patient.[40] On another occasion in November 1871 a horse jobber from Loughrea whose leg was broken by a kick from a pony at the Westport fair was admitted as a contributing patient.[41] Guardians regularly sought payment from individuals or patients' next of kin if they believed they were in a position to financially contribute to the upkeep of their family member. Those unwilling to pay were met with legal action, such as in

June 1871 when inmate John Nolan refused to pay for the maintenance of his wife, resulting in the guardians initiating legal proceedings against him. Nolan, who was a servant to the local parish priest, finally conceded to the board and offered to pay 2s 6d per month for his wife's maintenance.[42] Within the Westport workhouse a demarcation was made between paying and non-paying patients and those that were willing to pay received separate accommodation from the body of the sick poor.[43] The emergence of paying patients was an important reversal of the relationship between the poor and the Poor Law, and highlighted how the system was no longer merely for the relief of the destitute. Notwithstanding this, the majority of patients in the Westport workhouse hospital were still considered too poor to pay for the medical assistance that they received. As late as 1895, out of a total of thirty-nine inmates in the hospital, a mere three were designated as paying patients.[44]

Another significant development in relation to healthcare was the provision that allowed guardians to send those in need of medical attention that the workhouse medical official couldn't provide to extern institutions. This included the sending of blind and deaf and dumb inmates to specialised institutions and also moving patients to extern hospitals. Local Boards of Guardians enacted this measure to provide institutional medical relief outside their region. In 1869 Poor Law Boards countrywide expended £6,695 on the maintenance of individuals in other institutions; by 1889 this had increased to £13,581.[45] In Westport, during one week in April 1894 a total of eight individuals were in outside institutions whose cost was met by the guardians. Of this number only one was in a hospital, while the other seven were in blind and deaf and dumb asylums.[46] Applications to guardians for access to such specialised treatment often required some support from local individuals of influence, such as priests and nuns. This was demonstrated in August 1892 when the Westport Guardians consented to sending an eleven-year-old child to the Cabra Institution for the Deaf and Dumb on the recommendation of the Sisters of Mercy in Westport. The guardians also agreed to pay the cost of the child's father's train fare to Dublin; 'he being to poor to defray the expense himself'.[47] While such representations by clerical representatives to the board often helped to influence the willingness of guardians to expend such money, recommendations of the workhouse medical officials also sufficed. For example, in August 1894, the guardians sent a patient to the Mater Misericordiae Hospital in Dublin to receive attention for a urinary disease on the advice of the medical official and paid for his travelling expenses and medical costs.[48] Individuals could make representations themselves to the guardians to achieve such medical care, as was the case in November 1889 when during a meeting of the guardians an applicant named Denis Phelan was considered a most 'deserving case' and granted £2 to attend the Mater in Dublin.[49] Undoubtedly those that were granted assistance to receive medical attention outside of the union ascribed to the moralistic standards of the various respectable authorities including the clergy, doctors and the guardians themselves. The Poor Law at a local level also became intertwined in a wider network of medical care for the poor. In Westport patients and inmates that were deemed dangerous were frequently sent to the lunatic asylum in Castlebar.[50] Similarly, children in the town's industrial school who fell ill received medical attention in the workhouse infirmary.[51]

All these factors were important developments in the role of the Poor Law in providing medical relief. The emergence of paying patients represented a significant ideological break from the deterrence-based system and a sign that the remit had extended beyond the destitute. The provision of allowing patients to receive medical attention in institutions outside of the Poor Law indicated an important development in what can be referred to as the 'mixed economy of healthcare'. Patients were regularly sent by Boards of Guardians to hospitals outside of the Poor Law system, many of which were voluntary institutions run by religious orders. This allowed for the sick poor to receive specialised medical attention that was beyond the skill of workhouse medical officials. These developments altered the role of the Poor Law in local society and greatly blurred the boundaries of poor relief, helping to reduce the perceptions of pauperism. The more workhouses were seen as institutions for the sick, the more the stigmatisation of the Poor Law was diluted. The workhouse and Poor Law were increasingly important aspects of a wider network of welfare provision for the poor which involved other types of state-aided institution such as lunatic asylums and industrial schools.

The 1862 Act and the 1867 Act led to substantial reform in the role of workhouse infirmaries and the system of financing. The diversification of the financial base of the system was brought about by the introduction of paying patients and government grants to meet half the cost of the infirmaries' medical officer and medicines. Although such central government funding represented the undertaking of a greater responsibility from the state, the system was still largely reliant on the willingness and ability of guardians to raise finance, either through the rates or loans, to develop local Poor Law services. Such commitments from Boards of Guardians were central to the raising of the standard of care and conditions in workhouse infirmaries. The infrastructural development of buildings, the number of paid nurses and quality of provisions such as clothing, bedding and food all rested with the amount raised from local rates. The lack of government grants for improvements ensured that conditions within workhouses differed by union and by region. This was very evident in the west of Ireland whose economy for most of the latter part of nineteenth century was marked by cyclical economic depressions. In 1880, 1886, 1890-1, 1895 and 1898 central government introduced emergency measures to meet such periods of distress. These measures largely consisted of the extension of outdoor relief to the able-bodied, the opening up of relief works and the granting of loans for seed potatoes.[52]

The detrimental effect of such loans for the emergency relief of distress on the poorest western unions' finances was excessive. Under the Seed Supply Act of 1880, £598,306 was given in loans to Boards of Guardians to distribute seeds to small farmers and labourers whose crops had failed.[53] Although the initial intention was for the money to be repaid within two years, for the remainder of the decade local Poor Law Boards in the west struggled to collect the loans from small farmers and labourers. The difficulty repaying these loans presented to boards in impoverished districts, and the extra relief provided to help tackle subsequent periods of distress, ensured that Poor Law Unions in the west were under constant financial strain with few resources available for the development of other local services. The contrasting financial situation between Poor Law Unions in the west and in many

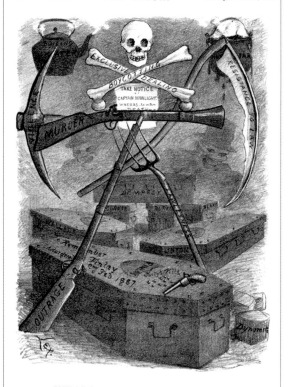

WEAPONS FROM WOODFORD.
To the Electors of Deptford.
VOTE FOR BLUNT, BOYCOTTING, and BLOODSHED.

1 The eviction of tenant leader, Francis 'Doc' Tully on the Clanricarde estate at Woodford in south east Galway during the Plan of Campaign in 1886. (L_Roy_02482, NLI)

2 Pro-landlord propaganda supporting the Marquis Clanricarde's campaign of evictions during the Plan of Campaign in Galway: English MP Wilfrid Scawen Blunt was a prominent supporter of the tenants and visited south Galway. (The Union, March 1888, 3A, NLI)

3 'Praise the Lord for here the tyrant's arm was paralyzed …' An effigy of landlord, Colonel John O'Callaghan, at a tenants meeting organised to resist evictions at Bodyke, county Clare, 1887. (EB_2665, NLI)

MEN OF CLARE!

The Lord of Inchiquin, lineal descendant of Murrough the Burner, and principal exponent of Toryism in Clare, is on the War-path again.

Once more he is bent on making way for the Bullock and the Sheep walk, and in his cruel eviction of James Sheehan from his farm in Ballygreen, thereby taking away his means of livelihood without giving him any fair chance of settling, he plainly shews what he & all his class will try and do when they think the people are weakened by division.

The last time he put the Battering-ram to work the people quickly let him see that the motto "LAUV LAUDER ENUCHTAR" belonged to them, not to any Landlord.

Again shew your power! Shew what the people united in their own interest can do: BOYCOTT SHEEHAN'S FARM IN BALLYGREEN.

Avoid those who will attempt to meddle wit it.

☞ WHAT IS SHEEHAN'S CASE TO-DAY, MAY BE YOURS ON TO-MORROW

GOD SAVE IRELAND.

4 A threatening notice warning farmers not to take the land of James Sheehan, evicted from his farm on the Murrough O'Brien estate in county Clare, c. 1887. (MS 45,201/6, NLI)

5 A tenant family pose outside their makeshift hut after being evicted from their cabin near Glenbeigh, county Kerry in 1887. (EB_2659, NLI)

6 Evicted tenants pose outside their cabins at Coomasaharn, near Glenbeigh, county Kerry in 1887. The cabin on the right has been destroyed and their sparse furniture stacked outside. (EB_2657, NLI)

7 Farm workers on the Clonbrock estate at Ahascragh in east Galway in the late nineteenth century. (CLON 472, NLI)

8 An effigy of the notorious Judge William Keogh at Castlebar, county Mayo. The men holding the figure are probably local Fenians. (WYN_13, NLI)

9 A group of local people on Achill Island in county Mayo at the end of the nineteenth century. Both Michael Davitt and James Hack Tuke endeavoured to develop fishing infrastructure on the island. (L_CAB_04151, NLI)

10 Fishermen and their families tend to their nets on Achill Island. (L_IMP_1289, NLI)

11 A group of children pose for James Hack Tuke and his colleagues in Connemara. They are wearing their best clothes but many are barefoot. (Tuke_37, NLI)

12 A 'village' or clachan settlement in Connemara visited by James Hack Tuke at the end of the nineteenth century. (Tuke_5, NLI)

13 A delegation from the Congested Districts Board is greeted by the clergy and local people in south Connemara at the end of the nineteenth century. (CDB_94, NLI)

14 A busy fair day in Roscommon town at the end of the nineteenth century. Cattle, hens, hay and foodstuffs are amongst the items sold in front of the town jail. (L_Roy_07344, NLI)

15 The rocky road to Castlebar, county Mayo in the late nineteenth century. (L_ROY_06093, NLI)

16 A view of Castle Street in Castlebar, county Mayo: A characteristically narrow western street at the end of the nineteenth century. (L_ROY_06035, NLI)

other parts of the country was demonstrated in 1885 expenditure levels. As depicted in the Table 1.1, during 1885 over 31 per cent of total expenditure of the Westport Poor Law Union was taken up with repaying loans under the Seed Supply Acts while over 22.1 per cent of the Connacht provincial expenditure involved repayment of loans under the same Act. This greatly contrasted to the overall average for the country, which stood at 4.9 per cent, and in the other three provinces where repayments made up an extremely low percentage of overall expenditure.

Table 1.1: Expenditure on loan repayments under the Seed Supply Act, total expenditure and percentage of total of the Westport Poor Law Union, each province and in Ireland as a whole in 1885

	Seed Supply	Total Expend	Percentage of Total
Westport	£1,572	£5,039	31.2 per cent
Connaught	£40,725	£184,126	22.1 per cent
Ulster	£6,109	£262,899	2.3 per cent
Munster	£14,672	£442,210	3.3 per cent
Leinster	£3,304	£434,040	0.8 per cent
Ireland	£64,810	£1,323,275	4.9 per cent

Source: *Annual report of the Local Government Board for Ireland, being the fourteenth report*, p. 177, HC 1886 [C.4728] [C.4278-1], xxxii.1, 49.

The financial position of western Poor Law Unions again became precarious in 1886 after the introduction of a £20,000 grant to relieve distress for six western unions, including Westport. Despite the attempt to limit the cost of relief, over £36,000 was spent by the local guardians who were in turn forced by the government to repay £16,000, which further indebted the board.[54] The cycle of government loans to relieve the frequent outbreaks of distress greatly undermined the financial stability of western unions and the Mayo Poor Law Boards of Belmullet and Swinford were dissolved in October 1887 and February 1888 respectively, and the unions administered by vice-guardians.[55] In other western unions the ability of local Boards of Guardians to maintain and develop the workhouses and welfare services was extremely restricted. Attaining loans from central government bodies such as the Board of Works was an important source of finance for the development of local infrastructure. In 1896 a total of £71,901 was outstanding in loans from local Boards of Guardians who had received loans 'for improvements and additions to workhouse buildings'. Of this figure a mere £993 was owed by Connacht Poor Law Unions, indicating the failure of local guardians to raise finance to invest in the upgrading of workhouses.[56] In turn, workhouse infirmaries developed at a much slower pace in the west than in many other regions of the country where Boards of Guardians had greater ability to finance the raising of standards in workhouses.

With the constant cycle of depression and the introduction of relief measures retarding the finances of western unions, conditions within many workhouses greatly deteriorated. This was evident in the Westport workhouse where the medical officer of the infirmary, Dr Johnston, frequently complained of poor conditions to the guardians and the LGB. In September 1894 he drew attention to 'bedsteads of the old wooden pattern, the bedding for the most part of straw in coarse canvas bags' and called on the guardians to replace them with 'woven wire and hair mattresses'.[57] A number of months later, in July 1895, Johnston reported to the LGB that extensive repairs were badly needed. He stated:

> The light and ventilation of the wards are imperfect, the iron widow sashes
> fit badly, thereby admitting the wind and rain in wet and stormy weather.
> Hospital wards are imperfectly ceiled, earth closets are required for heat-
> ing purposes, surface drains require to be repaired and the under-ground
> ones which are made of masonry ought to be remade with earthenware
> pipes.[58]

After receiving the report from the workhouse's medical officer, the Local Government Board called on the guardians to make the changes. In early 1896 the Westport Board of Guardians estimated that the improvements outlined would amount to over £3,000. The guardians were cognisant

that 'workhouses were very much changed from what they were originally intended for' and that while previously in order to 'prevent abuse,
it was necessary that [workhouses] should not be made too comfortable',
the emergence of 'the idiots, the aged, the infirm and the sick' as the most
prominent groups in receipt of indoor relief 'render[ed] the proposed
improvement and consequent outlay necessary'.[59] However, the guardians
were apprehensive about committing the ratepayers' money. The board
resolved that 'the union is the poorest in the country and could never be
taxed to such an extent 'and to undertake the proposed changes 'would be
ruinous to the ratepayers of the union'.[60] The guardians further highlighted
the lack of central government investment, stating that 'the government
have never spent anything on repairing the house since it was built in
1841'.[61] Indeed, the guardians were unwilling to expend the ratepayers'
money on the workhouse, with the chairman of the board, P.J. Kelly, stating
that 'we are unable to maintain our [workhouse]. We must admit that and
the sooner the government take its maintenance off our hands the better.
Otherwise the walls will crumble down.'[62] The board's chairman went
on to state that he 'did not think there was a sane man in Westport [that]
would say that the guardians of Westport had the slightest idea of spending
£3,000 of the ratepayers' money upon this workhouse, no; nor £50'.[63] In
Westport, the guardians were unwilling to invest any substantial amount
of money on the local workhouse hospital and attempted to force central
government to fund such development. However, the necessary funds were
not forthcoming from the central body and the Local Government Board
failed to push the matter any further, ensuring that the Westport workhouse infirmary remained in an unsatisfactory state.

The precarious financial condition of the union also retarded other
developments in the infirmary. The issue of 'pauper' and untrained
nursing was long a controversial issue in workhouse infirmaries. The
emergence of religious orders as nurses in workhouses was an important
development in increasing the standard of care. The practice of employing nursing sisters was a cheap alternative for guardians and began in
1861 when nuns were controversially appointed in the Limerick workhouse hospital. By 1895 sixty-three Boards of Guardians had placed
their workhouse infirmaries in the care of nuns; by 1903 that number

had increased to eighty-four.[64] The role of sisters as workhouse nurses was expected not only to improve the welfare of the sick, but also to influence the poor's spiritual and moral behaviour.[65] Their presence in workhouse infirmaries brought a degree of respectability and heightened the reputation of hospitals in their care. This was demonstrated in 1897 when an American reporter wrote of the Tuam workhouse infirmary, that 'the poor people are most fortunate in having for nurses those, kind, gentle self-sacrificing Sisters of Mercy' whose presence was believed to have been 'an unmixed blessing to the poor'.[66] Notwithstanding this, a large number of workhouse infirmaries, including Westport, didn't appoint any nuns as nurses ensuring that workhouse medical provision remained the sole responsibility of the ordinary officials and guardians at a local level.

Without any involvement from the religious orders, the Westport workhouse infirmary was reliant on the medical officer, one paid nurse and a number of 'pauper' nurses, which in 1881 amounted to ten for the infirmary and two for the fever hospital, along with a number of pauper ward attendants.[67] Although some union workhouses had no paid and trained nurses, the single nurse in Westport for an infirmary which had a weekly average of fifty-five patients represented a limited commitment on the part of the guardians. For example, the Swinford workhouse infirmary, which had an average of fifty-seven patients in 1881, had two paid nurses, while the Mallow workhouse in county Cork, with an average of fifty-nine patients, employed three nurses.[68] The Killarney workhouse infirmary in county Kerry, which was significantly larger and catered for an average of 164 patients, had six paid and fully trained nurses.[69]

From the early 1890s attempts by the LGB to force local guardians to employ trained nurses emerged. In 1890 the LGB issued a circular informing guardians that 'every inducement ought to be held out to the [sick poor] to seek in the workhouse hospitals the daily medical supervision and treatment calculated to alleviate their sufferings and to hasten their restoration to health'. Referring to the expectations of the poor themselves, the board stated that 'the sick cannot be expected willingly to seek treatment in workhouse hospitals if they have not confidence in the qualifications and

efficiency of the nurses in charge'.[70] The issue of 'pauper' nursing continued to raise controversy when the leading medical publication, the *British
Medical Journal*, undertook a series of investigative reports on Irish workhouse infirmaries, which condemned poor conditions and the persistence
of 'pauper' nursing. The journal advocated widespread reform in Irish
workhouses. In an 1897 article entitled 'Nursing in Ireland', the *B.M.J.*
highlighted how in voluntary or 'charitable' hospitals patients received 'all
the care that medical skill combined with nursing can supply'. However,
Irish workhouse infirmaries were castigated as 'meagre, squalid, and sordid'
with over-worked medical officials and the journal highlighted the continued 'presence of "pauper" nursing'.[71] The report ascribed to widely held
beliefs concerning the character of such 'pauper' nurses, describing them
as 'the poor atoms of humanity which have drifted into the workhouse
because elsewhere they are failures'.[72] In 1897 the Local Government
Board took definite action and ordered the stopping of 'pauper' nursing in
workhouses.[73] The campaign for the introduction of professional nursing in
hospitals began in England in the 1860s and '70s as a result of an Anglican
social reform movement which spread to the Dublin voluntary sector in
the 1880s. While this resulted from the need for more qualified and trained
nurses to keep abreast with developing medical science, it was also brought
about by the wish to establish a middle- and upper-class, morally upstand-
ing type of nurse who could direct the lower class onto a more moral
path.[74]

In Westport the attempts by the LGB to force the guardians to employ
fully trained nurses was met with considerable resistance. When in 1892
the LGB called for the appointment of a fully trained nurse in the fever
hospital, the Westport guardians refused on the grounds that they had
'strong women inmates of the workhouse' who discharged such duties.[75] In
contrast to the wider characterisations of pauper females as 'immoral', the
local guardians presented such women in a positive light in an attempt to
avoid the extra cost of employing paid nurses. Such local defence of pauper
employees was not restricted to nursing arrangements but also to paupers
working as ward attendants. When it emerged that a blind inmate was an
attendant in the hospital, the LGB enquired into his position. The medical
officer reported that although blind the inmate was resident in the house

for forty years and was 'an intelligent man'.[76] The master defended the attendant at a Board of Guardians meeting, stating that despite his blindness 'if you gave the man a key he could take you all over the house'.[77]

The guardians finally conceded to the demands of the LGB concerning the issue of 'pauper' nursing and appointed a non-pauper, although untrained, female as a night nurse in the institution.[78] However, the LGB refused to sanction her appointment on the grounds that she was not properly qualified.[79] The insistence of the LGB on the hiring of a trained nurse greatly frustrated the local guardians and the chairman complained: 'when we had no one at all here they told us we have to pay someone, and now when we pay a person they say she must be trained, while we had some of the paupers doing duty there for twenty or thirty years'.[80] Another guardian criticised the medical profession, claiming that 'the medical officers are getting a good deal out of this union'.[81] At another meeting a guardian claimed that a fully trained night nurse was not needed but that 'strong farmers' daughters' would suffice.[82] Notwithstanding the resistance from the guardians, three paid trained nurses were finally appointed in late 1897.[83]

Conclusion

When initially introduced, workhouses primarily provided a form of punitive and deterrence-based relief and were largely designed for the 'undeserving' able-bodied poor. However, in the post-famine period the state increasingly took on a greater responsibility for the medical welfare of the general population. This was evident in the introduction of the Irish dispensary service in 1851 and the opening up of workhouse infirmaries as general hospitals for the poor. While the central government initiated this development, a large degree of concern was expressed about the suitability of workhouses for the non-destitute. Importantly, such debate was centrally tied to wider societal notions of the 'deserving' and 'undeserving' poor and the potential degrading of the 'respectable classes' in workhouses. Despite such criticisms, the Poor Law Commissioners' ambitions to establish workhouse infirmaries as general hospitals for the poor was introduced under the 1862 Act. The introduction of a number of measures including the removal of the 'workhouse test' to receive medical relief, a system of paying patients and the ability of guardians to send patients to extern hospitals blurred the punitive image of the workhouse system. Although workhouses remained unattractive to many, and the number of middle-class patients undoubtedly remained limited, the reforms did appear to make the workhouse a more viable option for the general sick poor. This was evident in the Westport example where conditions in the workhouse infirmary were considered to be of a higher standard than in the rest of the workhouse, and the infirmary and was condoned by the clergy in the area.

The level of central government investment in local infirmaries was limited and the development of Poor Law services remained in the hands of local guardians. In Westport and throughout the west of Ireland, cyclical economic depression greatly weakened the financial stability of local Poor Law Boards. Emergency measures introduced to meet subsequent distress antagonised prominent ratepayers, which limited the ability of local boards to increase the standard of care in western workhouses. In turn, tensions arose as the reforming central government attempted to force local authorities into increasing workhouse infirmary standards. The unwillingness of either local or central authorities to commit the necessary finance ensured that conditions within the Westport infirmary remained poor. The issue of 'pauper' nursing further highlighted diverging opinions between the central and local authorities of the Poor Law system. The LGB's attempts to end the 'evil' of pauper nursing were influenced by a wider Victorian reforming agenda, which was centrally tied to notions of respectability and the moral education of the poor, along with the need to increase medical standards. Locally, the guardians rejected much of these concerns and presented 'pauper' nurses in a positive light in an effort to avoid the cost of professional nursing staff. While workhouse infirmaries had emerged as the largest form of institutional medical relief available to general poor, the weak financial base of the west, along with the unwillingness of the central government to support its reforming agenda with expenditure, ensured that Poor Law infirmaries remained unattractive for many within Irish society.

7

'A CLASS QUITE DISTINCT'

The Western Herds and their Defence of their Working Conditions

John Cunningham

EARLY IN 1892, Roger Richards, an agricultural expert who had previously investigated working conditions of employees on English farms, visited the Poor Law Union of Loughrea, county Galway, on behalf of the Royal Commission on Labour. Most farm workers in the district, he found, were in a pitiable state – only fitfully-employed, mal-nourished, and living in tumbledown hovels. There was one grouping, however, that did not match this pattern, or indeed any pattern known to Richards, since it formed 'a class quite distinct from any employed in any of the English districts visited, neither shepherds nor bailiffs, and yet a com-pound of both.'[1] He elaborated as follows:

> They are generally paid by 'freedoms,' the freedom consisting of so many 'collops.' A collop, the right to keep at the expense of the employer, and run-ning among his cattle:- one cow and one calf, or one mare and one foal (up to November); or three yearling calves; or four ewes with lambs; or six dry sheep. The cash equivalent of a collop is generally given as £5 or £6 accord-ing to the quality of the land.[2]

The workers described in this excerpt were known as 'herds' and they worked on estates and large-scale pasture farms, looking after cattle and sheep. Reasonably well-recompensed and with a reputation for being skilled, their social status was high – unlike the generality of agricultural labourers. In the words of an informant interviewed for a folklore project, the herd 'looked after the gentleman's stock and… was next to the gentleman himself.'[3] Roger Richards reported that herds 'have certainly the reputation for keeping the best horses, as I was assured in the fair that all the "long-tailed" horses, i.e., the best, were those of herds.'[4] A more substantial indication of the difference in status (and in the capacity to provide adequate dowries), between herds and ordinary labourers was provided by Samuel Clark, who found in a Roscommon marriage register of 1864-1880, that 70 per cent of herds' daughters married farmers' sons, while only 8 per cent of labourers' daughters married into farming families.[5]

But if herds' status was high, it was not secure, for it came under threat from two distinct sources. Many of the grazier employers regarded freedoms as anachronistic and they wished to replace them with weekly wages. For the leagues of the tenant farmers (especially the United Irish League (UIL), established 1898), the grazing economy which gave herds their livelihoods was immoral because its origins were in earlier clearances, and it was anti-social both because it gave little employment and it deprived 'congested' farm families of land.[6] Alert to the challenges facing them, west of Ireland herds established representative bodies – leagues, associations, trade unions – to protect and advance their interests. Some of these bodies were exceptionally durable by comparison with other rural labour organisations of the nineteenth century.

This article will describe the singular conditions under which the herds were employed and rewarded, and trace the origins of their occupation. It will closely examine the efforts of west of Ireland herds to regulate and standardise their earnings while retaining the time-honoured employment customs from which they derived their relative independence and their status.

The evidence gathered by the commissioners on the agricultural labourer is rich in detail with regard to conditions of Irish herds in the early 1890s. Four commissioners reported on thirty Poor Law Unions, including Castlerea, county Roscommon; Loughrea, county Galway; Westport, county Mayo; Dromore West, county Sligo; and Ennistymon, county Clare. A comparison of circumstances in western unions with those elsewhere indicates that Galway and Roscommon were exceptional in the extent to which strict rules applied in respect of remuneration governing collops and other matters.

'Collop' (Irish: *colpthach*) was a term which was in widespread use. The most significant of the herds' freedoms, it was a qualitative rather than a quantitative measure of land, and it was one which was also used in the allocation of shares in commonage and mountain-grazing. But if collops were the most significant of the herds' freedoms, they were by no means the only ones. According to Richards, each herd in the Loughrea area was also entitled to a house and several acres of tillage ground, the prevailing rate being either three collops and two acres for the first hundred of grazing land superintended, or two acres and three collops. Moreover, 'according to his conscience or worth,' the herd was permitted to keep a few pigs and some poultry on his employer's land.[7]

Richards's fellow assistant commissioner, Arthur Wilson Fox, was simultaneously making similar discoveries about the conditions of herds in the Castlerea union of county Roscommon. Carrying out detailed assessments of the monetary value of the emoluments of five Castlerea herds, he found considerable variation in their value, but concluded that a standard methodology was employed in their calculation. The annual value of the freedoms enjoyed by the herd employed by Mr Kelly of Castlerea, who was responsible for 200 acres, were estimated at £45, comprising a house and three or four acres of tillage land, £12; grazing for two cows and two calves, £16; grazing and hay for mare and foal, £16; keep of geese and pigs, £5. The estimated incomes of the other four varied between £31 10s for the herd of Mr Young of Harristown for looking after 100 acres, to £71 16s for the O'Conor Don's herd who looked after 400 acres.[8] It should be borne in mind that these figures were based on information provided by employers, and that the monetary value of freedoms varied with livestock and crop prices. Moreover, they did not always represent the return on the labour of a single individual. As Mr Sandford of Castlerea acknowledged, his herd was assisted by an adult son, and 'if he had not his son's help, he would have to pay an assistant £10 a year and keep him'.[9]

Collops were by far the most valuable of the freedoms, and when one employer, Lord Ashtown, changed the system of payment for his herds, he continued to provide a house and several acres of tillage ground. Instead of collops and informal indulgences, he paid £1 a week, or £52 a year, which points towards the true value to employees of the established system. Indeed, in exercising their freedoms to the maximum, herds had numerous opportunities to generate extra income, as Wilson Fox was advised in Castlerea:

> One of Mr Flanagan's herds told him that in 1892 that he got £40 for pigs. They also keep geese and poultry. Many herds are paid extra for saving hay and for attending fairs. They grow potatoes and vegetables and they consume milk and butter the value of which is impossible to estimate... Herds sell their calves say (15 months) at prices varying from £6 to £9, according to the sort of cows they breed them from, and this will depend on the quality of the land in possession of the employers... They manage if possible to have their cows calving in early spring so as to have their calves to sell in May year. The price of a calf greatly depends on the feeding it gets. In addition to feeding calves, the herds feed pigs on their land. They also make and sell butter. They mix linseed with the skim milk for feeding purposes. The herds breed better foals than small farmers, having better mares.[10]

There were certain similarities between the conditions enjoyed by east Galway and Roscommon herds and those of their colleagues of other parts of the country. Payment in kind, in part at least, was common, especially in mountain areas where contact between herds and their employers was infrequent and close supervision impractical. In more accessible places, perquisites were frequently allowed as indicated by the following from Naas, county Kildare – 'in the case of herds, in addition to a house, fuel, potatoes and milk may be allowed' – and from Cashel, county Tipperary – 'the grass of a cow is sometimes given by large farmers to herds or other confidential labourers'.[11] Contracts varied widely, however, and it was only from Ennistymon that there were any indications of the existence of standardised principles governing herds' emoluments similar to those obtaining in Galway and Roscommon.[12]

To better understand the economic position of west of Ireland herds, some comparison with the means of other contemporaries will be useful. If there was a labourer, employed full-time by the O'Conor Don, who earned £22 8s 5d in 1892, he was exceptional both in having regular work and in having an uncommonly considerate employer. (Evidently, the O'Conor Don was the only agricultural employer in Roscommon who paid his regular labourers when they were ill.) Annual earnings of labourers in the same county were more usually in the range £15 to £17, according to Wilson Fox.[13] A herd on 200 acres (assisted by a son, or a servant) would have earned three times as much, giving him an income close to that of a fully-employed urban tradesman, a rank-and-file policeman, or a female teacher.[14] But herds were exposed to risks not faced by others, in that they might be held responsible for any damage to livestock in their care due to their own negligence. According to Roger C. Richards, they were liable to make good any losses arising from 'scab or grub in sheep, injury to cattle from an open drain, or anything obviously out of order'; according to the pithy saying of the country, they were responsible for damage due to the depredations of 'hogs, bogs, dogs or thieves'.[15]

If the mechanism used to calculate the entitlements of herds were remarkably uniform in Galway and Roscommon, but not so elsewhere, this fact requires explanation. First, however, it is necessary to examine the earlier history of this 'quite distinct' occupational group.

The system of remuneration and the working condition of the western herds were manifestly archaic, and indeed elements of them may be traced to ancient times. The value of the *colpthach* or collop was defined in Brehon law (although it altered somewhat over the centuries), and the herd's duties in respect of restitution were also defined.[16] That the conditions were well established by the eighteenth century is suggested by an entry of 1741 in the diary of a substantial farmer from near Ennis, county Clare, setting down the responsibilities of herd and employer in respect of fairs, fences, and saving hay on the one hand, and the provision of necessary supports and freedoms on the other:

1st [May 1741] Friday. I agreed with John Higgins as a herd. He is obliged to herd Carhubranagh, Lurgo, Knockfluck and that part of Feninah held by Andrew Flanagan if I do not set it. He is also to save the hay of the meadows at Carhubranagh, Feninah, and Lurgo, with only the help of 6 men. I am obliged to give him horses to turn home hay and also to make it into a reek. He is also to leave my bounds in the same condition he gets them and to go or send the cattle in his care to fair or market. He's to get Thomas Connor's sheaf and Teige Connell's and the sheaf of Thomas Connor's soil that was tilled by Thomas Haly and to have the freedom of five collops.[17]

Some eighty years later, in his survey of agriculture in county Galway prepared for the Royal Dublin Society, Hely Dutton reported that because herds in the grazing districts of the county were 'servants of some responsibility, they have commonly many indulgences... a house, small garden, some tillage ground, and grass for a heifer, and generally keeping for a brood mare.' However, the advantage that the herd derived from running his own stock with those of the employer was of benefit also to the employer, because 'no person would take a herd without his possessing some stock, as they are frequently the only security from neglect or some misdemeanour.' A contemporary of Hely Dutton's remarked also on the prosperity of west of Ireland herds: 'many of the herdsmen here are able to give their daughters, when married, twenty guineas, and a feather bed, although the cabins in which they reside are apparently wretched, and seem to contain nothing but dirt, lumber, and rags.'[18]

If such nuggets convey a general impression, there is a more substantial record of the condition of herds in pre-famine Ireland in testimony collected for the *Poor Inquiry* of 1836. The testimony was generated by the following question which was part of a questionnaire circulated by the commissioners: 'Upon what terms are herds usually hired in your parish?' More than 15,000 responses were received, and they came from all counties. If the majority were submitted by clergymen, Catholic and Protestant, a considerable number came from employers of herds, and some of these provided quite detailed information.[19]

An examination of the responses shows that conditions broadly similar to those later found by Richards and Wilson Fox, and those earlier described by Hely Dutton, were widespread in the 1830s, but they did not apply everywhere (See Table 1). Almost universal in the five counties of Connacht and in Clare, they were also widespread in the major grazing counties of Meath and Westmeath, and in other counties to the east of Connacht and Clare. In the dairying and tillage counties of the south, and in Ulster, with the exception of some mountain areas, such herding as took place was carried out by farm servants, by boys, or by old men not fit for heavier work, and it was poorly rewarded.[20]

In county Galway, however, even on barren Árainn where there were 'but two persons' employing herds, payment was almost always in freedoms.[21] That their value varied from one part of the county to another is indicated by the contrasting information provided by T.N. Bagot, of Kilcroan, near the Galway-Roscommon border – 'Herds have a house, two acres of land and grass for two cows, for taking care of the stock, &c., of a farm of 100 acres; and pretty much in that proportion for a larger farm,' – and by James Kirwan of Tuam – 'They generally get an acre of land and the grazing of a cow or horse for the care of 100 acres, and so on in proportion.'[22] Revd E. Mahon of Strokestown, county Roscommon suggested that the herd's consideration was less than it had been: 'Some get an acre of land, and the grass of a cow; some two acres and the grass of two cows; only half of what used to be given.' There were as many as forty herds in the parish of Baslisk, according to the parish priest, John O'Callaghan, and they each had one and a half or two acres of tillage, and the grazing of two or three cows.[23] Around Ahascragh, Ballinasloe, Revd Henry Hunt reported that herds generally got 'a free house, garden, and two or three acres of land and sometimes the grass of three collops (a collop means a cow or three calves, or three sheep), about £20 per annum, but he answers for losses from bog, dog, or thief'. Incidentally, variations of the latter phrase as an explanation of the herd's liabilities (mentioned above, and recorded within the past decade from an oral informant) appeared also in responses from Kildare, King's County and Meath.[24] For his part, the Bishop of Killala drew an idyllic pen picture of the lifestyle of his own herd:

> My herd I find here, he had served my predecessors more than 30 years; he has a cabin in repair by me; three acres of land for oats, potatoes and flax; permission to keep two cows on the demesne, and rear their young; he has no wages; the heads of the beasts and sheep fatted for my house are his; a present at Christmas as he deserves or wants.[25]

Table 1: Form of remuneration for herds in four Irish Counties, by parish, mid-1830s

	Freedoms Mainly	Wages & Prequisits	Good Wages	Labourer's/ Servant's Wage	Boys & Old Men	No Herds	Unclear
Galway (51)	82%	2%	4%	–	–	8%	4%
Kildare (33)	33%	28%	9%	18%	–	6%	6%
Cork (191)	3%	2%	1%	30%	15%	41%	8%
Down (120)	2%	1%	3%	5%	11%	75%	3%

Source: Interpretation of information provided to *Poor Inquiry*, 1836, Appendix C, pt. 1.

A remark of James McHale, parish priest of Robeen, Kilcommon, county Mayo, that herds were 'the most comfortable' among the lower orders in his parish was echoed by respondents throughout Connacht and Leinster, although Charles Kelly of Churchtown, county Westmeath qualified his comment by stating that they were also 'in general the greatest rogues'.[26] A statement from Robert Martin, a resident of the parish of Killanin and Kilcummin on the western side of Lough Corrib, shows that there were herds who were paid in 'freedoms' in rundale farming: 'Landholders of large farms pay herds, generally, by allowing pasture for so many head of cattle and some tillage land; and villages employ herds, and pay them in like manner.' Other early nineteenth-century sources confirm that this was not an isolated instance.[27]

Labourers, it should be pointed out, were only very rarely paid in freedoms in the 1830s. According to evidence from the same questionnaire, they were paid either cash wages or a notional daily amount which was set against conacre or farm rent.[28]

Pastoral farming was long-established as the predominant economic activity of east Connacht and north Leinster,[29] with Ballinasloe's October fair being the principal venue where store animals raised west of the Shannon were sold for fattening on the plains of Meath and places adjacent. Annual returns from the fair of Ballinasloe show that the trade was expanding at the time of the Poor Inquiry, and that it continued to expand during the following decade, providing employment for herds but reducing the space available for more labour-intensive agricultural activity.[30] In the post-famine period, economic and social conditions continued to favour grazing. There was demand for food from industrialising Britain, but due to competition from the United States after the repeal of the Corn Laws, meat was much more profitable than grain. With famine clearances and encumbered estates legislation facilitating the shift to pasture, cattle and sheep numbers doubled during the second half of the nineteenth century. The grazing element was reinforced by speculative newcomers: solvent middling farmers wishing to expand, as well as by shopkeepers and professionals seeking profitable investment opportunities. The newcomers typically rented farms of 100 acres and upwards, from year to year. Under the eleven-month system, the renter gained no tenancy rights, which suited landlords, as did the relative ease of extracting rent from a one large tenant grazier as opposed to a multiplicity of impecunious smallholders.[31]

Among the more successful of the *arriviste* graziers was Joseph Hardy, a small mill-owner at Killimor, county Galway, in the late 1830s, who 'commenced to take land for grazing,' by his own account, in 1846. His name was routinely mentioned in reports of fairs in the region – at the Ballinasloe fair of 1861, for example, he sold 170 two-year-old heifers – and he was renting 6,000 acres by 1880, 90 per cent of them in county Galway, from several owners, including Lords Dunsandle and Clonbrock. Although owning no land, he won admission to gentry society, living in the splendid

Dartfield House, near Kilrickle, serving as a Justice of the Peace, Poor Law Guardian, and Grand Juror, and becoming a leading light in the Ballinasloe Agricultural Show Society. A self-made moderniser and shrewd in business, Hardy nonetheless continued to pay his herds in the traditional way, in collops and tillage ground.[32]

During 1881-2, conflicts arose between herds and their employers in mid-Roscommon and east Galway which would have long-lasting consequences. This was a period of intense political commotion in Ireland, encompassing the banning of the Land League and the arrest of its leaders, the formation of the Ladies' Land League, the release of the imprisoned leaders and the publication of the terms of the 'Kilmainham Treaty', the Phoenix Park assassinations and the Crimes Act, the public declaration by Michael Davitt of his support for land nationalisation, and a strike by members of the Royal Irish Constabulary.[33]

That conflict involving herds broke out in east Connacht, and indeed was largely confined to this region, is not surprising if the occupational distribution is considered. (See Table 2) Almost one-fifth of Irish 'shepherds' – the census category in which were placed those styling themselves 'herds', 'herdsmen' or 'shepherds' – were to be found in an east Connacht region encompassing seven adjoining Poor Law Unions: Loughrea, Tuam, Mountbellew, Ballinasloe, Castlerea, Roscommon and Strokestown. Herds were present throughout this region in numbers sufficient for an *esprit de corps* to develop among them and to sustain their own associations. Another factor facilitating organisation was that traditional conditions of employment for herds survived in this region to a greater extent than elsewhere. The evidence suggests that herds' contracts in the great grazing zone of north Leinster were being 'modernised' even in the pre-famine period, and while there were instances there where remuneration was in freedoms, the consideration was usually in cash wages – though calculated in widely-varying ways. As Roger Richards observed of the Balrothery union in county Dublin, 'the greatest diversity is found in the payment of herds'.[34] There were grazing employers in Connacht who had changed from freedoms to cash, and others who wished to do so,[35] but western herds did not wish to be 'proletarianised' – with an associated loss in independence and in status – so when the Land War created the conditions for collective action, they acted to extend their freedoms and to retain their freedom.

Table 2: Distribution of shepherds, 1891, by province, by selected country, and by selected PLU

Connacht	Leinster	Munster	Ulster	Total
2594 (41 %)	2394 (38%)	884 (14%)	461 (7%)	6333

Galway	Roscommon	Mayo	Sligo	Meath
1221 (19%)	624 (10%)	529 (8%)	179 (3%)	776 (12%)

Loughrea	Ballinasloe	Mountbellew	Tuam	Castlerea	Roscommon	Strokestown
226 (3.5%)	169 (2.6%)	124 (2%)	216 (3.5%)	164 (2.5%)	176 (2.8%)	91 (1.5%)

Source: 1891 Census.

A Herds' Association was formed in Roscommon early in late 1881/early 1882, in a context of unrest among subaltern elements in the area. With

the Land League proclaimed since the previous October, there were efforts
to establish alternatives and successors, and a Labour League gave voice to
popular sentiment on a range of issues, just as cognate bodies were doing
in Leinster and Munster.[36] It was in this milieu that the Herds' Association
emerged into public view at a meeting of over 400 people on 2 March
1882, on the 'historic hill of Carn,' near Tulsk, a site that tradition associated with the O'Connor kings. In the choice of meeting place there was
an assertion of the nationalist and 'popular' credentials of the herds, and
this disposition was also evident in the tenor of the resolutions adopted.
Among them was one demanding the release of the nationalist prisoners and another insisting that the grazier employers support that same
demand.[37] At a subsequent meeting in Tulsk, at which there were representatives from throughout Roscommon, resolutions of a vocational character
were adopted (which were subsequently printed a on membership card),
serving notice on employers that members would withdraw their services from any employer who had not complied by 18 May with the herds'
demands for two acres, for the grazing of two cows, and for £10 per eighty
acres herded. The meeting further committed the association's members to
exclusively 'peaceful and legal means'.[38]

From the reported speeches, it is apparent that the Roscommon herds
were intent upon establishing a national organisation. The Tulsk branch, led
by seventy-five-year-old James Scott, was described as 'the central branch',
in line with the organisational model of the Land League and the Ladies'
Land League. Routine meetings were held at 'their rooms in Tulsk'. Despite
receiving national press coverage, notably in *The Nation*, the association
never extended far beyond county Roscommon, and the only affiliated
branch outside the county was in Ballymote, county Sligo. Representatives
from other places did attend particular meetings – from Moate, county
Westmeath, and from Lansborough, county Longford, and adjacent parishes in county Galway. More generally, Roscommon developments had a
considerable effect in Galway, as will be shown below.[39]

Alarmed, Roscommon employers also became organised. A meeting
held to form a Grazing Landholders' Association was advised of steps already
taken on behalf of 'flockmasters' by the Property Defence Association (a
'physical force organisation', in the words of London's *Times*, established

by leading Irish landlords in December 1880 to prosecute the Land War on behalf of their own class).[40] Seventy-one responses, evidently, had been received to advertisements in Scottish newspapers seeking replacement herds. A skirmishing fund was opened and those present acquiesced in a resolution denouncing the herds' combination as 'a moonlight society under a false name', and declaring their determination to put it down.[41]

At a herds' meeting in Ballintubber just after the strike deadline, it was announced that while eight employers had conceded the association's claim, a majority remained opposed to concession or compromise. Condemning the recent Phoenix Park assassinations, the herds passed a further resolution eschewing violent methods in prosecuting their own dispute. Evidently, they were more united than their employers, for a report of an ensuing meeting suggested that there were further defections from the graziers' camp. Strike action was taken on a few farms, sums were voted for the support of those involved, and in one instance, it was reported that labourers had walked out in sympathy with a striking herd.[42]

The herds' association's commitment to strictly legal methods was accepted neither by the employers nor by the authorities. For the employers, the association was a cat's-paw of the banned Land League, and the real objective of the strike was not to secure the outrageous increases sought but rather to bring an end to the grazing system itself.[43] Whether graziers genuinely believed this is unclear, but it was assuredly in their interest to represent the herds' association as an element of the general agrarian disorder.

The allegations that the herds' association was indeed a 'moonlight society' seemed confirmed when one of its leading members, William Gilhooly, faced serious charges in August, charges brought under the 'Crimes Act', passed in response to the Phoenix Park assassinations. Gilhooly's prominence is confirmed by the fact that he was called to the chair at the earliest reported 'monster meeting' in March, and at another in July.[44] John Neilan testified to having dismissed Gilhooly, who had worked for his family for several decades, and having him evicted from his cottage at Holywell in the parish of Kilbride, when he went on strike in May, despite being 'better paid than most herds'. It proved difficult, however, to get a replacement. Neilan recalled making a bargain with a man called Morgan 'at three times the ordinary salary,' but the man withdrew on receiving a threatening letter and on learning that 'the country people had gathered in hundreds' to build a new house near Holywell for the dismissed herd. Others initially interested declared themselves 'afraid of being shot'.

Three months passed before Patrick Mannion, a local small farmer described as 'very poor but very brave', took charge of the holding, having first inquired from Gilhooly whether he wished to return to his former employment. Neilan's second-hand account of the dismissed man's response was as follows: 'No, I will never herd a day for a man of his name; neither will any other man, for the man who would take it would be shot. The Herds' League have subscribed to a fund to pay for the shooting of any man who takes another man's place.'[45] Undeterred by this, and by a subsequent similar conversation, Mannion evidently fulfilled his responsibilities towards Neilan's animals until he was confronted by Gilhooly while repairing a stone wall. From that point, Mannion insisted upon police protection, and swore information against his predecessor, in whose coercive behaviour he also implicated James Scott of Tulsk. Allegations against Scott were withdrawn in the course of the subsequent trial, but Gilhooly was convicted of intimidation, and sentenced to six months with hard labour. An appeal was lodged, with legal fees borne by the Herds' Association.[46]

That a *de facto* curfew was imposed on herds and that tensions arose from that and from the Gilhooly prosecution is apparent from a resolution passed on the hill of Rathcroghan in September at a meeting attended by 'large contingents, including a very good sprinkling of the fair sex' from 'Ballintubber, Baslisk, Ballinagar, Ballymote, Kiltrustan, Ballybroughan, Kilglass, Cloonfinlough, Kilbride, Elphin, Mantua, Oran, Tulsk, Killyfin, Roscommon, Fuerty, Athleague, Rahera, Lanesborough and Tisaragh':

> That whereas our employers should hold us responsible for any accident
> that may occur through our negligence on their respective farms, we wish
> to point out that we will not in future hold ourselves responsible for
> anything that may happen to the flocks in our charge from an hour after
> sunset till sunrise, as some of our members have already been interfered

with by the constabulary and cautioned not to be caught out during that time.[47]

In the event, Gilhooly's appeal was unsuccessful. While he served his sentence in Mullingar, his family was supported by his comrade herds, who continued to deny that their association had a secret set of rules which permitted recourse to violence.[48] Notwithstanding the repeated denunciations of violence, Patrick Mannion continued to feel threatened. Reputedly an educated man, he must, nonetheless, have been surprised to find on the whitewashed walls of the cottage provided for him by Neilan, alongside 'a picture of a gun, a pistol and a revolver,' a message pencilled in Latin: *Jacobus Neilan, Jacobus Kilkelly* [the resident magistrate], *Jacobus Becketta, Patria Mannion: pro fidelibus defunctis.*[49]

Clearly, the efforts of the authorities to curb 'moonlighting' had consequences for the graziers, and those still holding out against the demands of their herds found it hard to recruit replacements. The vaunted 'Scotch herds' did not arrive, and eventually the employers as a body decided to concede their herds' demands in full. This occurred before March 1883, if an allusion at a herds' meeting at Fourmilehouse to the 'time of the settlement' is an indication. No other contemporary reference to the settlement was located, although there were concurrent allegations that some graziers were reneging on commitments given.[50] These problems were evidently resolved, for almost ten years later Wilson Fox reported that an agreement dating from 1883 was still observed, more or less, notwithstanding the dissolution of the Roscommon Herds' Association. Upon agreement being reached, he reported:

> The herds' league and the masters' defence fund immediately ceased to exist, and it is satisfactory to be able to say that any friction which existed at the time of the strike has long ago died away. A large employer of labour who took an active part in obtaining the settlement said to me, 'We are just as good friends as ever,' and a herd who belonged to the league said, 'Masters and men are very friendly now.'[51]

No references were discovered to any Herds' Association activity in Roscommon between 1883 and 1904. At this last date, a local paper reported on 'herds' agitation' in Castleplunkett, Ballinagare, Clashganny and Kilmurry, prompted by concern among herds about the prospects of those involved under the terms of the recent Wyndham Act.[52]

Herds in county Galway had followed with interest the fortunes of their comrades in Roscommon, and during May and June 1882 there was a series of meetings of herds at Killimor, Kilconnell, Loughrea and Bullaun. The mobilisations, the police discovered, were prompted by agitational material sent by James Scott of Tulsk. Because these events in the Loughrea area have been treated in detail elsewhere, a summary will suffice.[53]

At the Kilconnell meeting, veteran Patrick Connolly complained that freedoms were the same as when he started in his career. 'Artisans, mechanics, and labourers had their wages greatly increased in the last ten years,' he continued, 'but the shepherds of Ireland have made no progress; they receive the same miserable wages as their fathers.'[54] Preparations for a large meeting at Bullaun on 8 June 1882 alarmed employers, and one of them alerted the authorities to what was taking place. In terms very similar to those used by the Roscommon graziers, he advised that herds were 'for the most part content,' and that their movement was not what it seemed, that it in fact represented 'an attack on the grass farms of this county veiled in this manner'.[55]

If the Galway herds were influenced by proceedings in Roscommon, so were the graziers, for they quickly established a Galway Grazing Landholders' Association. Following Roscommon precedent further, the new association established a 'defence fund' and prepared to face down a strike – despatching its secretary to 'the North of Ireland' to arrange for the recruitment of substitute herds there, and ruling out any negotiations with herds' representatives.[56]

Joseph Hardy, at Dartfield, acted as recommended by his association when a representative of his own herds approached him for improved conditions. He dismissed the man, Thomas Broder, had him evicted from his house, and introduced 'scab' labour, provided by the graziers' association when his other herds went on strike in protest. As it transpired this was an ill-considered approach, and it would place at risk Hardy's lifetime's achievements in pastoral agriculture. The eviction, the introduction of 'emergencymen' from Armagh, the arrival of police reinforcements, was all too suggestive of the

'Land War' tactics of landlords to be accepted by the community. Moreover, Hardy was already notorious in Killimor for having evicted a herd's widow in the townland of Lurgan in 1880 – the house was subsequently burned by agrarian incendiaries.[57] Smaller graziers, consequently, felt pressurised to concede. At a Herds' Association meeting in Killimor, where Hardy's 'emergencymen' were bivouacked, a grazier announced that he was accepting the herds' terms. Others followed suit. Isolated, Hardy summoned herds' representatives to Dartfield, where he conceded the demands of three collops, two acres, and £10 for each 100 acres herded. He further agreed to have a new cottage built for each of his herdsmen.

Five years later, Hardy was in a reduced condition, grazing less than a third of his former acreage. He blamed his difficulties on the strike – that the settlement was 'most extravagant'; that the graziers agreed to continue paying in freedoms rather than in cash; that he personally 'had been obliged for years to have protection'. He continued to believe that the herds' agitation was fomented by the Land League, and that the strike of 1882 was organised for the benefit of the Land League: 'Everything proceeds from the Land League or National League – they have absorbed everything into them, and while the government allows them to exist, and doesn't put down its foot and stop it, you will never have things as they ought to be.'[58]

By the early 1890s, there are no indications that any of Richards's or Wilson Fox's informants believed that the Land League had fomented the herds' agitation of 1882. By that point, indeed, it was widely accepted that the objectives of tenant farmers and of herds were incompatible. How then did the notion of Land League influence over the herds gain such wide currency? Firstly, as has been pointed out above, graziers promoted this interpretation in order to secure more intensive policing of herd militancy. Secondly, the speeches of herds' leaders supported this interpretation. Conscious that the type of farming in which they were engaged was anathemised by elements of the agrarian movement, herds supported tenant farmers' demands and likened their own predicaments to those of farmers. In speaking the language of the Land League, it is not surprising that it was considered to be part of it. Finally, and most importantly, there was evidence from one part of the country of Land League manipulation of herds. In 1880, a year before the Roscommon and east Galway agitation,

Oughterard and adjacent branches of the Land League adopted resolutions demanding that herds 'give up herding so that the land might become waste... and the owners forced to divide it into small farms'. Fifteen 'outrages' against herds in north Connemara were recorded during 1880, the objective being to force those targeted to give up their herdings. While a 'Shepherds' Association' claimed responsibility for the attacks, the pattern of the violence would suggest that it was instigated on behalf of tenant farmers, rather than by the small number of herds in that district (there being six times as many herds in the Poor Law Unions of Loughrea and Ballinasloe as in the Poor Law Unions of Oughterard and Clifden).[59]

If the authorities were credulous in 1882 of assertions of Land League manipulation of the herds' associations, it was because when such a body had previously come to their attention, it had been transparently a Land League creation. The Roscommon and east Galway mobilisations, however, clearly had as their objective the winning of improved working conditions. Significantly, the terms agreed in 1882 were still observed in Galway ten years later, just as they were in Roscommon.[60]

Although suspicions of tenant farmer manipulation of the herds' movement were allayed, there remained in the official mind a belief that organised herds continued to achieve their objective through violence. A leading historian of rural labour, moreover, has accepted that theirs was among 'the most violent societies of the countryside'.[61] The calculated use of violence would explain the effectiveness of this rural labour body, but the evidence for it is arguably somewhat slender. In the first place, it seems certain that the most sustained violent episode attributed to herds – in Connemara in 1880 – was not perpetrated by herds at all but by militant advocates of the cause of tenant farmers. And even if one chooses not to accept at face value the repeated disavowals of violence by representatives of Galway and Roscommon herds, there is little enough to connect their associations with strategic violence. It is true that William Gilhooly was convicted of threatening strike-breaker Patrick Mannion, but the evidence against him was not that strong. Even if the alleged threats were made, the circumstances suggest that they reflected the anger of an individual rather than the *modus operandi* of an association. Certainly threats were made in the heat of battle, intimidatory meetings were held, and there were incidents of 'drumming' or 'rough music' outside the houses of notorious individuals but the evidence indicates nonetheless that moral suasion was far more important in the assertion of the herds' claims than any physical force.[62]

The disputes of 1882-3 were the only widespread herds' disputes although, unlike their Roscommon comrades, the herds of Galway remained organised during the following two decades. In May 1884, a great meeting of the county Galway Shepherds' Associations was held at Cappataggle to protest the dismissal and imminent eviction of Matthew McKeague by his employer, Mr Longworth. McKeague said that his difficulties began two years previously when he acted as a representative for the association: 'Because I attended meetings, the landlord is wreaking vengeance on me.'[63] During the following decade, there were other such indignation meetings at Killimor, Kiltormer, and Loughrea in response to individual grievances.[64]

By the early 1890s, the Galway association had divided into two, one headquartered in Loughrea, the other in Tuam. At a meeting of the latter in November 1891, James Pender of Kilrickle, a representative of Loughrea, reported that his association had 400 members. Encouraged by this information, those present agreed that: 'the Shepherds' Associations of Athenry, Milltown, Tuam, Dunmore, Kilconnell, Oranmore, and Claregalway... be amalgamated with the Loughrea branch and deposit funds in the Hibernian Bank'.[65] Insofar as it reveals that the Tuam Association – the St Patrick's Herdsmen Association – extended twenty miles east, twenty miles west, and ten miles north of its headquarters, the resolution is of interest. It was not acted upon, however, and, three years later, a similar resolution was discussed in Tuam. By then, St Patrick's was claiming 400 members itself. Evidently, it was in a strong financial position, for the authorities discovered it had £250 to its credit in the bank.[66]

Only in one of the other thirty unions investigated by the agricultural labourer commissioners was there any suggestion of an organisation of herds. This was in Ennistymon, county Clare, where herds received generous freedoms and where they had 'in recent times [i.e. in the early 1890s] entered into some form of combination which renders it now impossible for farmers to fill the places of any of them that it may have been found necessary for any reason to remove'. An intelligence report confirmed that there was an association 'to prevent interference with the interests of herdsmen' in the same district at that time, noting it had 'no connection' with the Galway movement.[67]

The St Patrick's Herdsmen Society carried out the useful service for future historians of providing the most comprehensive extant set of rules of any of the herds' associations. Published in a local newspaper in 1891, there were twenty rules in all providing for the conduct of the Association's internal affairs: for terms and conditions of employment, for herds' duties to their employers, for the friendly benefits payable to members in adversity, for the duties of members towards one another ('to assist each other at fairs and markets', to contribute five shillings each to the widow or family of a deceased member, to boycott any employer wrongfully dismissing a member).[68]

Arguably, the most important of the Tuam rules was the following: 'That none but a qualified herdsman be admitted as a member.' What constituted qualification was not defined, but the matter of eligibility was discussed at several meetings, so it is possible to discern what was intended. Only herds who had held their position for five years were admitted to membership at the founding of the association in Loughrea in 1882; a decade later it was a requirement that the prospective member should have been in position in 1882.[69] There was provision for succession rights, however, in the Tuam rules' facility for honorary membership for 'a son, a brother, or friend [i.e., relative; in-law] living with him on the farm'. Succession indeed was fought for, and there were several instances when the associations defended the right of the widow of a member to continue in occupancy – on the basis usually that she hired an assistant until a son was able to take over. For example, in a resolution adopted at a 'large and enthusiastic' meeting called to consider the removal of 'Widow Egan and her son' from a farm at Aggard, Craughwell, herds pledged to 'sustain young Egan on the land of his birth where his father worked for forty years'.[70] Generally, rights of tenure for herds were asserted on the same basis as those of tenant farmers, so while contracts of employment generally included a clause obliging the herd 'to give up possession of cottage by one month's notice,' the prevailing attitude was that no herd should be removed without grave reason.[71]

The attention to eligibility for membership arose from a desire to exclude potentially controversial individuals, who might place their association in conflict with tenant farmers' leagues. Thus, the Tuam rule prohibiting members from acting 'as bailiff, rent warmer, or caretaker, unless the land be conacred'. A key objective of herds was to have their position accepted in the community, notwithstanding the public opprobrium that surrounded grazing itself. Their associations, therefore, cheerfully endorsed the policies of the farmers' leagues, even to the extent of being critical of grazing itself on occasion. They certainly did not wish to have to protect members who offended against popular notions of propriety with regard to land, notions they themselves might have shared. While there were certainly herds who accepted unpopular and controversial responsibilities, herds' associations excluded such people, regarding them in the same light as unionised artisans regarded 'colts' or *gobáns*. Resolutions adopted at herds' meetings and statements in the local press confirmed the cultural orthodoxy of the members by reflecting the political language of the tenant movements. Dismissed herds, therefore, were 'evicted herds'; those who took on dismissed herds' responsibilities were 'herd grabbers'.[72]

But if the herds' associations adapted well to rural circumstance, they were highly conscious of the need to guard their own particular interests. A resolution adopted at a meeting in Bullaun marking the tenth anniversary of the association in that area stressed its independence, the legitimacy of its members' position, and its commitment to broader national and agrarian, as well as labour, causes: 'That working as an independent body for the past ten years, side by side with the tenant farmers, labourers and mechanics who desire a native parliament, we claim an honest recognition by the Irish Parliamentary Party.' Several other rural labour bodies that had emerged at the same time as the herds' association had been absorbed by the tenant-dominated nationalist movement and had their own particular agendas ignored.[73]

Two years later, at Bullaun, the recognition demanded was given when two nationalist land-warrior MPs, John Roche of east Galway, and David Sheehy of south Galway, were 'the first MPs ever to stand on a platform of the Shepherds' Association'. Impressed by this achievement of their 'South Galway brethren,' the Tuam herds resolved to invite their own MP, Colonel Nolan, to attend a demonstration.[74] Police reports during the following years confirmed the continuing existence of a herds' association,[75] attributing its relative quiescence to the fact that the 'principles for which it was formed have not hitherto been seriously meddled with'.[76]

Renewed activity in 1899 was prompted by the emergence of the UIL. Just as its predecessor had done with labourers' organisations in 1882, it urged the herds to throw in their lot with it, but the herds were determined to remain independent. For the authorities, up to then concerned about the herds' movement, it now represented a 'certain antidote' to the redistributionist impulse of the new tenant movement, and in November 1900, a police officer predicted that a 'clash' between the two bodies was inevitable. This did not transpire. Rather, William Duffy, David Sheehy's successor as MP for south Galway, spoke at a meeting of herds at Kilrickle in the following month, urging them to join the UIL.[77] They did not do so immediately but there was cooperation between herds and the UIL in the Woodlawn area when Lord Ashtown replaced his own herds with Scotsmen.[78]

There was a final flurry of meetings of herdsmen in 1903-04, in response to the important Wyndham Act, which facilitated the transfer of land ownership from landlord to tenant, while making provision for certain estate workers. Both before and after the legislation was introduced, there were meetings in east Galway, in north Mayo, and in Roscommon, where demands were made that herds not be overlooked – that they be 'put on the same footing as tenant farmers'.[79] The absence of further reports suggests that the herds abandoned their own associations at that point, and that they began to assert their claims to share in the land reform through the UIL. The process was a difficult and protracted one, and local papers as well as police reports contain many accounts of attacks on herds, as the people of rural Ireland competed for scarce acres.[80] Generally, the victims of such attacks were individuals who were acting as rent warmers or bailiffs on controversial properties, rather than the more settled category of herds represented by herds' associations. In the grazing heartland of eastern Connacht, established herds successfully made the transition to farmer in the following decade or so. According to tradition, moreover, they did well as far as the allocation of land was concerned, generally getting 'a big farm out of the landlord's property,' in the words of one informant.[81] In their new role, herds continued to place their attested skills in veterinary matters and in the judging of animals at the disposal of their neighbours. Many of them (and their descendants), evidently, became noted breeders of cattle and sheep.[82]

The herds of Galway and Roscommon were remarkable in many respects. They were not the only rural workers who acted to maintain archaic working methods – harvesters in the south-east had smashed reaping machines and scythes fitted with 'cradles' in 1858 in a vain effort to protect the sickle from obsolescence[83] – but they were singularly unsuccessful in this regard. Indeed, not only did they keep their collops and their freedoms but through sustained organisation and collective action, they were able to standardise and to considerably improve their value. Their associations were also able to protect individual members from victimisation by employers. In both respects they were unusual among Irish rural trade unions in the nineteenth century, which were characteristically 'spontaneous, fragile and ephemeral'.[84] The herds' success was clearly attributable to their capacity to organise, but why were herds, especially those in county Galway, better at maintaining their organisations than almost all other rural workers? The main reason was that their bargaining position was much better than that of ordinary labourers, so there were clear benefits to be derived from organisation. Herds were unusually skilled, and could not be easily replaced, and in this respect they benefitted from solidarity in rural Ireland, among one another most importantly, but also from small and middling farmers. It was by no means inevitable that herds should have had the sympathy of tenant farmers, for, given their position in the rural economy, they might have been pushed into the landlord/grazier camp in the course of the Land War. Their associations were careful therefore to ensure that the membership was restricted to those conforming with the 'unwritten law' of the countryside. At the same time, and unlike most other rural bodies, they remained independent of the tenant farmers' leagues until the 1903 Land Act meant that this was no longer expedient. In terms of organising themselves, herds also benefited from a confidence that came with status and from routinely exercising responsibility in their employment. Moreover, by comparison with rural labourers, herds' working conditions and relatively high living standards facilitated an organisational culture among them. They could come and go without getting permission from an employer, and most of them owned a horse to take them to and from meetings.

8

'OUR DESTITUTE COUNTRYMEN ON THE WESTERN COAST'

Relief and Development Strategies in the Congested Districts in the 1880s and '90s

Carla King

The problem of poverty and the west of Ireland

THE WESTERN coastline was a byword for backwardness and poverty throughout the nineteenth and indeed much of the twentieth century. Nationalists in the early twentieth century, may have idealised it as the repository of all things authentically Irish, in terms of language, rugged lifestyle, clothing, and so on, but no one could get away from the fact that the west was plagued by recurrent famine and near-famine, typhus epidemics and misery. This chapter will discuss a transition in approach from sporadic efforts at famine relief in the face of specific crises to addressing the difficulties in a more structured way, to provide sustainable living for the people of the area; in other words – focussing on development rather than relief. This may seem an obvious step to us today, where the idea of 'development' is ubiquitous but in the nineteenth century it was a very new concept. The prevailing wisdom envisaged remedies in terms of the market or charity; it was not seen as the role of government to get involved in encouraging sectors or areas of the economy, at least in these islands, although already the French government under the Third

Republic from the 1870s was busy setting up professors of agriculture in every department and agricultural colleges to help modernise its farming.[1]

The problems of the coastal counties of the west were largely structural. Farms were too small and land too poor to yield a rent and yet the population was relatively high and in the absence of other sources of income, tenants were in sharp competition for land, and therefore ready to offer unrealistic levels of rent (which would have to be supplemented by income from migratory labour or indeed from emigrants' remittances to secure holdings). In the 1960s there was a debate about the extent to which the west was or was not commercialised in the nineteenth century, beginning with the publication of Patrick Lynch and John Vaizey's *History of Guinness's Brewery in the Irish Economy* (1960), in which they postulated a conceptual division of early nineteenth-century Ireland into two geographically and economically separate zones – a commercial zone in the east and a subsistence zone in the west.[2] This idea was challenged by J.J. Lee, who argued that the western subsistence zone was in fact penetrated by a cash economy.[3] It might be argued that the issue was always a little artificial and more a case of degree, because once tenants were paying rent in money the economy began to be commercialised and until Ó Gráda's article on 'Supply responsiveness in Irish agriculture' in 1975, there was no clear definition of what was meant by subsistence in the Irish context anyway.[4] Four years after the publication of Lynch and Vaizey's book, S.H. Cousins argued that even after the Great Famine, many parts of the west remained in a pre-famine state, in that they were still heavily dependent on potato cultivation with subdivision continuing.[5] The region was distant from markets, communications were very poor, landlords were largely absentees and there were no local industries that might have supplemented farm incomes. Nevertheless, Michael Cuddy and Chris Curtin who analysed the returns for sixteen Poor Law Unions in the Congested Districts Board's Baseline Reports for 1890 concluded that all farms except the very smallest in the 1-5 acre category were quite highly commercialised.[6] This may seem conclusive until one takes into account that the average holding in the congested districts was four acres.[7]

Nevertheless, if the economy was commercialising, the process was a difficult one and there was a great problem of rural indebtedness, as noted by the Richmond Commission in 1881.[8] Hence the emergence of that other great hate figure in Irish popular opinion, along with the landlord and his agent, the gombeen man – the rural moneylender, who, as Liam Kennedy has argued, if he charged high (some would argue extortionate) interest rates, played a part in modernising the economy.[9] There was still considerable seasonal migration from the poorer parts of the west for harvest work in England, by which a tenant might earn £8 or £10 to pay the rent.[10] Ó Gráda estimates numbers in 1880 to have been as high as 38,000, although they fell fairly steadily thereafter.[11] Reflected in the term 'congested districts' the perception was that these areas were over-populated and since the decades before the Great Famine, assistance when offered, was largely seen in terms of assisted emigration. Some philanthropic landlords, such as Robert Gore Booth and Lord Palmerston had provided assisted emigration schemes prior to the Great Famine[12] and in its aftermath this was the favoured approach.

Relief efforts in the 1870s and '80s

Attention turned to the west with the near famine of the late 1870s, a crisis in which the islands off the Galway and Mayo coast suffered most, owing to the collapse of the kelp industry coinciding with very adverse weather conditions and a recurrence of potato blight.[13] The Poor Law was insufficient to meet the crisis because the poorer unions were incapable of raising sufficient rates. In the event, the Local Government Board provided loans to the Poor Law Unions to purchase seed potatoes to distribute but these would have to be repaid. Four voluntary relief organisations stepped into the breach – the Mansion House Relief Committee, the Duchess of Marlborough Relief Committee, the New York Herald Relief Committee and the Land League.[14] There was lack of coordination and duplication of effort but these charities did manage to save lives. Some £2 million was spent during the crisis by these organisations, mainly in the west. However, apart from a donation of $100,000 from the Canadian government used to develop fishing and construct harbours, at this point there was relatively little thought given to long-term solutions to the problem. For example, the only suggestions the Mansion House Committee could make in their report on the distress was to alter the system under which each Poor Law union had to support their own poor (they didn't suggest how this might be achieved) and 'some redistribution of the population', whether by emigration or migration.[15] These remedies were reiterated by the Bessborough Commission of 1881 and the Cowper Commission of 1887.[16] Allen Warren has pointed out that in its response to this crisis Beaconsfield's government concentrated on 'the specific and distinctive features of the west of Ireland', laying down a pattern for all subsequent economic policy in relation to Ireland.[17]

One man who had a great influence on policies concerning the west was James Hack Tuke, a Quaker philanthropist and banker. He had first visited Ireland during the Great Famine, accompanying W.E. Forster on two tours of famine-stricken areas.[18] He remained in touch with Ireland and played an important part during the near-famine of 1880. At W.E. Forster's request (now Chief Secretary), Tuke spent two months in the west early in the year, distributing funds privately subscribed by Quakers. As his prescription for the problem, expressed in letters to *The Times*, articles in the journal *Nineteenth Century* and his pamphlet, *Irish Distress and its Remedies: A Visit to Donegal and Connaught, February, March and April 1880,* he urged land reform, promotion of local industries (particularly fishing), and the construction of light railways, all of which were later adopted by the Congested Districts Board. Tuke also strongly advocated state-funded family emigration to relieve congestion[19] and Forster included a clause to this effect in the 1881 Land Bill. When Forster's initiative failed, Tuke organised his own committee (commonly referred to as 'Mr Tuke's Fund') which by 1884 had assisted some 9,482 emigrants to travel to America and Canada. However, opposition from the Irish bishops and others to the policy of assisted emigration led to the closing down of the fund in June 1884.[20]

There has been a general tendency to perceive policy on land problems solely in terms of the nationalist struggle for peasant proprietorship versus policies of constructive unionism, such as those fostered by Arthur and Gerald Balfour and Horace Plunkett. Although this view bears much truth, it is an over-simplification. Some nationalist leaders did address wider development issues, whereas there was also a significant degree of interaction between the two sides and converging views of where the problems lay and even on how to address them. However, while most nationalists tended to see solutions in terms of Home Rule and peasant proprietorship, constructive unionists such as Tuke and Horace Plunkett emphasised economic solutions. In *The Condition of Donegal*, Tuke wrote:

> ...the evils which affect the people can alone be removed (if at all) by economic measures, and not by political changes, however wide their scope. Under whatever form of Government Ireland may in the future exist, these evils will perpetually confront it, and demand a recognition and solution.[21]

Despite efforts by the Prime Minister, W.E. Gladstone in 1881 to ameliorate the land situation, Ireland faced an economic downturn in the mid-1880s, brought about by a wider depression in agricultural prices. The crisis that overtook tenants on the western seaboard was far more severe than elsewhere, bringing the poorest once again to the brink of famine. The potato crop, on which much of the population was dependent for subsistence, failed. Moreover, the effect of the agricultural depression in Britain sharply depressed the availability of employment for migrant labourers.[22] Many tenants, who relied on this income to pay their rents, defaulted and faced eviction. News of serious destitution in the west began to emerge at the end of 1885, and the *Freeman's Journal* had already reported on the issue in a series of six articles entitled 'How things are in the west', published in November and December 1885.[23] Unfortunately, the articles appeared in the midst of election fever, even more prolonged in the 1880s than today, as the polling was extended over several weeks. In January 1886, Davitt, in receipt of letters describing the distress, wrote to the paper, suggesting that the urgency of the issue was being overlooked 'owing to the excitement over the Home Rule question' and advocating that steps should be taken immdiately 'to prevent starvation occurring through want of warning or neglect'.[24] Shortly afterwards he decided to see for himself, while privately suspicious that the priests of the area were exaggerating the difficulties.[25] He travelled on 22 January, braving harsh weather to reach the islands and what he saw convinced him of the gravity of the situation. From Westport he travelled by horse and car to Achill Sound, where he took a leaky ferry to Achill Island.

On his arrival, the jarvey was drunk and upset the car into a ditch, landing Davitt up to his knees in icy water. At last he reached his destination, the parochial house, where Revd Patrick O'Connor awaited his arrival.[26]

Davitt spent a week touring Achill, Clare Island, Inishturk and Inishboffin, compiling detailed notes of the homes he visited and the condition of the people, and finishing up with a visit to Westport workhouse.[27] This was an area of recurrent food shortage, and the situation in 1886 was desperate. He went from cabin to cabin, later observing '...The squalor and wretchedness of these huts it would be impossible to describe,' hearing accounts of shortage, witnessing half-starved, barefoot children and their anguished parents, and noting rent levels, which were high for the barren, boggy land.[28] The failure of the potato crop meant starvation not only for the human population but also for their livestock, as their fodder had been supplemented with potatoes. With little to feed them, it became impossible to sell stock. The people had eaten even the seed potatoes, which meant there was nothing left to sow in the coming season. The local shopkeepers could no longer obtain supplies from the merchants in Westport as everyone, tenants and grocers, was now in debt.

On 28 January the *Freeman's Journal* published an article entitled 'The Distress in Achill', in which Davitt described what he had seen and predicted trouble in the months ahead, the paper's editorial calling on the government to intervene in the crisis.[29] Further reports from Davitt appeared in the paper on 1-4 February, detailing conditions in the western islands.[30] He followed this up, on his return from a lecture tour in Wales, with an open letter to the Liberal Chief Secretary, John Morley, drawing his attention to distress in Achill, Inishturk, Inishboffin and the Aran Islands, calling for the government to extent 'some kind of relief to prevent starvation during the next five months,' and in particular, the provision of healthy seed potatoes to the next season's planting.[31] The situation on Achill was taken up by nationalist MPs in the House of Commons on 8 March, in questions to the Chief Secretary. Morley's response was reassuring: 'My attention was called to this subject at the first moment of my taking office, and I lost no time in consulting the authorities in reference to it.'[32] He had contacted James Hack Tuke, who undertook to organise the delivery of seed potatoes to the area. Tuke and the local clergy were to report to the Chief Secretary on the situation by the end of that week and the Local Government Board made its own recommendations.[33] Tuke visited Achill in March, discovering, as had Davitt two months earlier, scenes of desperate poverty[34] for which he raised a relief fund of over £5,000 and supervised the purchase and distribution of seed potatoes along the west coast, publishing his recommendations in *Achill and West of Ireland: Report of the Distribution of the Seed Potato Fund* (1886) and in letters to *The Times*, published collectively in *The Condition of Donegal* (1889).[35] Assistance was also forthcoming from Irish-America. Letters from Davitt describing the distress in the west were published in Patrick Ford's *Irish World*, appeals in the paper over the following year elicited over $12,000.[36] There were also subscriptions in response to Davitt's appeals from Britain and Ireland – he received the sum of £3,852 from this source in the first seven months.[37] The funds collected were sent directly to Davitt, who distributed them over the next four years, generally through the priests of the area, whom he requested to write to the papers to acknowledge receipt of assistance.

Like many nationalists, Davitt was very uncomfortable about seeking temporary relief measures, as he believed that the only lasting solution would be provided by self-government. But such was the desperation of the situation he found in the west that he felt compelled to step in. Moreover, while other nationalist leaders did subscribe privately to the fund, the relief effort appears to have been mainly Davitt's with little support from the movement as a whole. As soon as possible, he looked to a longer-term project, and proposed that some of the money collected be put into providing larger boats for the fishermen of the region, in order to build up a fishing industry. He had noted the potential of the area on his visit to Achill:

> …if small breakwater could be built from Illenawnbeg [sic] to Sparrow Island, distance of about 400 yards, a splendid harbour of refuge for fishing boats would be constituted… Best fishing ground opposite this island. Stone on spot. Need not cost much.[38]

The currachs used by the fishermen of the islands were too light to use in heavy seas and Davitt hoped to build a large hooker for the Achill islanders to supplement one provided by Thomas Brady, the Inspector of Fisheries for the Aran Islands. More ambitiously, Davitt pointed out that if a small steamer could be purchased, it could tour the islands collecting fish from the local fishermen and bring them to Westport, for transport by train to the market in Dublin.

Eventually the administration stepped in: seed potatoes were provided and government relief works set up. On a return visit in June 1886, Davitt reported the situation greatly improved, although he noted with regret that the some of the works had been suspended owing to mismanagement by nationalist Boards of Guardians, providing work for their friends, rather than assistance to those in real need.[39] He was also dismayed by the fact that some of the clergy through whom the relief funds were disbursed had encouraged tenants to use them to pay rent arrears. In view of the recovery he urged that the relief fund be closed at the end of the month,[40] although the Western Islands Fishing Boat Fund continued in existence until 1893, when its remaining funds were disbursed.[41] J.J. Louden, a barrister and former Land League campaigner based in Westport, from whom Davitt sought advice on conditions in the area in the summer of 1886, wrote outlining the situation and pointing out the inter-relationship between agricultural problems, indebtedness and landlord–tenant issues:

Dear Davitt,

You ask me for my candid opinion on the present condition of things in the Westport Union. I shall give it to you. The pressure of distress is now over; but nearly the whole population stands on the brink of ruin. At present the people who were in receipt of relief have either new potatoes, money which they receive from England or funds from one source or another; but they will have little or nothing to meet their obligations in the fall. They are hopelessly insolvent. In the past they relied almost entirely on the price of their cattle to pay rent, taxes and shop debts. When the price of cattle was high they barely managed to make ends meet; but when, owing to American competition, the value of Irish cattle went down – as it did three years ago 10 per cent, two years ago 20 per cent, and last year 40 per cent, where it now remains – they began to go in debt until the spring of this year when credit was suddenly stopped. It was this sudden and unforeseen stoppage of credit,

brought about by the service in a huge scale of ejectment and civil bill processes on the part of the landlords... which necessitated on the part of the
Guardians the action which they found themselves compelled to pursue. The
people now have few cattle. The livestock in their possession would not pay
50 per cent of their shop debts (meal account) much less taxes and rent. The
landlords will commence the extermination of the tenants at the November
Sessions, and the winter will witness scenes as dreadful and as sad as those
which took place in '47. For remember – there is now no Land League to
protect the poor – Mr Parnell has taken good care of that...'[42]

Davitt retained a continuing interest in the development of the western
seaboard. In 1887, he and his wife, Mary Davitt, attended the opening
of a bridge linking Achill Island to the mainland named after him.[43]
He visited the Aran Islands with a journalist from the *New York Sun* early in
1888 following another potato failure and participated on an Aran Relief
Committee set up to provide immediate assistance to the area, the government eventually agreeing to provide more seed potatoes.[44] When on 14
June 1894 a hooker carrying harvesters from Achill sank, with the loss of
thirty-two young people, an appeal was raised for assistance to the bereaved
families and Davitt coordinated the investment in annuities for regular
assistance to those affected.[45] It is worth noting that there was a considerable degree of consensus among commentators over what solutions
they proposed regarding the west – building up fisheries, handicrafts and
improving communications among them, and in these they anticipated the
policies of the Congested Districts Board – although differences emerged
over issues of assisted emigration and land redistribution.

In early 1886, alongside the debate over Gladstone's first Home Rule
bill, came an exchange of views over solutions to the land question, to
which both Davitt and Tuke contributed. This was initiated by Sir Robert
Giffen, assistant secretary at the Board of Trade in an article in *The Statist*,
in which he proposed the purchase by the state of the land held by tenants in Ireland, which would be paid for in consols, and recouped from
the former tenants, through the projected Home Rule government.
In a response in *The Times*, Sir James Caird, an agricultural economist and
statistician, pointed out that in view of the agricultural depression about

five-sixths of Irish tenants were unable at that time to pay any economic rent at all.[46] Davitt welcomed Giffen's suggestion in a detailed response in *The Contemporary Review* but Tuke argued that ownership alone would not solve the issue of poverty. Pointing out that some 200,000 families existed in Ireland on holdings of an annual valuation of £4 or less, their conversion into smallholders would make little material difference to them:

> Should we not merely be face to face with 300,000 impoverished owners instead of 300,000 impoverished tenants? ... The disease which afflicts Ireland is no merely sentimental or political malady. Behind Mr Parnell, behind Mr Davitt, behind even Archbishop Croke, stands another figure – the gaunt form of Poverty. Truly wrote the wise man of old, 'The destruction of the poor is his poverty'.[47]

The Congested Districts Board

The decision to establish the Congested Districts Board has to be seen against the background of the Plan of Campaign and indeed, the Special Commission on Parnellism and Crime. Although relentless in his determination to crush the Plan of Campaign, in private the Chief Secretary, Arthur Balfour, recognised that this was insufficient in itself. He argued that the Irish question was not one but at least four questions and that the problems of constitutional reform, landholding, long-standing poverty and political agitators were all essentially independent of each other.[48] Andrew Gailey in his study of constructive unionism, *Ireland and the Death of Kindness*, has made a strong case for Balfour's policy as having been driven primarily by English, rather than Irish considerations, specifically, at keeping the Liberal Unionists loyal to their alliance with the Conservatives.[49] Nevertheless, while this may have played a major part in Balfour's thinking, he appears to have brought a thoroughness and determination to bear on the worst examples of regional poverty equal to that with which he harried the Plan of Campaign.[50] In this, he was influenced by the findings of the Cowper and Allport Commissions, established by Lord Salisbury in 1886. The former, tasked with investigating the workings of the 1881 Land

Act, emphasised, among other things, the need for concerted state action to address the problems of the west of Ireland because it was acknowledged that local political and financial resources were inadequate to the task. The second concentrated on public works in Ireland, and advocated greater state involvement in developing Ireland's economic infrastructure, including railways, facilities for deep-sea fishing, tramway construction and efforts to provide more labourers' housing.[51]

When the potatoes failed once more in the autumn of 1890, Balfour, after repeated denials in parliament that there was any threat of food shortage,[52] organised extensive public relief to the stricken areas and in October toured the affected regions. He came to the conclusion that only emigration and land purchase offered a permanent solution to the problems of the west. In 1889 he had written to his Under-Secretary, Joseph West-Ridgeway, recognising the intractable nature of the problem but uncertain as to how to deal with it:

> Without doubt the congested districts supply us with the most insoluble part of the Irish difficulty. In other parts of Ireland it would probably be enough to restore obedience to the law and to facilitate the acquisition of the freehold of their tenancies by the farmers – in the congested districts something more is required, and what that something more shall be is a most perplexing question. Railways, no doubt will produce some benefit, but the chief advantage I anticipate from them is that of providing employment in the districts through which they are constructed, and thus tiding over the interval which must elapse before any more permanent beneficial scheme can come into operation.[53]

Tuke's proposals had included the gradual establishment of peasant proprietorship by means of state-aided land purchase, the construction of light railways in remote districts and the fostering by the government of fishing and other local industries.[54] For the smallest and poorest tenants he urged a scheme of 'family emigration' under the auspices of a government department set up to coordinate and facilitate it.[55] As subsidiary proposals he advocated measures for the improvement of agriculture and the cleansing of houses.[56] All these projects were ultimately among those undertaken by the Congested Districts Board. However, Tuke's proposals

had envisaged only a series of separate government measures for dealing with the problem of congestion in the west. Balfour's legislation, on
the other hand, established one body with the responsibility of offering
'paternal assistance to districts which were too poor to help themselves,
acting as a very wealthy and benevolent landlord might act towards an
estate in which he found people sunk in great difficulties from which
they were quite incapable of extricating themselves'.[57] According to
Plunkett's diaries, Balfour's initial bill had been quite vague and he and
Tuke had amendments inserted as it was passing through the House, to
more clearly define the role of the new body. Both men were to serve
on the Congested Districts Board, Tuke travelling to Dublin for monthly
meetings until his death in 1895. Plunkett, a landlord by background
(third son of Lord Dunsany) was a dedicated reformer who had established the Irish agricultural co-operative movement and would be the
founder and first vice-president of the Department of Agriculture and
Technical Instruction (DATI).[58] Although a moderate unionist, he sought
common action with nationalists of all sides on economic reform and
sometimes achieved it. The Parnellites, John Redmond and T.P. Gill in
particular, were willing to participate in the co-operative movement and
on the Recess Committee, which pressed for the establishment of the
DATI.[59] Even Davitt, who deeply mistrusted Plunkett, was willing to col-
laborate with him on scheme to provide support by the CDB to a granite
quarrying venture at Blacksod Point in Belmullet in 1897.[60]

The Board, charged with the general development of an area and given a
grant of money and a wide definition of its duties, represented a significant
innovation in British administrative policy. By defining a region and delim-
iting it on a map, measures could be taken within it that departed from
laissez-faire policy on the grounds that the extreme conditions obtaining
there necessitated and excused them in the light of orthodox economics.
The people of the congested districts, it was argued, were so acutely disad-
vantaged that special assistance would be needed to raise them to the level
of the remainder of the country, at which time they would be treated like
the rest of the population. The precedent was followed up with the creation of the Scottish Congested Districts Board in 1897, the forerunner of
the Highlands and Islands Board.[61]

The definition of a congested district was one in which the rateable valuation divided by the number of inhabitants was less than thirty shillings. The original area defined as 'congested' included districts in counties Donegal, Leitrim, Sligo, Roscommon, Mayo, Galway, Kerry and west Cork. The 'congested districts' were less densely populated than the rest of the country, the term 'congested' reflecting the belief that the land was overpopulated in relation to its capacity to support its population. When its jurisdiction was further expanded under Birrell's Land Act in 1909, it comprised the whole of counties Donegal, Leitrim, Sligo, Roscommon, Mayo, Galway and Kerry and parts of counties Clare and Cork. The Board's committee, made up of the Chief Secretary, a land commissioner and five members appointed by the Chief Secretary, were given wide powers. On its staff was a secretary, an assistant secretary and outdoor staff which had risen to 84 people by 1912.[62]

The functions of the CDB as laid down in the Purchase of Land and Congested Districts Act allowed it to:

- purchase a tenant's interest in his holding
- aid emigration or migration of tenants
- provide seed potatoes or oats to tenants
- aid the fishing industry
- assist agriculture by 'encouraging and developing knowledge of practical and scientific agriculture and improvement of the breed of livestock and poultry'
- improve and develop 'weaving or spinning or any other industrial resources.

However, the Board soon came to exceed these functions and to add new ones unforeseen by the Act. Having established the condition of the eighty-four districts under its jurisdiction, in detailed surveys called the Base Line reports, the CDB went about introducing reforms. These were very wide ranging, including areas such as agricultural instruction, provision of improved breeds of livestock and poultry, fertiliser and higher grade seeds at reduced prices, grants to farmers to drain their land, etc. There were also efforts to build up the fishing industry by constructing piers, introducing larger boats, setting up curing stations, providing instructors, and even undertaking the purchase and resale of fish, guaranteeing a minimum price. It fostered domestic industries, such as knitting, weaving crocheting and lace-making, employing instructors and distributing orders for those trained to carry out in their homes.[63] Plunkett, who served on the industries sub-committee of the CDB, questioned the usefulness of fostering handicraft industries in the west, arguing that they might provide a supplementary source of income:

> But in conditions which are themselves at root uneconomic, and where the industries cannot become permanent and self-supporting, I have grave doubts as to the wisdom of regarding these industries as more than a temporary expedient. The great majority of those who conduct them regard them as a means of bettering their condition, not in Ireland, but in America, where, as far as I can learn, they seldom pursue the craft they have learned at home.[64]

Davitt had been involved in an effort initiated by Ada Yeates, a former member of the Ladies' Land League, in 1882, to assist the poverty-stricken people of Carraroe by training the women in handicrafts. He went on to found the Irish Woollen Manufacturing and Export Company but this folded in 1896. As Joanna Bourke has observed 'home industries were adopted because they conformed to the reformers' idealised image of the Irish rural community'.[65] They allowed women to work in the domestic environment and it was believed that the skills developed in lace-making, knitting etc., would transfer into making home life more comfortable and help to prevent emigration. In fact, for a whole range of reasons domestic handicraft production was never economically successful and as the Board itself recognised in 1905, the women tended to use the income from their produce to enable them to emigrate.[66] However, Ciara Breathnach argues that the CDB was never intended to be a capitalist institution intent on making a profit – its aim was more focused on raising living standards and improving overall social conditions.[67] The CDB also assisted two woollen factories established by the Sisters of Charity in Mayo and Roscommon, which provided regular waged employment to people of the area. The Board's reform efforts even reached to the level of individual homes with its Parish Committee Scheme, under which tidying up houses, removing dung-heaps from the front of houses, planting shelter belts of trees, and fruit and flower gardening were encouraged by grants and prizes. Plunkett, a dedicated member of the Board, nevertheless was frequently critical of its paternalistic approach and concerned that if measures were undertaken on behalf of the population by an outside body, it would evoke only their passive participation. He urged that they should be encouraged to organise themselves along co-operative lines and take more responsibility and initiative, an approach that tends to be favoured by development agencies today.[68]

Nevertheless, despite all the efforts of the Board, it could not prevent the recurrence of crisis and shortage, at least in the first decade of its existence. In 1898, despite a police report that rents had generally been paid in full in 1897,[69] a Special Commissioner of the *Daily Post* described scenes of misery around Westport, and William O'Brien, in a letter to the *Freeman's Journal*, pointed out cases of hardship and eviction in the same area, asking 'Is there any denying the fact that it is the very districts where the Congested Districts Board have been trying their minor experiments most actively for the last ten years that are at this moment in the direst state of destitution?'[70]

Some aspects of the initial plan for the CDB never worked. One example is assisted emigration. It had been envisaged that the Board would undertake state-funded assistance to emigrants. Horace Plunkett, a member of the committee, had been interested in the prospects for emigrants since he had spent his experience in Wyoming as a cattle rancher. In September 1891 he investigated the prospects for emigrants in the United States and Canada, interviewing both government officials and Irish settlers and returning with an optimistic report.[71] However, while he was conducting his investigation adverse newspaper reports appeared in the English and Canadian press alleging that he had gone to organise a huge scheme of Irish emigration on behalf of the British government and whole scheme was dropped.[72]

Another example of a provision that failed is the purchase of tenants' interest in their holdings if they were leaving the area, to facilitate the expansion of neighbouring holdings. However, the outgoing tenants invariably passed on the holding to other family members and were completely unwilling to sell their interest. This made the Board's intention of increasing the size of holdings impossible unless an alternative means was found of acquiring land. The CDB's solicitor, Sir George Fottrell (also secretary to the Land Commission) hit upon a solution by which the Land Commission might buy entire estates on behalf of the CDB, which would then rearrange them, redistribute any grazing land to tenants and sell the holdings to the tenants under the provisions of the Ashbourne Land Act. Thus began what was to become the most important function of the Board – the purchase and resale of estates – although it had not been foreseen in the act establishing the Board. Moreover, it called for a great deal more money than had been previously envisaged but under the Land Law (Ireland) Act, 1896 it was permitted to borrow from the Land Commission to purchase estates, which it would then rearrange, consolidating holdings, fencing and possibly draining the land and building new houses, after which the holdings would be sold to tenants.[73] The slow pace of this process often gave rise to frustration on the part of the tenants. Indeed, it could be argued that the existence of this opportunity – in the shape of the purchase and redistribution of land – played an important part (among others) in calling forth the United Irish League in 1898.

The United Irish League

William O'Brien did not initiate the protests against large graziers which first emerged at the end of 1895 in west Mayo and he was not involved in the first meetings but within six months he had become the coordinator of the new movement. He had been living in Westport since 1891 and in 1895 he retired from parliament as a result of being declared bankrupt, leaving him more time to devote to local issues. Graziers emerged with the switch from tillage to pasture in the post-famine decades, a grazier, who was frequently also a shopkeeper, held tracts of land on an eleven-month letting, often purchasing calves and young cattle from small farmers and reselling them to larger fatteners in the east, prior to their export to British markets. However, the land occupied by graziers, who could easily afford high rents to landlords, deprived their smallholding neighbours of land. Raymond Crotty has pointed out that insecurity of tenure was an inescapable effect of the orientation of Irish agriculture away from tillage and towards dry cattle and sheep production, which created a more fluid rental market in land.[74] The Land League had already drawn attention to the grazier issue and the need for land redistribution in the west.[75] However, the UIL revived the issue, linking the problem of distress to the issue of small farmers being squeezed out of the land market by graziers. Thus, in the inaugural meeting of the United Irish League in Westport on 23 January 1898 it was urged that:

> The most effective means of preventing the frequent cries of distress and famine in the so-called congested districts would be the breaking up of the large grazing ranches with which the district is cursed and the partition of them amongst the smallholders who were driven into the bogs and mountains.[76]

Davitt was invited by the Liberal Chief Secretary, John Morley, to serve on the CDB in 1892 but refused, probably owing to unwillingness among nationalists to accept government posts.[77] However, William O'Brien readily cooperated with the Board on several projects. He raised a fund of £500, much of it his own contribution, to purchase three boats for fishermen in Murrisk, in Clew Bay, to help them build up a fishing industry. He and the Archbishop of Tuam acted as joint guarantors to the Land Commission in the purchase of Clare Island to prevent the islanders from being evicted. He also proposed a project to build a road through the Doolough Pass to try to develop a tourist industry there.[78] O'Brien had been keen that the CDB be provided with compulsory powers to purchase land from graziers and landlords and was critical of the tardiness of the Board and in its early phase the United Irish League must be seen not only as a means of reuniting Irish nationalism, which had been divided into three warring factions since the Parnell split, but also of putting pressure on the CDB. In a speech in Westport at the inaugural meeting of the UIL Executive Council in January 1898, O'Brien asserted that the agitation against grabbers and graziers was designed to assist the work of the Board in land distribution. Claiming that the Congested Districts Board had money assigned to buy grass farms for division among small farmers, he alleged that the graziers were coming in and bidding up the price, urging that the people united would 'put the fear of God into the heart of the man, whoever he may be, that puts his own selfishness and greed before the interest of the community'.[79]

The anti-grazier focus of the UIL provided a new and potentially divisive issue for the nationalist movement. Whereas the Land League had managed to hold together a coalition of larger and smaller tenant farmers, and even agricultural labourers, in a campaign against landlords, the later movement, while it aimed to pressure owners of estates to sell, also targeted graziers who leased large tracts of land. But quite a few leaders of the Land League in the west, including James Daly and James J. Louden, were themselves graziers.[80] Moreover, many Catholic priests also held grazing land or would have had social or family links with graziers. Nevertheless, they gradually came around to support the UIL. Bishop O'Donnell of Raphoe, a member of the Congested Districts Board, and John Joseph Clancy, Bishop of Elphin, were important in turning the tide of opinion, and at a meeting in Tuam on 26 September 1899, the six Catholic bishops of Connacht[81] called upon Balfour to settle the province's problems by extending the powers of the CDB to purchase grazing land for the purpose of enlarging holdings in the most impoverished districts and to increase the range of the Board's activities throughout Connacht.[82] While no reference was made to the UIL, this request was in accordance with its policy. Indeed, many clergy supported the League to the extent of holding open branch meetings in chapel yards and committee meetings in sacristies.[83]

Initially, although Balfour had favoured including compulsory purchase powers in the Land Act of 1891 to be used against recalcitrant landowners,[84] the members of the CDB were divided over the issue. Plunkett favoured them and supported an unsuccessful bill sponsored by the Irish Parliamentary Party to that effect in 1898.[85] The new movement was launched in Westport in January 1898 and even before it was formally begun it was pressing for the compulsory expropriation of estates and large grazier farms and their redistribution among tenants. The Board was clearly worried that if it were seen to concede to such demands agitation would spread, and it issued a statement that no purchases would be carried out in areas where the UIL was active.[86] At first the UIL grew slowly – indeed in February 1898, the police described it as being confined to 'a very limited area', namely 'a small area about 10 miles square comprising the Parishes of Burrishoole, Kilmeena, Kilmaclasser and Islandeady'.[87] O'Brien had some difficulty in gaining support from the Irish parliamentary leaders, especially from his old colleague in the Plan of Campaign, now leader of the anti-Parnellites, John Dillon. Davitt, however, was willing to assist O'Brien, addressing meetings in Mayo and raising issues concerning the UIL in parliament.[88] In February 1899 he introduced a bill in the House to allow for compulsory purchase by the county boards to enable the enlargement of holdings.[89] When O'Brien was ill in late 1899 and early 1900, Davitt took over running the UIL. However, he left for the Boer War in April and after his return he and O'Brien quarrelled. O'Brien himself stepped back from the UIL from the middle of 1900 and the movement altered as it became a national one and emerged as a replacement for the Irish National League. However, this meant that to a large degree it lost some of its initial focus on the problems of the west. On the other hand, as Donald Jordan and Philip Bull have discussed, the United Irish League, following a pattern set by the Land League and Irish National League, established elements of a shadow state, most tangibly in the organisation of league courts to settle land disputes.[90] In Heather Laird's words, they 'attempted to fill a gap created by an official system of law which rarely sought and never attained the kind of widespread support that its successful administration required'.[91] By September 1898, O'Brien recorded that some graziers were signing requisitions to the Congested Districts Board asking them to take over their lands.[92] An example of how this worked is cited in the evidence of P.A. Meehan to the Royal Commission on Congestion. Explaining about a case in Garryglass, county Roscommon, he recounted that 300 acres of untenanted land was divided among four graziers who already held other land: 'A protest was made, and one surrendered all his allotment to the Estates Commissioners; and another had since done so, and it was hoped that the others would follow'. The transaction was carried out by the local branch of the United Irish League, who negotiated the sale through the Estates Commissioners, acting on behalf of the local small farmers.[93]

Support for the CDB came from all sides, despite frequent criticism over the tardiness of its procedure. In *The Fall of Feudalism in Ireland*, Davitt praised Balfour's action in establishing it:

Though opinions differ as to the amount of good done by this body, there can be no doubt that much benefit has been conferred by its labours upon several districts comprised within the area of its operations. It has purchased a few estates and carried out improvements upon the holdings before reselling them to the tenants. The Lord Dillon estate in Roscommon and Mayo counties was acquired (1898) in this way, and the marked improvement that is now seen (in 1903) in the homes and the tillage of the small tenants on this property bear strong testimony to the excellent results of the board's efforts. This result causes much regret that the powers and income of the board are not adequate to the carrying out of large schemes for acquiring Connaught grazing ranches on which to 'plant' tenants with larger holdings and better land than the great majority of the Western peasantry live upon at the present time.

The power exercised by the congested districts board is that of an enlightened state socialism, and the credit due to the initiation of the plan of operations, where its benevolent and practical work was most called for in Ireland, belongs to Mr Arthur Balfour.[94]

This is not to suggest that the work of the Board was uncontroversial or that there were not disputes among its members. Indeed, the membership of the Board displayed a careful balancing of interests which sometimes clashed and Horace Plunkett's diaries suggest heated exchanges.[95] Unfortunately, the papers of the Congested Districts Board, which were available in the 1980s, have since been closed to researchers for reasons best known to the administrators of the Land Commission.

Conclusion

To summarise, it has been argued here that the extreme conditions of the west forced new thinking about economic development in general, notably a move away from *laissez faire* approaches into the idea of a government board charged with economic reform on a regional basis. It is further argued that nationalist organisation and government policies need to be seen as much more interrelated than is often the case.

Perhaps inevitably the issue of development of the west became politicised – while both nationalists and the government sought to assist the population, and their ideas about what needed to be done were not greatly dissimilar, they found it almost impossible to work together. By the end of the nineteenth century there was a widespread consensus that the only real solution to western poverty was a policy of land redistribution that would have to come by reallocating land occupied by graziers. However, after the Ranch War (1904-8) the Irish Parliamentary Party's leadership discouraged a renewal of land agitation, believing it would hinder their efforts to obtain land legislation at Westminster. A further round of Land War broke out in the period 1918-23 but it achieved relatively little in terms of ameliorating the situation of small farmers and agricultural labourers.[96] Moreover, the question must be asked whether land redistribution alone would really have solved the question of economic underdevelopment. Both Plunkett and Henry Doran, a civil engineer and farmer employed as a surveyor by the CDB felt strongly that it would not. Plunkett recognised that peasant proprietorship would create an extremely immobile system which would inhibit good farming practices.[97] Eventually, with the termination of the CDB in 1923, their broader approach, which had been faltering anyway, was abandoned.

William Lawson Micks, Secretary of the Board throughout its existence, strongly defended its work in his evidence to the Royal Commission on Congestion and in his history of the CDB, published in 1925.[98] In 1908 he pointed out that Teelin in county Donegal was so improved since the Board began operations that people now had money to buy potatoes in case of crop failures and that the work of the Board had 'changed the whole face of the country' in the Teelin district.[99] However, he complained that the Board had always been short of funds and that by 1908, 'nineteen-twentieths of the Board's work was land purchase' but that the other twentieth part, what we would now term development work, should be enlarged, that it was the real work of the Board, with the land-purchase functions taken over by the Estates Commissioners.[100]

Catherine Shannon sought to assess the success of the CDB, suggesting that government expenditure on relief works fell dramatically. Whereas the government spent £565,014 on relief works in the twelve years before 1891, they laid out only £100,000 during the Board's existence. Moreover, the number of paupers in Connacht fell from one in fifty-four to one of every seventy-seven, while Post Office savings deposits saw a nine-fold increase between 1881 and 1912.[101] However, if there was a significant amelioration of a bad situation, it was not sustained growth, or anything like it. With the achievement of peasant propri-etorship came in Raymond Crotty's memorable phrase, 'a new era of stability, amounting, indeed to stagnation'.[102] In fact, the Post Office savings that Shannon refers to as an indicator of increased wealth also resulted from the fact that investment in agriculture was very low as the country – the west of Ireland included – settled into a pattern of cattle and some sheep farming, with low inputs and relatively low returns. This type of agriculture, which requires relatively little labour, largely accounts for the continued patterns of emigration from rural areas. Nevertheless, for those who remained, there was a marked improve-ment in living standards in the early decades of the twentieth century, but this was countrywide and not specific to the congested districts, so it is difficult to assess the contribution of the Congested Districts Board to the pattern in the west.[103]

For political reasons, the CDB's efforts to assist emigration had been abandoned, but this did not mean its cessation. Certainly the numbers emi-grating declined, from 15,468 leaving from Connacht in 1887, to 11,533 in 1902, a decade after the CDB's work had commenced. But this is in line with a general reduction in the numbers emigrating from Ireland. The numbers leaving from Connacht as a proportion of the total emigrat-ing from the country rose, from 20.4 per cent in 1887 to 28.5 per cent in 1902.[104] The point is that had a state agency been allowed to assist those who continued to emigrate, it might have made their lives a lot easier. The Congested Districts Board was closed down in 1923 but there was a near famine in Connemara in the mid-1920s. This would suggest, in the first place, that there was still a need for some kind of structured assistance and in the second, that the CDB's work had not been as successful in prevent-ing the recurrence of distress as had been hoped.

On the nationalist side, both the Land League and the United Irish League emerged out of attempts to grapple with land issues in the west, but in each case in developing into nationwide movements the issues of distress among small farmers and labourers from which they sprang eventually became submerged in wider political issues. In fact, neither the British government nor the Irish government that succeeded it (at least in the first four or five decades of its existence) ever really overcame the problem of underdevelopment in the west.

NOTES

Chapter 1

1 Mary E. Daly, *The Famine in Ireland* (Dublin, 1986), p. 1; For a local study of the famine of 1822, see Gerard MacAtasney, *The Other Famine: The 1822 Crisis in Leitrim* (Dublin, 2010).

2 Samuel Clark, *Social Origins of the Irish Land War* (New Jersey, 1979), p. 21.

3 For an overview of pre-Famine society during this period in Galway see, Richard McMahon, 'The Court of Petty Sessions and Society in Pre-Famine Galway' in Raymond Gillespie (ed.), *The Remaking of Modern Ireland 1750-1950: Beckett Prize Essays in Irish History* (Dublin, 2004), pp 101-31.

4 Joel Mokyr, *Why Ireland Starved: A Quantitative and Analytical History of the Irish Economy, 1800-1850* (London, 1985), p. 6.

5 *Ibid.*, pp 6-10.

6 K.H. Connell, *The Population of Ireland, 1750-1845* (Oxford, 1950), pp 144-6.

7 James S. Donnelly Jnr, *The Land and the People of Nineteenth Century Cork: The Rural Economy and the Land Question* (London, 1975), p. 17.

8 Cormac Ó Gráda, *Ireland: A New Economic History, 1780-1939* (Oxford, 1994), p. 16; Mokyr quoted in Ó Gráda, p. 98.

9   T.P. O'Neill, 'The 1822 Famine' (Unpublished, MA Thesis, UCD, 1965), p. 1.

10   John Cunningham, 'Compelled to their Bad Acts by Hunger: Three Irish Urban Crowds, 1817-1845' in *Éire-Ireland*, 45 (Spring/Summer 2010), pp 128-51.

11   *Select Committee on the State of Disease and Condition of the Labouring Poor in Ireland: Second Report, Minutes of Evidence and Appendix* [Reprint of 1819], p. 21, HC, 1829 (HC; 347), vol. iv, p. 451.

12   *Ibid.*, p. 97.

13   L.M. Cullen, *An Economic History of Ireland Since 1660* (London, 1987), p. 100.

14   For an overview of the commercialisation of the rural economy during this period, see Raymond D. Crotty, *Irish Agricultural Production, its Volume and Structure* (Cork, 1966), pp 35-46; Donnelly Jnr, *The Land and the People of Nineteenth Century Cork*, pp 9-73; Cormac Ó Gráda, *Ireland Before and After the Great Famine: Explorations in Economic History, 1800-1925* (Manchester, 1988), pp 1-35.

15   See Crotty, *Irish Agricultural Production, its Volume and Structure*, pp 35-46.

16   *Report of the Select Committee on the State of the Poor in Ireland being a Summary of the First, Second and Third Reports of Evidence Taken Before that Committee Together with an Appendix of Accounts and Papers*, pp 7-8, HC, 1830 (HC; 667), vol. vii, p. 1.

17   Connell, *The Population of Ireland, 1750-1845*, p. 15.

18   T.P. O'Neill, 'Rural Life' in R.B. McDowell (ed.), *Social Life in Ireland, 1800-45* (Cork, 1973), pp 40-52.

19   Figures listed in Table 1 for Cork, Galway and Limerick do not include the statistics for the urban areas of Limerick city, Cork city and Galway city.

20   Clark, *Social Origins of the Irish Land War*, p. 28.

21   *Roscommon and Leitrim Gazette*, 4 May 1822.

22   *Freeman's Journal*, 7 May 1822.

23   Mokyr, *Why Ireland Starved*, p. 24.

24   *Condition of the Labouring Poor in Ireland and Application of Funds for Their Employment: Report From the Select Committee on the Employment of the Poor in Ireland, Minutes of Evidence and Appendix*, p. 4. HC, 1823 (HC; 561), vol. vi, p. 331.

25   *Freeman's Journal*, 7 May 1822.

26 *Roscommon and Leitrim Gazette*, 4 May 1822.

27 *Connacht Journal*, 24 Mar. 1823.

28 *Roscommon and Leitrim Gazette*, 11 May 1822.

29 *Condition of the Labouring Poor in Ireland and Application of Funds for their Employment: Report from the Select Committee on the Employment of the Poor in Ireland, Minutes of Evidence and Appendix*, p. 5. HC, 1823 (HC; 561), vol. vi, p. 331.

30 Henry Comyns to Ross Mahon, correspondence dated 15 Nov. 1822 (NLI, Mahon Papers, MS 47,843/3-5).

31 *Freeman's Journal*, 26 Jun. 1822.

32 *Report of the Committee for the Relief of the Distressed Districts in Ireland, Appointed at a General Meeting Held at the City of London Tavern, on 7 May 1822* (London, 1823), p. 39.

33 *Freeman's Journal*, 1 Jul. 1822.

34 *Freeman's Journal*, 6 Jul. 1822.

35 *Freeman's Journal*, 13 Jun. 1822.

36 *Report of the Committee for the Relief of the Distressed Districts in Ireland*, pp 150, 348-52.

37 *Ibid.*, p. 161.

38 *Ibid.*, p. 162.

39 T.P. O'Neill, 'The 1822 Famine', pp 1-35.

40 *Employment of the Poor in Ireland: Copies of the Reports Made to the Irish Government by the Civil Engineers Employed During the Late Scarcity in Superintending the Public Works, Account of Appropriation of Sums Expended to Provide Employment for Irish Poor*, pp 28, 48, 76, HC, 1823 (HC; 249), vol. x, p. 437.

41 *Ibid.*, pp 44-6.

42 *Ibid.*, p. 44.

43 *Ibid.*, p. 4.

44 *Ibid.*, p. 5.

45 *Ibid.*, pp 44-8.

46 *Ibid.*, p. 53.

47 *Clare Journal and Ennis Advertiser*, 18 Apr. 1822.

48 *Limerick Chronicle*, 5 Jun. 1822.

49 *Hansard 2, i [etc.], HC Deb. 17 June 1822, vol. 7, cc.* 1123, *Mr. V. Fitzgerald.*

50 *Limerick Chronicle*, 5 Jun. 1822.

51 *Connacht Journal*, quoted in *Roscommon and Leitrim Gazette*, 25 May 1822.

52 *Connacht Journal*, 20 Mar. 1823.

53 *Connacht Journal*, 20 Mar. 1823.

54 *Hansard 2, i* [etc.], *HC Deb. 29 April 1822, vol. 7, cc.* 146, Sir E. O'Brien.

55 *Connacht Journal*, 3 Feb. 1823.

56 *Connacht Journal*, 24 Mar. 1823.

57 *Connacht Journal*, 24 Mar. 1823.

58 *Connacht Journal*, 10 Apr. 1823.

59 *Clare Journal and Ennis Advertiser*, 18 Apr. 1822.

60 *Clare Journal and Ennis Advertiser*, 25 Apr. 1822.

61 *Clare Journal and Ennis Advertiser*, 2 May 1822.

62 *Limerick Chronicle*, 19 Jun. 1822.

63 *Limerick Chronicle*, 5 Jun. 1822.

64 *Limerick Chronicle*, 19 Jun. 1822.

65 *Limerick Chronicle*, 19 Jun. 1822.

66 *Limerick Chronicle*, 13 Jul. 1822.

67 *Limerick Chronicle*, 27 Jul. 1822.

68 Virginia Crossman, *Politics, Pauperism and Power in Later Nineteenth Century Ireland* (Manchester, 2006), p. 7.

69 *Roscommon and Leitrim Gazette*, 25 May 1822.

70 *Roscommon and Leitrim Gazette*, 27 Apr. 1822.

71 *Report of the Select Committee on the State of the Poor in Ireland being a Summary of the First, Second and Third Reports of Evidence Taken Before that Committee Together with an Appendix of Accounts and Papers*, p. 7, HC, 1830 (HC; 667), vol. vii, p. 1.

72 Cullen, *An Economic History of Ireland Since 1660*, pp 114–5.

73 *(Four) Reports from the Select Committee on the State of Ireland, with References to Disturbances: Report, Minutes of Evidence and Index*, p. 42, HC, 1825 (HC; 129), vol. viii, p. 1.

74 *Ibid., Minutes of Evidence*, Denis Browne, p. 33.

75 Members of the committee included Malachy Kelly, Ross Mahon, James Mahon, Mr Cobbett, Dr Chambers, William Trench, William Kelly, Thomas Bermingham, Revd Seymour, Revd Cowen, Eyre Lynch, Lewis Ward, Dr Bird, Thomas Davis, Alexander Lynch, Mr Daly Esq.

76   Minutes of the Committee to Prevent Pauperism in North Galway, unpaginated (NLI, Mahon Papers, MS 47,844/6).

77   *Ibid.*

78   *Ibid.*

79   *Ibid.*

80   *Ibid.*

81   *Ibid.*

82   *First Report from the Select Committee on the State of Ireland, 1825.* HC, 1825 (HC; 129), Minutes of Evidence, Denis Browne, p. 28.

83   *Report of the Select Committee on the State of the Poor in Ireland being a Summary of the First, Second and Third Reports of Evidence Taken Before that Committee Together with an Appendix of Accounts and Paper,* p. 4, HC, 1830 (HC; 667), vol. vii, p. 1.

84   Weekly Labour Returns for the Castlegar Estate, 1824 and 1825 (NLI, Mahon Papers, MS 47,824/2-4).

85   *Report of the Select Committee on the State of the Poor in Ireland being a Summary of the First, Second and Third Reports of Evidence Taken Before that Committee Together with an Appendix of Accounts and Paper,* p. 6, HC, 1830 (HC; 667), vol. vii, p. 1.

86   *Ibid.,* p. 7.

87   *(Four) Reports from the Select Committee on the State of Ireland, with References to Disturbances: Report, Minutes of Evidence and Index,* p. 36, HC, 1825 (HC; 129), vol. viii, p. 1.

88   *Ibid.,* p. 38.

89   See Kevin J. James, *Handloom Weavers in Ulster's Linen Industry, 1815-1914* (Dublin, 2007).

90   *Connacht Journal,* 2 Jun. 1823.

91   *Roscommon and Leitrim Gazette,* 13 Jul. 1822.

92   *Roscommon and Leitrim Gazette,* 13 Jul. 1822.

93   *Connacht Journal,* 20 Mar. 1823.

94   *Connacht Journal,* 20 Mar. 1823.

95   *Roscommon and Leitrim Gazette,* 31 Aug. 1822.

96   *Limerick Chronicle,* 1 Jun. 1822.

97   *Hansard 2, i* [etc.], *HC Deb. 17 June 1822, vol. 7, cc.* 1125, Mr. John Smith.

98   *Hansard 2, i* [etc.], *HC Deb. 17 June 1822, vol. 7, cc.* 1125, Mr. Spring Rice.

99   *Hansard 2,* i [etc.], *HC Deb. 17 June 1822, vol. 7, cc.* 1123, *Mr. Secretary Peel.*

100   Clark, *Social Origins of the Irish Land War,* p. 33.

101   Resolution of the Principal Parishioners of Tarmonbarry, dated 22 May
      1822 (NLI, Mahon Papers, MS 47,844/1).

102   *Correspondence and Accounts Relating to the Different Occasions on Which*
      Measures were Taken for the Relief of the People Suffering from Scarcity In Ireland
      Between the Years 1822 and 1839, p. 3, HC, 1846 ([Command]; 734), vol.
      xxxvii, p. 1.

103   *Report of the Select Committee on the State of the Poor in Ireland Being a*
      Summary of the First, Second and Third Reports of Evidence Taken Before that
      Committee Together with an Appendix of Accounts and Papers, p. 8, HC, 1830
      (HC; 667), vol. vii, p. 1.

Chapter 2

1   Samuel Clark, *Social Origins of the Irish Land War* (New Jersey, 1979), pp
     36-7.

2   *Ibid.,* p. 38.

3   *Ibid.,* p. 37.

4   Oliver MacDonagh, 'Politics, 1830-1845' in W.E. Vaughan (ed.), *A New*
     History of Ireland, V, Ireland Under the Union I, 1801-70 (Oxford, 1989), p. 219.

5   Clark, *Social Origins of the Irish Land War,* pp 28-30.

6   Joel Mokyr, *Why Ireland Starved: A Quantitative and Analytical History of the*
     Irish Economy, 1800-1850 (London, 1983), pp 17-26, 213-15; R.D. Collison
     Black, *Economic Thought and the Irish Question, 1817-70* (London, 1960), pp
     18, 32-3.

7   *Condition of the Labouring Poor in Ireland and Application of Funds for their*
     Employment: Report from the Select Committee on the Employment of the Poor
     in Ireland, Minutes of Evidence and Appendix, p. 4. HC, 1823 (561), vi, p. 331.

8   *Ibid.,* p. 6.

9   *Ibid.,* pp 5-6.

10   G.L. Lampson, *A Consideration of the State of Ireland in the Nineteenth*
     Century (London, 1907), pp 566-8, 589-90.

11   Maria Edgeworth, *The Absentee* (London, 1896), p. 246.

12 Edgeworth, *The Absentee*, p. 246.

13 Lady Morgan, *The Wild Irish Girl* (New York, 1979), p. 12.

14 Charles Lever, *St Patrick's Eve* (London, 1845), pp 15, 72; Lady Morgan, 'Dramatic Scenes', in *Mount Sackville* (New York, 1979), pp 53-5; Anthony Trollope, *The Kellys and the O'Kellys* (Oxford, 1859), p. 341; Pádraig G. Lane, 'Connacht Agrarian Unrest in Fiction *c*. 1800-1850', in *Journal of Galway Archaeological and Historical Society*, vol. 58 (2006), pp 42-52.

15 Trollope, *The Kellys and the O'Kellys*, pp 259-60.

16 Jonathan B. Trotter, *Walks Through Ireland in the Years 1812, 1814 and 1817 Described in a Series of Letters to an English Gentleman* (London, 1819), pp 404-13, 472.

17 William Makepeace Thackeray, *The Irish Sketchbook of 1842 with Numerous Engraving on Wood by the Author* (Dublin, 1990), pp 204-49.

18 Johann G. Kohl, *Travels in Ireland* (London, 1844), p. 34.

19 MacDonagh, *Politics and Society, 1830-1845*, p. 222.

20 Jonathan Binns, *The Miseries and Beauties of Ireland* (London, 1837), pp 337-9, 374-5.

21 *Ibid.*, pp 6-23.

22 Asenath Nicholson, *Ireland's Welcome to the Stranger or an Excursion Through Ireland in 1844 and 1845 for the Purpose of Personally Investigating the Condition of the Poor* (London, 1837), p. 242.

23 Henry Blake, *Family Letters from the Irish Highlands of Cunnemarra* (London, 1825), pp 251-73.

24 *Evidence Taken Before Her Majesty's Commissioners of Inquiry into the State of the Law and Practise in Respect to the Occupation of Land in Ireland (Devon Commission)* HC 1845 (616), xx, pp 185, 389, 247-66, 381-95, 425, 453-79.

25 *Ibid.*

26 *Ibid.*, Pt. 2, pp 271, 366, 399, 468, 479.

27 *Ibid.*, Pt. 2, pp 185, 399.

28 James S. Donnelly Jnr, *The Land and the People of Nineteenth-Century Cork: The Rural Economy and the Land Question* (London, 1975), p. 13.

29 Clark, *Social Origins of the Irish Land War*, p. 31.

30 Kerby A. Miller, *Emigrants and Exiles: Ireland and the Irish Exodus to North America* (Oxford, 1985), pp 285-9.

31 Oliver MacDonagh, 'Irish Emigration to the United States of America and the British Colonies During the Famine,' in R.D. Edwards and T.D. Williams (eds), *The Great Famine: Studies in Irish History 1845-52* (Dublin, 1994), pp 319-40; Christine Kinealy, *This Great Calamity: The Irish Famine, 1845-52* (Dublin, 1994), p. 217.

32 Alexander Somerville, *Letters from Ireland During the Famine of 1847: With an Introduction by K.D.M. Snell* (Dublin, 1994), pp 75-82.

33 Mary E. Daly, 'Farming and the Famine' in Cormac Ó Gráda (ed.), *Famine 150 Commemorative Lecture Series* (Dublin, 1997), p. 40.

34 Cormac Ó Gráda, *Was the Great Famine Just Like Modern Famines? Working Paper Series, University College Dublin, Centre for Economic Research*, WP 95/12 (Dublin, 1995), p. 26.

35 Ó Gráda, *Was the Great Famine Just Like Modern Famines?*, p. 5.

36 *Ibid.*

37 Daly, 'Farming and the Famine', p. 40.

38 *Ibid.*, p. 41.

39 *Ibid.*, p. 43.

40 Miller, *Emigrants and Exiles*, pp 284-96; MacDonagh, 'Irish Emigration to the United States of America and the British Colonies during the Famine', p. 319.

41 MacDonagh, 'Irish Emigration to the United States of America and the British Colonies during the Famine', p. 327.

42 Mokyr, *Why Ireland Starved*, pp 263-9; Harriet Martineau, *Letters from Ireland* (London, 1852), pp 182-3; William Bullock Webster, *Ireland Considered as a Field for Investment* (London, 1852), p. 47.

43 Henry Grant, *Ireland's Hour* (Dublin, 1850), pp 84-5; Sydney G. Osborne, *Gleanings in the West of Ireland* (London, 1850), p. 223; *Dublin Evening Post*, 18 Apr. 1853.

44 *Dublin Evening Post*, 18 Apr. 1853 (from *Mayo Constitution, Castlebar Telegraph, Galway Vindicator*).

45 *Mayo Constitution*, 5 Apr. 1853.

46 *Western Star*, 10 Sep. 1853.

47 *Galway Packet*, 8 Apr. 1854.

48 *Dublin Evening Post*, 9 Jan. 1855 (from *Western Star*).

49 MS 7,600, MS 7,613, Larcom Papers, NLI; *Clare Journal*, 26 Aug. 1853

(from *Freeman's Journal*); MacDonagh, 'Irish Emigration to the United States of America and the British Colonies during the Famine', pp 327-8.

50 MS 7,783, MS 7,784, MS 7,785, Larcom Papers, NLI; CSORP, 17715,1860, 9769, NA; *Copies of All Reports Received by the Poor Law Commissioners in Ireland from their Inspectors and Medical Inspectors During the Months of December 1861 and January and February 1862 Relating to the Condition of the Poor in the Counties of Mayo and Galway* HC 1862 (HC; 667), xlix, reports 3, 13, 17, 22.

51 Henry Coulter, *The West of Ireland, Its Existing Condition and Prospects* (Dublin, 1862), pp 97-8, 209.

52 *Bessborough Commission, Report of the Commission of Inquiry into the Working of the Landlord and Tenant (Ireland) Acts, Representative Digest and Minutes of Evidence Appendix, Index 1881* [C. 2779-1], xviii, p. 1, vol. 2., pt. 1, p. 708.

53 *Royal Commission on Agriculture: Preliminary Report of the Commission (Richmond Commission)*, HC 1881, [C. 2778-1], xv, p. 75, Minutes of Evidence, vol. li, pp 445, 494, 502, 526, 861, 879.

54 *Cottages and Plots of Land: Select Committee on Agricultural Labourers (Ireland): Report, Proceedings, Minutes of Evidence, Appendix and Evidence*, HC, 1884 (HC; 317), viii, p. 245, Minutes of evidence, Mr Henry Robinson, p. 1.

55 *Ibid.*

56 Michael Davitt, *The Fall of Feudalism in Ireland* (New York, 1904), p. 964.

57 *Cottages and Plots of Land: Select Committee on Agricultural Labourers (Ireland): Report, Proceedings, Minutes of Evidence, Appendix and Evidence*, HC, 1884 (HC; 317), viii, p. 245, pp 50-1/1008-1041.

58 *Report and Tables Relating to Migratory Agricultural Labourers in Ireland, 1893 (Bee-Keeping Sstatistics, 1892)* HC 1894 (C.; 7264), *ci*, p. 483.

59 *United Ireland*, 1 Dec. 1883, 19 Jan. 1884, 27 Feb., 9 Oct. 1886, 28 Feb. 1891.

60 For a discussion on the significance of the Land League, see Joseph Lee, *The Modernisation of Irish Society 1848-1918* (Dublin, 1973), pp 89-105.

61 See Paul Bew, *Land and the National Question in Ireland 1858-82* (Dublin, 1978), pp 217-32; idem, 'The Land League Ideal: Achievements and Contradictions' in P.J. Drudy (ed.), *Irish Studies 2: Ireland: Land, Politics and People* (Cambridge, 1982), pp 77-92.

62 Clark, *Social Origins of the Irish Land War* (New Jersey, 1979), pp 31, 185-9; Miller, *Emigrants and Exiles*, pp 290-1; John Newsinger, 'A Great Blow

Must be Struck in Ireland: Karl Marx and the Fenians', in *Race and Class*, vol. xxiv (Oct. 1982), pp 151-67; Brian Griffin, 'Social Aspects of Fenianism in Connacht and Leinster, 1858-1870', *Eire-Ireland* (Spring, 1986), xxi, pp 16-39; CSORP, 11368, 1855, NA.

63 Pádraig G. Lane, 'Perceptions of Agricultural Labourers after the Great Famine, 1850-70', in *Saothar*, no. 19 (1994), pp 14-25; 'Notes Towards a History of Agricultural Labour Organisation in Mayo', in *Cathair na Mart* (2011), pp 77-83; CSORP, 11960, 1869: 1800, 1870, NA.

64 *Reports from Poor Law Inspectors on the Wages of Agricultural Labourers in Ireland*, HC 1870 (C.; 35), Vol. XIV, p. 1; *Reports from the Poor Law Inspectors on the Subject of Labourers' Dwellings*, HC, 1873 (C.; 764), xxii, p. 615.

65 Clark, *Social Origins of the Irish Land War*, pp 249-51; Godfrey Locker Lampson, *A Consideration of the State of Ireland in the Nineteenth Century* (London, 1907), p. 372.

66 *Freeman's Journal*, 28 Aug. 1879.

67 *The Queen Against Parnell and Others, Printed Reports of Meetings* (London, 1880), vols. i-iv, 3 May, 11 Jul., 8 Aug., 24 Oct., 28 Nov. 1880.

68 *Ibid.*

69 CSORP, 6295, 14033, 15979, 19771, 1880, NA.

70 Lee, *The Modernisation of Irish Society 1848-1918*, p. 92.

71 Bew, *Land and the National Question in Ireland 1858-82*, pp 222-3.

72 Folklore Commission, 70/135; 238/97; 434/154.

Chapter 3

1 See Paul Bew, *Ireland: The Politics of Enmity, 1798-2006* (Oxford and New York, 2007), p. 234, in which he claims that 'Connaught's participation in the Tenant League was to be strikingly restrained, weak, indeed to the point of being almost non-existent.' As this paper will show, this claim is an exaggerated one, although it contains an element of truth.

2 James S. Donnelly Jnr, *The Great Irish Potato Famine* (Stroud, 2002), p. 140.

3 See Donnelly, *Great Irish Potato Famine*, p. 156 and Donald Jordan, *Land and Popular Politics in Ireland: County Mayo from the Plantation to the Land War* (Cambridge, 1994), p. 113.

4   Donnelly, *Great Irish Potato Famine*, p. 156.

5   See Jordan, *Mayo*, pp 105-8.

6   Brian Jenkins, *Sir William Gregory of Coole: A Biography* (Gerrards Cross, 1986), pp 86-7.

7   K.T. Hoppen, *Elections, Politics and Society in Ireland, 1832-1885* (Oxford, 1984), p. 92.

8   The distressed unions in the province of Connacht were Ballina, Ballinrobe, Castlebar, Castlerea, Clifden, Galway, Gort, Roscommon, Sligo, Swinford, Tuam and Westport. See Christine Kinealy, *This Great Calamity: The Irish Famine, 1845-52* (Dublin, 1994); See John Joseph Conwell, 'Clanricarde and the Great Famine' in Joseph Forde, Christina Cassidy, Paul Manzor and David Ryan (eds), *The District of Loughrea, i; History, 1791-1918* (Galway, 2003), p. 231.

9   There is a good short account of the early history of the Tenant League in Joseph Lee, *The Modernization of Irish Society, 1848-1918* (Dublin, 1973), pp 39-41. See also J.H. Whyte, *The Tenant League and Irish Politics in the Eighteen-Fifties* (Dundalk, 1966), pp 6-8.

10 See Whyte, *Tenant League and Irish Politics*, pp 8-9.

11 K.T. Hoppen, *Ireland Since 1800: Conflict & Conformity* (Harlow, 1989 edition), p. 189.

12 For a discussion of the origins of the tenant agitation in Ulster, see Paul Bew and Frank Wright, 'Agrarian Opposition in Ulster Politics' in Samuel Clark and J.S. Donnelly (eds), *Irish Peasants: Violence and Political Unrest 1870-1914* (Manchester, 1983), pp 194-200. See also Frank Wright, *Two Lands on One Soil: Ulster Politics before Home Rule* (Dublin, 1996), pp 165-207.

13 W.E. Vaughan, *Landlords and Tenants in Mid-Victorian Ireland* (Oxford, 1997), p. 76.

14 *Freeman's Journal*, 12 Apr. 1850.

15 Lucas to MacHale, 27 Apr. 1850, quoted in Bernard O'Reilly, *John MacHale, Archbishop of Tuam: His Life, Times, and Correspondence*, 2 vols. (New York, 1890), ii: pp 230-1.

16 Lucas to MacHale, 15 May 1850, quoted in O'Reilly, *MacHale*, ii, p. 232.

17 For an analysis of popular attitudes to MacHale, with particular reference to county Mayo, see Eugene Hynes, *Knock: The Virgin's Apparition in Nineteenth-Century Ireland* (Cork, 2008), pp 70-90.

18 Donal Kerr, *Peel, Priests and Politics* (Oxford, 1982), p. 26.

19 John MacHale, *The Letters of the Most Rev. John MacHale, D.D., under the Signature of Hierophilos; John, Bishop of Maronia: Bishop of Killala; Archbishop of Tuam* (Dublin, 1847), pp 609-24.

20 MacHale to John O'Connell, 4 May 1850, quoted in O'Reilly, *MacHale*, ii, pp 225-6.

21 For a detailed report of the Castlebar meeting, see the *Freeman's Journal*, 13 May 1850.

22 *Freeman's Journal*, 1 Dec. 1847.

23 Hoppen, *Elections, Politics and Society*, pp 101-2; Hoppen, *Ireland Since 1800*, pp 111-2.

24 See, for example, the accounts of the Tenant Right meetings held in Mullingar and Navan in April/May 1850 in Paul Connell, *The Diocese of Meath under Bishop John Cantwell, 1830-66* (Dublin, 2004), pp 170-3.

25 *Freeman's Journal*, 31 May 1850.

26 For Lavelle's career, see Gerard Moran, *A Radical Priest in Mayo: Fr Patrick Lavelle, the Rise and Fall of an Irish Nationalist* (Dublin, 1994).

27 *Ballina Chronicle*, 28 Aug. 1850.

28 See Hoppen, *Elections, Politics and Society*, pp 371-3 and T.W. Moody, *Davitt and Irish Revolution, 1846-82* (Oxford, 1982), p. 566.

29 Moody, *Davitt*, p. 566.

30 For a comparison of the social basis of both organisations, see Hoppen, *Elections, Politics and Society*, pp 480-2. See also Samuel Clark, *Social Origins of the Irish Land War* (Princeton and Guilford, 1979) and idem, 'The Importance of Agrarian Class Structure and Collective Action in Nineteenth-Century Ireland' in P.J. Drudy (ed.), *Irish Studies 2: Ireland: Land, Politics and People* (Cambridge and New York, 1982), pp 11-36.

31 For detailed reports of both meetings, see the *Freeman's Journal*, 14 and 20 Jun. 1850.

32 See Liam Bane, *The Bishop in Politics: Life and Career of John MacEvilly* (Westport, 1993), pp 96-9.

33 For Duggan's later support of the Land League, see Moody, *Davitt*, p. 191.

34 Lucas to MacHale, 27 Oct. 1851, quoted in O'Reilly, *MacHale*, ii, p. 231.

35 *Freeman's Journal*, 28 Jan. 1850.

36 See MacHale to Lucas, 2 May 1850, in *Freeman's Journal*, 11 May 1850.

37 *Freeman's Journal*, 9 Aug. 1850.

38 See Whyte, *Tenant League and Irish Politics,* pp 8-9.

39 See Whyte, *Tenant League and Irish Politics*, pp 8-9.

40 R.F. Foster, *Modern Ireland, 1600-1972* (London, 1988), p. 375.

41 *Freeman's Journal*, 31 May 1850.

42 For a detailed report of the Ballinrobe meeting, see *Freeman's Journal*, 23 Aug. 1850.

43 See Jordan, *Mayo*, pp 175-7.

44 See *Freeman's Journal*, 22 Jul. 1850.

45 See *Freeman's Journal*, 16 and 22 Jul. 1850.

46 *Freeman's Journal*, 6 Sep. 1850.

47 *Telegraph or Connaught Ranger*, 4 Sep. 1850.

48 *Telegraph or Connaught Ranger*, 4 Sep. 1850.

49 In its return of the contributions to the Tenant League in 1851, *The Nation* of 7 February 1852 recorded the contributions from Connacht as being zero. This figure does not seem to have included individual subscriptions, as *The Nation* of 13 Sep. 1851 had published a letter from Fr Thomas Hardiman, the parish priest of Ballinrobe, including a subscription of £1 for the League's funds. Hardiman had recently been at the Tenant League conference of that year.

50 Lee, *Modernisation*, pp 39-41.

51 See J.H. Whyte, *The Independent Irish Party, 1850-9* (Oxford, 1958), pp 30-8.

52 *Freeman's Journal*, 5 Mar. 1852. It is also significant that the copious correspondence which took place between George Henry Moore and Archbishop John MacHale in 1850 and 1851 was concerned almost exclusively with the controversy over the Ecclesiastical Titles Act and includes few references to the agitation for Tenant Right. See, for example, Moore to MacHale, 2 Apr. 1851 and MacHale to Moore, 3 Apr. 1851 in the George Henry Moore papers (NLI, MS 891).

53 See Donnelly, *Great Irish Potato Famine*, pp 194-9.

54 The seven Independent Party MPs elected for Western constituencies were Anthony O'Flaherty and Martin Blake for Galway city, Thomas Bellew for Galway county, Richard Swift for county Sligo, Oliver Grace for county Roscommon and George Henry Moore and Ouseley Higgins for county Mayo. Most of these MPs, with the notable exception of George

Henry Moore were later to revert back to their previous support for the Whig–Liberal party.

55 See O'Reilly, *MacHale*, ii, pp 260–9. For Moore's later political career, see M.G. Moore, *An Irish Gentleman: George Henry Moore, his Travels, his Racing, his Politics* (London n.d.).

56 Whyte, *Independent Irish Party*, pp 142–9.

57 *Ibid.*, p. 147.

58 See Ulick Bourke, *The Life and Times of the Most Rev. John MacHale: Archbishop of Tuam and Metropolitan* (New York, 1883), pp 171–81.

59 See Jordan, *Mayo*, pp 176–7.

60 See R.V. Comerford, 'Churchmen, Tenants and Independent Opposition, 1850–56' in W.E. Vaughan (ed.), *A New History of Ireland: v: Ireland Under the Union, 1801-70* (Oxford, 1989), p. 408.

61 See Whyte, *Tenant League and Irish Politics*, p. 17.

62 See for example the report of the subscription of £5 to the League by the clergy of Dunmore, county Galway, in *The Nation*, 3 Jun. 1854, the declaration in favour of Tenant Right by the Tuam clergy in *The Nation*, 15 Dec. 1855 and the report of the subscription of £5 to the League by the clergy in the Tuam archdiocese in *The Nation*, 25 Apr. 1857.

63 See Jordan, *Mayo*, pp 175–7; O'Carroll, *Paul Cardinal Cullen*, pp 129–39 and Patrick Corish, *The Irish Catholic Experience: A Historical Survey* (Dublin, 1985), pp 198–9.

64 See Whyte, *Independent Irish Party*, p. 154. For the brief revival of the Independent party in 1865–66, see Comerford, *Fenians in Context: Irish Politics and Society 1848-82* (Dublin, 1985), pp 139–42.

65 Hoppen, *Ireland Since 1800*, p. 86.

66 Lee, *Modernisation*, p. 40.

67 See Vaughan, *Landlords and Tenants*, pp 230, 279.

68 Moody, *Davitt*, p. 564.

69 See, for example, the reports of the tenant right meetings in Tuam in early 1854 in the *Tuam Herald*, 28 Jan. 1854, the similar meeting at Castlebar reported in the *Tuam Herald*, 3 Feb. 1855 and the reports of the banquet held in Castlebar in January 1857 in honour of George Henry Moore in the *Tuam Herald*, 24 Jan. 1857. On that occasion, Archbishop MacHale himself was one of the principal speakers.

70   For Moore's political career, see Moore, *Irish Gentleman*. See also Whyte, *Independent Irish Party*, passim.

71   George Henry Moore to John MacHale, 22 February 1848, George Henry Moore papers (NLI, MS 891).

72   Moore, *Irish Gentleman*, p. 123.

73   Quoted in Hoppen, *Elections, Politics and Society*, p. 247.

74   See Bourke, *Life and Times*, pp 170-81.

75   It was this circumstance that led to Parnell's later contention that 'Fintan Lalor might have founded his Land League in the eighteen-forties if railways had been available to bring his message to the people.' See Patrick Maume, *The Long Gestation: Irish Nationalist Life, 1891-1918* (Dublin, 1999), p. 7.

76   Hoppen, *Ireland Since 1800*, p. 112.

Chapter 4

1   Paul Bew, *Land and the National Question in Ireland, 1858-82* (Dublin, 1979); Samuel Clark, *Social Origins of the Irish Land War* (Princeton, 1979); Donald E. Jordan, *Land and Popular Politics in Ireland: County Mayo from the Plantation to the Land War* (Cambridge, 1994); Fergus Campbell, *Land and Revolution: Nationalist Politics in the West of Ireland, 1891-1921* (Oxford, 2005); Philip Bull, 'The formation of the United Irish League, 1898-1900: The Dynamics of Irish Agrarian Agitation,' *Irish Historical Studies*, xxxiii, no. 132 (Nov. 2003), pp 404-23.

2   Philip Bull, *Land, Politics and Nationalism: A Study of the Irish Land Question* (Dublin, 1996), pp 69-70.

3   For James Daly, see Gerard Moran, 'James Daly and the Rise and Fall of the Land League in the West of Ireland, 1879-82' in *Irish Historical Studies*, xxxix, no. 114 (Nov. 1994) pp 189-207. While there is no separate study of Matthew Harris, his role in the land agitation has been examined in Bew, *Land and the National Question; Clark, Social Origins of Irish Land War*, but in particular in T.W. Moody, Davitt and Irish Revolution, 1846-82 (Oxford, 1981).

4   For discussion on estate clearances and evictions during the Great Famine see, James S. Donnelly, Jnr, *The Great Irish Potato Famine* (Stroud, 2001),

pp 134-68; Tim P. O'Neill, 'Famine Evictions' in Carla King (ed.), *Famine, Land and Culture in Ireland* (Dublin, 2000), pp 29-70.

5   See Samuel Clark, 'The Social Composition of the Land League,' in *Irish Historical Studies*, 17, no. 68 (Sep. 1971), pp 447-23; idem, 'The Importance of Agrarian Classes: Agrarian Class Structure and Collective Action in Nineteenth-Century Ireland' in *British Journal of Sociology*, 29, no. 1 (Mar. 1978), pp 22-40.

6   See Gerard Moran, 'The Emergence of Popular Politics in county Limerick, 1868-1874' in Liam Irwin, Gearóid Ó Tuathaigh and Matthew Potter (eds), *Limerick: History and Society* (Dublin, 2009), pp 457-82.

7   David Thornley, *Isaac Butt and Home Rule* (London, 1964), p. 274.

8   See Mitchell Henry's letter to *Tuam Herald*, 26 Oct. 1876.

9   Rules of the Ballinasloe Tenants' Defence Association (NLI MS 47,373/3, Sweetman papers).

10   *Connaught Telegraph*, 5 May 1877.

11   *Report from the Select Committee on the Irish Land Act, 1870: Together with the Proceedings of the Committee, Minutes of Evidence and Appendix*, HC, 1878 (249), xv, I, p. 270, 4987-8.

12   *Report of Her Majesty's Commissioners of Inquiry into the Working of the Landlord and Tenant (Ireland) Act, 1870, and the Acts amending the same*, HC 1881, xviii (2779-iii), p. 692, 20998-21005 (hereafter cited as *Bessborough Commission*).

13   *Bessborough Commission*, p. 650, 20,936; *Connaught Telegraph*, 13 May 1879; *Western News*, 9 Nov. 1878.

14   Bew, *Land and the National Question*, p. 59.

15   R.V. Comerford, *The Fenians in Context: Irish Politics and Society, 1848-82* (Dublin, 1985), pp 214-5.

16   Gerard Moran, 'The Changing Course of Mayo Politics, 1868-74' in Raymond Gillespie and Gerard Moran (eds), *A Various Country: Essays in Mayo History, 1500-1900* (Westport, 1986), pp 149-53; Jordan, *Land and Popular Politics in Ireland*, pp 187-9.

17   Clark, *Social Origins of Irish Land War*, pp 272-3

18   See Gerard Moran, 'The Land War, Urban Destitution and Town Tenant Protest' in *Saothar*, 20 (1995), pp 17-31.

19   Bew, *Land and the National Question*, p. 57.

20 *Tuam Herald*, 4 Nov. 1876.

21 *Connaught Telegraph*, 20 Oct. 1877.

22 *Ibid.*, 12 Jan. 1878.

23 *Connaught Telegraph*, 31 Mar. 1877; *Bessborough Commission*, p. 653, 21026-7.

24 *Western News*, 8 and 15 Feb. 1879.

25 *Connaught Telegraph*, 26 Jan. 1878.

26 *Ibid.*, 9 Nov. 1879.

27 *Ibid.*, 5 Aug. 1876.

28 *Ibid.*, 8 Jul. 1876.

29 *Ibid.*, 30 Sep. 1876.

30 *Ibid.*, 30 Sep. 1876.

31 *Ibid.*, 12 May 1877.

32 On the issue of local newspapers in the post-Famine period see Marie-Louise Legge, *Newspapers and Nationalism: The Irish Provincial Press, 1850-92* (Dublin, 1999).

33 *Connaught Telegraph*, 12 Aug. 1876. John Callanan was a native of Ballinasloe and worked for the *Connaught Telegraph* until 1877 when he left to establish the *Western News*, which was based in Ballinasloe.

34 *Connaught Telegraph*, 1 Jul. 1876.

35 *Ibid.*, 22 Dec. 1877.

36 *Ibid.*, 26 Aug., 11 Nov. 1876.

37 *Connaught Telegraph*, 3 Feb. 1877; *Tuam Herald*, 3 Feb. 1877; *Connaught Telegraph*, 1 Feb. 1879.

38 See Moran, 'James Daly and the Rise and Fall of the Land League in the West of Ireland', pp 191-2; Jordan, *Land and Popular Politics in Ireland*, pp 210-2.

39 Jordan, *Land and Popular Politics in Ireland*, p. 209.

40 *Connaught Telegraph*, 24 Jun. 1876.

41 *Report from the Select Committee on the Irish Land Laws, 1870; together with the proceedings of the committee...*, p. 271, 5003-7; p. 273, 5029.

42 *Bessborough Commission*, p. 562, 21013. While Kilmartin held a large farm, much of it was waste or marginal land and he did not consider himself a grazier.

43 *Connaught Telegraph*, 5 May 1877. The O'Donoghue tended to be radical on the agrarian question, but adopted a more independent approach on most other political issues.

44 *Ibid.*, 15 Sep. 1877.

45 *Ibid.*, 16 Mar. 1878; 6 Apr. 1878.

46 *Ibid.*, 13 Apr. 1878.

47 *Bessborough Commission*, p. 651, q. 20951.

48 *Connaught Telegraph*, 20 Apr. 1878.

49 *Western News*, 1 Mar. 1879.

50 *Connaught Telegraph*, 20 Apr. 1878.

51 On the internal crisis within the Land League in early 1880 see Moran, 'James Daly and the rise and fall of the Land League in the west of Ireland', pp 200-6; Bew, *Land and the National Question*, pp 102-4.

52 *Connaught Telegraph*, 22 Sep. 1877. This attack was directed at MPs such as The O'Conor Don, Charles French, Sir Patrick O'Brien and The O'Donoghue.

53 *Western News*, 2 Nov. 1878.

54 *Ibid.*, 8 Feb. 1879.

55 *Connaught Telegraph*, 3 Jun. 1876.

56 Jordan, *Land and Popular Politics in Ireland*, p. 212.

57 *Connaught Telegraph*, 9 Nov. 1878, 23 Aug. 1879.

58 *Western News*, 14 Jun. 1879; *Nation*, 14 Jun. 1879.

59 *Western News*, 5 Apr. 1879; see also Moran, 'James Daly and the rise and fall of the Land League in the West of Ireland', pp 191-2.

60 See Robert Kee, *The Laurel and the Ivy: The Story of Charles Stewart Parnell and Irish Nationalism* (London, 1993), p. 177, 181.

61 *Connaught Telegraph*, 9 Nov. 1878.

62 See *Western News*, 17 May 1879. The evidence of the resolutions passed at the council meetings and demonstrations is to be found in the local newspapers.

63 *Connaught Telegraph*, 7 Dec. 1878.

64 For the background to the New Departure see T.W. Moody, 'The New Departure in Irish Politics' in H.A. Cronne, T.W. Moody and D.B. Quinn (eds), *Essays in British and Irish History in Honour of James Eddie Todd* (London, 1949), pp 303-33.

65 Moody, *Davitt and Irish Revolution*, pp 275-6.

66 *Ibid.*, pp 193-4.

67 *Western News*, 21 Jun. 1879.

68 *Ibid.*, 26 Jul. 1879.

69 *Ibid.*, *Western News*, 21 Jun. 1879; *Nation*, 28 Jun. 1879; *Tuam Herald*, 7 & 28 Jun. 1879.

70 *Connaught Telegraph*, 14 Jun. 1879.

71 *Tuam Herald*, 24 May 1879.

72 Bew, *Land and the National Question*, p. 94.

73 *Bessborough Commission*, p. 650, 20937-40.

74 Moody, *Davitt and Irish Revolution*, p. 342. Moody questions O'Sullivan's abilities as an office administrator and organiser.

Chapter 5

1 T.M.P. Flynn, *History of Leitrim* (Dublin, 1937), pp 53-8; Miriam Moffitt, *The Church of Ireland Community of Killala & Achonry* (Dublin, 1999), pp 15-19.

2 The populations of Leitrim and Roscommon in 1881 were 90,372 and 132,490 respectively.

3 Miriam Moffitt, *The Church of Ireland Community of Killala & Achonry*, pp 24-7.

4 Moffitt, 'The Protestant Experience of Revolution in county Leitrim', *Breifni Journal*, xxii, no. 26 (2011), pp 303-23.

5 *Census of the Population of Irish Free State on 18th April 1926, Preliminary Report*, Vol. III, Part 1, tables 20 and 22. The numbers of Protestant/Catholic farms in 1926 were Leitrim (771/10,265), Sligo (760/10,721), Roscommon (206/14,921), Mayo (349/28,231) and Galway (216/24,525).

6 *Irish Times*, 9 Nov. 1880.

7 *Freeman's Journal*, 9 May 1889, *Irish Times*, 4 May 1889.

8 Lord Massereene to Archbishop Logue, 23 May 1889, reproduced in *Report of the Commissioners Appointed to Inquire into the Estates of Evicted Tenants* [C6935-I], HC 1893-94, xxxi, vol. ii, p. 195b.

9 *Irish Times*, 10 Sep. 1908.

10 Quoted in Philip Bull, *Land, Politics and Nationalism, a Study of the Irish Land Question* (Dublin, 1996), p. 119.

11 Moffitt, *Clanricarde's Planters and Land Agitation in East Galway, 1886-1916* (Dublin, forthcoming [2011]), p. 31.

12 *Report of the Proceedings of the Grand Orange Lodge of Ireland at the Half Yearly Meeting*, Dec. 1881, pp 44-5.

13 In county Sligo, three lodges were opened during the land war and two dormant lodges revived: Lissadell (LOL 2040, 1881-1901 and LOL 7, est. 1880), Skreen-Ballisodare (LOL 1959, 1885-1901), Riverstown 'No Surrender' (LOL 1733, est. before 1875, revived 1881), Coolaney (LOL 1759, 1852-1901, revived 1887) and warrants had been issued for six pre-existing lodges in the county: Ballisodare (LOL 465, 1874-1901), Ballymote (LOL 795, est. before 1875-1913), Collooney (LOL 786, 1872-92), Drumcliff (LOL 235, est. 1874), Sligo (LOL 464, no foundation date and LOL 562, 1879-1901). In county Leitrim, three lodges were opened during the Land War era: Manorhamilton (LOL 866, 1882-94 and LOL 478, est. 1881), Newtowngore (LOL 243, 1885-1905) and warrants had been issued for fifteen pre-existing lodges in the county: Ballinamore (LOL 332, no foundation date), Carrick-on-Shannon (LOL 397, 1877-1905), Carrigallen (LOL 309, est. 1876; LOL 387, 1875-93; LOL 679, no foundation date; LOL 865, est. 1877; LOL 1581, no foundation date), Glencar (LOL 19, no foundation date), Manorhamilton (LOL 586, 1870-94 and LOL 395, 1870-1905), Newtowngore (LOL 863, est. 1874 and LOL 396, 1874-1905), Gortinar (LOL 764, 1871-1905), Killegar (LOL 545, 1875-1905) and Dromahaire (LOL 477, no foundation date). In addition to these lodges, a number of lodges functioned in the adjoining counties of Roscommon and Longford: Rockingham (LOL 2071, est. 1882), Boyle (LOL 2041, est. 1881), Ballinalee (LOL 830, est. 1888), Kilglass (LOL 842, 1889-94), Granard (LOL 843, est. 1889), Kenagh (LOL 844, est. 1889), Longford (LOL 1595, 1885-1903 and LOL 1530, before 1875-1891), Edgeworthstown (LOL 1614, before 1875-1891), Ballymahon (LOL 1615, before 1875-1891), Liscryan (LOL 1626, 1854-1891). MS listing of lodges, 1875, 1891 (Archives of the Grand Orange Lodge of Ireland, Belfast) and *Report of the proceedings of the Grand Orange Lodge of Ireland*, 1850-1900.

14 For example, Revd Joseph Mayne of Lurganboy was Grand Chaplain of County Leitrim Grand Orange Lodge in 1883, assisted by three Deputy Chaplains (Revds George Clarke of Killegar, George Grierson

of Manorhamilton and Richard Clarke of Ballinamore) while in county Sligo, the same year, Grand Chaplain, Revd Thomas Cosgrove of Lissadell was assisted by five Deputy Chaplains (Revds Thomas Heaney of Calry, Thomas Walker of Ballymote, Francis Burke of Ardcarne, James Todd of Ahamlish and Frederick Austin, curate at Lissadell). *Report of the Proceedings of the Grand Orange Lodge of Ireland*, 1883, pp 21-2.

15 *Report of the Proceedings of the Grand Orange Lodge of Ireland*, Dec. 1881.

16 Robert Taylor, Thomas Beattie, Robert Lawson, *Report of the Proceedings of the Grand Orange Lodge of Ireland*, Dec. 1882; John Thompson of Ballymote *Report of the Proceedings of the Grand Orange Lodge of Ireland*, Dec. 1886.

17 *Irish Times*, 19 Jan. 1909.

18 *Irish Times*, 1 Jan. 1909.

19 Letter from Revd Robert Weir in file of Charles Rainsberry (PRONI, MS D989/B/3/12).

20 *Freeman's Journal*, 23 Jan. 1884, article headed 'Another Plantation'; *Westmeath Examiner*, 9 Feb. 1884; *Irish Times*, 4 Feb. 1884.

21 Revd J. Allan French, Drumcliff, Sligo.

22 *Westmeath Examiner*, 9 Feb. 1884.

23 *Report of the Proceedings of the Grand Orange Lodge of Ireland*, Dec. 1886.

24 TNA, CO 762/173/23.

25 See, for example, IG report, Sep. 1901 (NAI, MS IGCI/2) which stated that all rents were withheld throughout the Morley and Fausset estates in Leitrim in an effort to force a sale.

26 Fergus Campbell, *Land and Revolution, Nationalist Politics in the West of Ireland 1891-1921* (Oxford, 2005), p. 16-17.

27 *Leitrim Observer*, 4 May 1907 (evidence of James McCartan, Ballinamore to the Royal Commission on Congestion).

28 *Leitrim Observer*, 14 Sep. 1907.

29 *Church of Ireland Gazette*, 13 Aug. 1920 (editorial).

30 *Sligo Champion*, 25 Jun. 1904.

31 IG Report, Sep. 1901 (NAI, MS IGCI/2).

32 IG Report, Jan. 1904 (NAI, MS IGCI/5).

33 *Irish Protestant*, Oct. 1902.

34 *Notes from Ireland*, Mar. 1908.

35 *Leitrim Observer*, 8 Feb. 1908.

36 *Irish Times*, 10 Sep. 1908.

37 *Irish Times*, 24 Sep. 1908.

38 *Grievances from Ireland*, Sep. 1906, p. 513.

39 *Leitrim Observer*, 5 Oct. 1907.

40 *Leitrim Observer*, 11 Apr. 1908.

41 *Anglo Celt*, 5 Mar. 1910, *Irish Times*, 12 May 1910.

42 CI report, Leitrim, Mar. 1902 (NAI, MS IGCI/2).

43 *Anglo Celt*, 18 Jan. 1908.

44 CI report, Leitrim, Jan. 1908 (NAI, MS IGCI/13).

45 CI report, Leitrim, Feb. 1908 MS IGCI/13 (NAI).

46 CI report, Leitrim, Jun. 1908 MS IGCI/13 (NAI).

47 CI report, Cavan, Jan. 1910 (TNA, MS CO 904/83).

48 Joseph McCordick of Stroke, Ballinamore was boycotted for years for occupying an evicted farm until he surrendered the holding in Feb. 1909. See, for example, IG Report, Apr. 1894, MS CO/904/58; CI report Leitrim, July 1902, CO 904/76; CI Report Leitrim, July 1902 (TNA CO 904/75); CI Report Leitrim, Feb. 1909 (TNA, CO 904/77A); *Roscommon Herald*, 11 Apr. 1908.

49 CI report, Leitrim, Jul. 1908 (NAI, MS IGCI/14).

50 CI report, Leitrim, Aug. 1908 NAI, MS IGCI/14).

51 CI report, Leitrim, Feb. 1910 (TNA, MS CO 904/80).

52 CI report, Leitrim, Aug. 1908 (NAI, MS IGCI/14).

53 CI report, Leitrim, Dec. 1909 (TNA, MS CO 904/79).

54 CI report, Leitrim, Jan. 1910 (TNA, MS CO 904/80); *Irish Times*, 4 Jan. 1910.

55 *Anglo Celt*, 5 Mar. 1910.

56 *Roscommon Herald*, 29 Jan. 1910.

57 CI report, Cavan, Feb., Mar. 1910 (TNA, MS CO 904/80).

58 *Irish Times*, 5 Mar. 1910.

59 *Hansard*, HC, 10 Mar. 1910, vol. 14, c1786W; *ibid.*, HL, 6 Jul. 1910 vol. 5, cc1092-148.

60 CI report, Cavan, Oct., Nov. 1910 (TNA, MS CO 904/82).

61 CI report, Leitrim, Sep. 1912 (TNA, MS CO 904/88).

62 CI report, Leitrim, Jun. 1910 (TNA, MS CO 904/80).

63 *Irish Times*, 13 May 1910.

64 *Anglo Celt*, 19 Jun. 1909.

65 *Report of the Proceedings of the Grand Orange Lodge of Ireland*, Dec. 1908, Dec. 1911. Revd Frederick Woods was rector 1908-11, Revd John Blaney 1911-16.

66 TNA, MS CO/762/159/11.

67 TNA, MS CO 904/121/208, 215.

68 *Anglo Celt*, 29 May 1920.

69 TNA, MS CO 904/121/215.

70 CI report, Leitrim, May 1921 (TNA, MS CO 904/115).

71 TNA, MS CO/762/38/14.

72 NAI, MS FIN/1/1034.

73 TNA, MS CO/762/173/12.

74 *Irish Times*, 14 May 1909.

75 'Riverstown Conspiracy Case' (TNA, MS CO 904/121), pp 155-7.

76 *Freeman's Journal*, 14 May 1909.

77 *Irish Independent*, 14 Nov. 1908.

78 'Riverstown Conspiracy Case'.

79 *Irish Times*, 19 Nov. 1908.

80 'Riverstown Conspiracy Case'.

81 *Irish Times*, 6 Nov. 1908.

82 *Irish Times*, 20 Nov. 1908.

83 *Irish Times*, 14 May 1909.

84 For details of this extensive campaign of intimidation against the following persons (Elizabeth Meredith, Edward Harte, Thomas Harte, John Harte, Charles O'Connor, William Clifford, Henry Bright, George Middleton, James Bright, Thomas Higgins, James Allen, James Johnston (senior), James Johnston (junior), Thomas Morrison, Thomas Rowlette), see *Irish Times*, 7 Feb, 14 May 1909; *Sligo Champion*, 6 Feb. 1909.

85 *Sligo Champion*, 22 May 1909.

86 *Irish Times*, 5 Feb. 1909.

87 *Irish Times*, 15 May 1909.

88 *Irish Times*, 8 Nov. 1909.

89 *Sligo Champion*, 3 Jan. 1912.

90 *Sligo Champion*, 2 Dec. 1911.

91 *Sligo Champion*, 3 Jan. 1912.

92 *Sligo Champion*, 3 Jan. 1912.

93 *Irish Times*, 30 Mar. 1912.

94 *Sligo Independent*, 29 Jun., 23 Nov. 1912.

95 *Sligo Independent*, 16 May, 4 Jul. 1914.

96 *Report of the Proceedings of the Grand Orange Lodge of Ireland* (Dublin, 1913), p. 25.

97 *Irish Times*, 13 Jul. 1911.

98 *Sligo Champion*, 20 Jan. 1912.

99 *Church of Ireland Gazette*, 13 Aug. 1920 (editorial).

100 *Irish Protestant*, Oct. 1902.

101 In the twentieth century, lodges operated at Carrigallen, Dromahair (Bohey), Newtowngore, Ballinamore and Manorhamilton.

Chapter 6

1 Anna Clark, 'Wild Workhouse Girls and the Liberal Imperial State in Mid-Nineteenth Century Ireland' in *Journal of Social History*, xxxix, no. 2 (Winter, 2005), p. 391.

2 Virginia Crossman, 'The New Ross Workhouse Riot of 1887: Nationalism, Class and the Irish Poor Laws' in *Past & Present*, no. 179 (May 2003), pp 135-59; Virginia Crossman, Georgina Laragy, Donnacha Seán Lucey and Olwen Purdue, 'Sources for the History of the Irish Poor Law in the Post-Famine Period' in Ciara Breathnach and Catherine Lawless (eds), *Visual, Material and Print Culture in Nineteenth-Century Ireland* (Dublin, 2010), pp 198-220.

3 For an examination of the regional trends of the Poor Law in the west of Ireland, see Donnacha Seán Lucey, 'Regional Practices in Poor Relief in the West of Ireland, 1861-1911' in Virginia Crossman and Peter Gray (eds), *Poverty and Welfare in Ireland, 1838-1948* (Dublin, 2011), pp 37-52.

4 For an outline of the development of voluntary hospitals in Ireland see Catherine Cox, 'Institutionalisation in Irish History and Society' in Mary McAuliffe, Katherine O'Donnell and Leeann Lane (eds), *Palgrave Advances in Irish History* (London, 2009), p. 174.

5 Jonathan Reinarz, 'Receiving the Rich, Rejecting the Poor: Towards a
 History of Hospital Visiting in Nineteenth-Century Provincial England'
 in Graham Mooney and Jonathan Reinarz (eds), *Permeable Walls:
 Historical Perspectives on Hospital and Asylum Visiting* (Amsterdam, 2009),
 p. 35.

6 For an exploration of the Dublin hospital system see Gary A. Boyd,
 Dublin, 1745-1922: Hospitals, Spectacle and Vice: The Making of Dublin City
 (Dublin, 2006); Also see, G.M. Fealy, *A History of Apprenticeship Nurse
 Training in Ireland* (London, 2006).

7 Ruth Barrington, *Health, Medicine and Politics in Ireland, 1900-70* (Dublin,
 1987), p. 4.

8 *Thom's Directory* (Dublin, 1862).

9 J.P. Murray, *Galway: A Medico-Social History* (Galway, 1994).

10 *Index to the Report from the Select Committee on Poor Relief (Ireland)*, p. 28,
 HC 1861 [408], x. 1.

11 *Ibid.*

12 R.D. Cassell, *Medical Charities, Medical Politics: The Irish Dispensary System
 and the Poor Law, 1836-1872* (Suffolk, 1997), p. 104.

13 Jonathan Reinarz, 'Investigating the "Deserving" Poor: Charity and the
 Voluntary Hospitals in Nineteenth-Century Birmingham' in Anne Borsay
 and Peter Shapely (eds), *Medicine, Charity and Mutual Aid: The Consumption
 of Health and Welfare in Britain, c. 1550-1950* (Hampshire, 2007), pp 111-33.

14 For an examination of the registration of children under the Poor Law
 see, Mel Cousins, 'Registration of the Religion of Children Under the
 Irish Poor Law, 1838-1870' in *The Journal of Ecclesiastical History*, vol. 61,
 no. 1, Jan. 2010, pp 107-24. For the boarding out of children by Boards of
 Guardians see, Virginia Crossman, 'Cribbed, Contained, and Confined?
 The Care of Children Under the Irish Poor Law, 1850-1920' in *Eire-Ireland*,
 44: nos. 1&2 (Earrach/Samhradh/Spring/Summer, 2009), pp 37-61.

15 For an examination of the emergence of the dispensary system see,
 Laurence Geary, *Medicine and Charity in 1718-1851* (Dublin, 2004).

16 For the most recent work on dispensaries see Catherine Cox, 'Access and
 Engagement: The Medical Dispensary Service in Post-Famine Ireland'
 in idem and Maria Luddy (eds), *Cultures of Care in Irish Medical History,
 1750-1970* (London, 2010), pp 57-78.

17 For an outline of the workhouse test see, Helen Burke, *The People and the Poor Law in Nineteenth Century Ireland* (Dublin, 1987), p. 22.

18 *Index to the Report from the Select Committee on Poor Relief (Ireland)*, p. 28.

19 Poor Law (Ireland). Copies of reports received by the Poor Law Commissioners in Ireland from their inspectors and medical inspectors during the months of December 1861, and January and February 1862, relating to the condition of the poor in the counties of Roscommon, Sligo, Galway, and Mayo, p. 5, HC 1862 [111], xlix, pt. 1. 629.

20 *Index to the Report from the Select Committee on Poor Relief (Ireland)*, p. 185.

21 *Ibid.*, p. 184.

22 *Ibid.*

23 Cousin, 'Registration of Children under the Irish Poor Law', p. 113.

24 *Index to the Report from the Select Committee on Poor Relief (Ireland)*, p. 30.

25 Arlene Young, 'Entirely a Woman's Question?: Class, Gender, and the Victorian Nurse' in *Journal of Victorian Culture*, vol. 13 no. 1 (Mar. 2008), p. 19.

26 G.M. Fealy, *A History of Apprenticeship Nurse Training in Ireland* (Oxon, 2006), p. 20.

27 *Ibid.*, p. 30.

28 *Poor Law (Ireland) Amendment Act* (23 & 26 Vic., c. 83).

29 *Annual Report of the Commissioners for Administering the Laws for Relief of the Poor in Ireland*, p. 61, HC, 1863 [3135], xxii. 341.

30 Barrington, *Health, Medicine and Politics*, p. 6.

31 Alysa Levene, 'Between Less Eligibility and the N.H.S.: The Changing Place of Poor Law Hospitals in England and Wales, 1929-39' in *Twentieth Century British History*, vol. 20, no. 3 (2009), p. 323.

32 For a comprehensive study of the origins of the Irish Poor Law, see Peter Gray, *The Making of the Irish Poor Law, 1815-43* (Manchester, 2009).

33 Martin Gorsky and Sally Sheard, 'Introduction' in *Financing Medicine: The British Experience Since 1750* (Oxon, 2006), p. 5.

34 *Annual Report of the Commissioners for Administering the Laws for Relief of the Poor in Ireland*, HC, 1872 [c. 577], xxix. 1.

35 For further analysis of the economy and society of county Mayo during this period see, Donald E. Jordan *Land and Popular Politics in Ireland: County Mayo from Plantation to the Land War* (Cambridge, 1994), pp 103-69; Cormac O'Grada, 'Seasonal Migration and Post-Famine Adjustment in the

West of Ireland' in *Studia Hibernica*, 13 (1973), pp 48-76.

36 For an outline of relief practices in Westport see, Donnacha Seán Lucey, 'Relief Practices in the Westport Poor Law Union, 1850-1880', Seminar Presentation, Oxford Brookes University (Feb. 2008), http://www.esrc.ac.uk/my-esrc/grants/RES-062-23-0181/read; Gerald Moran, 'Famine and the Land War: Relief and Distress in Mayo, 1879-1881, part I' in *Cathair na Mart: Journal of the Westport Historical Society*, vol. 5, no. 1, 1985; idem 'Famine and the Land War: Relief and Distress in Mayo, 1879-81, part II' in *Cathair na Mairt: Journal of the Westport Historical Society*, vol. 6, no. 1, 1986, pp 111-28; T.P. O'Neill 'Minor Famines and Relief in Galway, 1815-1925' in *Galway: History and Society: Interdisciplinary Essays on the History of an Irish County* (Dublin, 1996), pp 465-72.

37 J.J. Louden, the editor of the Land League mouthpiece in the 'west', the *Connaught Telegraph*, sat on the board; for an exploration of the wresting of control by nationalist guardians from their landlord counterparts see, W.L. Feingold, *The Revolt of the Tenantry: The Transformation of Local Government in Ireland* (Boston, 1984); Virginia Crossman, *Politics, Pauperism and Power in Late Nineteenth-Century Ireland* (Manchester, 2006), pp 36-70; Donnacha Sean Lucey, *The Irish National League in Dingle County Kerry, 1885-92* in Maynooth Local History Series (Dublin, 2003), idem, 'Power, Politics and Poor Relief During the Irish Land War, 1879-82' in *Irish Historical Studies*, Nov. 2011 (forthcoming).

38 Westport Board of Guardians Minute Book (hereafter WBGMB), 29 Nov. 1865, MS 12,635 (National Library of Ireland).

39 WBGMB, 8 May 1890, MS 12,668.

40 WBGMB, 22 Mar. 1866, MS 12,635.

41 WBGMB, 2 Nov. 1871, MS 12,646.

42 WBGMB, 21 Sep. 1871, MS 12,646.

43 WBGMB, 18 Nov. 1897, MS 12,678.

44 WBGMB 18 Jul. 1895, MS 12,676.

45 *Annual Report of the L.G.B.*, p. 15, HC 1890 [C. 6094], xxxiv. 361.

46 WBGMB, 4 Apr. 1894, MS 12,674.

47 WBGMB, 6 Aug. 1892, MS 12,673.

48 WBGMB, 9 Aug. 1894, MS 12,674.

49 WBGMB, 7 Nov. 1889, MS 12,668.

50 Committals from the Westport Workhouse to the Lunatic Asylum were common occurrences, for example see WBGMB, 8 May 1890, MS 12,668.

51 WBGMB, 30 Nov. 1893, MS 12,674.

52 The relief of distress in the 'west' has been the focus of much research see, Virginia Crossman, *Politics, Pauperism and Power*, pp 106-43.

53 *Annual Report of the L.G.B.*, pp 127-9, HC 1881 [C. 2926] [C. 2926-1], xlvii, 269, 305.

54 For an examination of the 1886 Relief of Distress Bill and the controversy arising from the guardians' over-expenditure, see Virginia Crossman, 'The Charm of Allowing People to Manage their Own Affairs: Political Perspectives on Emergency Relief in Late Nineteenth-Century Ireland' in D. George Boyce and Alan O'Day, *Ireland in Transition, 1867-1921* (London, 2004), pp 193-208.

55 *Ibid.*, p. 207.

56 *Annual Report of the L.G.B.*, p. 21, HC 1896 [C. 8153], xxxviii. 1.

57 WBGMB, 13 Sep. 1894, MS 12,675.

58 WBGMB, 18 Jul. 1895, MS 12,676.

59 *Connaught Telegraph*, 22 Feb. 1896.

60 *Connaught Telegraph*, 22 Feb. 1896.

61 *Connaught Telegraph*, 22 Feb. 1896.

62 *Connaught Telegraph*, 22 Feb. 1896.

63 *Connaught Telegraph*, 22 Feb. 1896.

64 Maria Luddy, 'Angels of Mercy: Nuns as Workhouse Nurses, 1861-1898' in *Medicine, Disease and the State in Ireland, 1650-1940* (Cork, 1999), p. 103.

65 *Ibid.*, p. 107.

66 *Connaught Telegraph*, 9 Oct. 1897. Reprint of an article that appeared in the *Western Catholic News* (USA).

67 *Return of the Average Number of Sick Persons Tended in Each Union Workhouse in Ireland… and Showing the Number of Paid Nurses, and Unpaid or Pauper Assistants in Charge of Such Persons… during the Year Ended 30th June 1881*, p. 19, HC 1881 (433), lxxix. 199.

68 *Ibid.*

69 *Ibid.*

70 *Annual Report of the L.G.B.*, p. 68, HC 1890-91 [C. 6439], xxxv. 1.

71 'Nursing in Ireland' in the *British Medical Journal*, 23 Jan. 1897, p. 231.

72 *Ibid.*, p. 23273 *Annual Report of the L.G.B*, p. 67, HC 1898 [C. 8958], xli. 1.

73 *Annual Report of the L.G.B.*, p. 67, HC 1898 [C.8958], xli. I.

74 Fealy, *A History of Apprenticeship Training in Ireland*, p. 20.

75 WBGMB, 11 Aug. 1892, 29 Sep. 1892, MS 12,673.

76 WBGMB, 19 Mar. 1896, MS,12,676

77 *Connaught Telegraph*, 14 Mar. 1896.

78 WBGMB, 14 May 1896, MS,12,676.

79 WBGMB, 14 Jan. 1897, MS 12,678.

80 *Connaught Telegraph*, 16 Jan. 1897.

81 *Ibid.*

82 *Connaught Telegraph*, 20 Nov. 1897.

83 WBGMB, 18 Nov. 1897, MS 12,679.

Chapter 7

1 *Royal Commission on Labour: The Agricultural Labourer, vol. iv, Ireland*, pt. iii, Report on the Loughrea Union by Roger C. Richards, 1893-94, House of Commons, vol. xxxvii, p. 21.

2 *Ibid.*

3 J. Forde *et al*, *The District of Loughrea, vol. ii: Folklore, 1860-1960*, Loughrea History Project, 2003, p. 255.

4 *Royal Commission on Labour*, Richards report, p. 23.

5 Samuel Clark, *Social Origins of the Irish Land War* (Princeton, 1979), p. 118.

6 Paul Bew, *Conflict and Conciliation in Ireland, 1890-1914: Parnellites and Radical Agrarians* (Oxford University Press, 1987), passim; D.S. Jones, *Graziers, Land Reform, and Political Conflict in Ireland* (Washington DC, 1995), pp 176-84; J. Cunningham, *Labour in the West of Ireland: Working Life and Struggle, 1890-1914* (Belfast, 1995), pp 42-6.

7 *Royal Commission on Labour*, Richards's report, p. 21.

8 *Ibid.*, pt. iv, report of Arthur Wilson Fox on the Castlereagh union, p. 97.

9 *Ibid.*

10 *Ibid.*, p. 92.

11   *Ibid.*, reports of W.P. O'Brien on Naas Union, p. 44, and on Cashel Union, p. 65.

12   *Ibid.*, O'Brien report on Ennistymon, p. 53.

13   *Ibid.*, Wilson Fox report, pp 90, 92, 97.

14   John Cunningham, *Unlikely Radicals: Irish Post-Primary Teachers and the ASTI, 1909-2009* (Cork, 2009), p. 7.

15   Series of conversations with Tom Glynn (1916-2003), whose father and his antecedents were herds for O'Rourkes at Mullaghmore, Moylough, county Galway.

16   According to P.W. Joyce (*Social History of Ancient Ireland*, Phoenix, Dublin 1903, vol. ii, pp 281-3), animals were classified in Brehon law as follows with regard to the regulation of grazing rights, 'the cow being taken as the unit': two geese are equivalent to a sheep; two sheep to one *dairt* or one year old heifer; two *dairt*s to one *colpthach* or two-year-old heifer; two *colpthach*s to one cow; a cow and a *colpthach* to one ox.' See also F. Kelly, *Early Irish Farming: A Study Based Mainly on the Law Texts of the 7th and 8th Centuries A.D.* (Dublin, 1997), pp 182-7, 442-4. I am indebted to Dáibhì Ó Cróinín for these references.

17   B. Ó Dálaigh, 'The Lucas Diary, 1740-41,' *Analecta Hibernica*, no. 40 (2007), p. 118.

18   H. Dutton, *A Statistical and Agricultural Survey of the County of Galway, with Observations on the Means of Improvement* (Dublin 1824); E. Wakefield, *An Account of Ireland, Statistical and Political*, 2 vols (London, 1812), vol. ii, p. 749. I am indebted to Cathal Smith for this reference.

19   *Poor Inquiry (Ireland)* Appendix D. 'Baronial Examinations Relative to Earnings of Labourers... and Supplement Containing Answers to Questions 1 to 12 Circulated by the Commissioners,' House of Commons, 1836, vol. xxxii.

20   *Ibid.*, passim.

21   *Ibid.*, p. 2.

22   *Ibid.*, p. 3.

23   *Ibid.*, pp 31, 37.

24   *Ibid.*, pp 6, 64, 65, 86, 104.

25   *Ibid.*, p. 29.

26   *Ibid.*, pp 24, 136. See also pp 7, 25, 33.

27 *Ibid.*, p. 13; A.T. Lucas, *Cattle in Ancient Ireland* (Kilkenny, 1981), pp 20-1.

28 Responses to Q. 11 of the *Poor Inquiry* supplement: 'Are Wages Usually Paid in Money, or Provisions, or by Conacre? Or in What Other Way?'

29 Kevin Whelan, 'Settlement and Society in Eighteenth Century Ireland,' in G. Dawe and J. Wilson (eds), *The Poet's Place* (Belfast, 1991), pp 45-62.

30 Jones, *Graziers*, pp 32-41.

31 *Ibid.*, pp 42-61, 139-58.

32 *Irish Times*, 9 Oct. 1861; P. Melvin, 'Estates and Gentry around Loughrea,' in Forde *et al*, *Loughrea History*, pp 46-47; John Cunningham, '"A Spirit of Self-Preservation": Herdsmen Around Loughrea in the Late Nineteenth Century.' Forde *et al*, *The District of Loughrea, vol. i: History, 1791-1918* (Loughrea History Project, 2003), pp 464-66; Mark Thomas, 'Dartfield House,' in 'Abandoned Ireland', http://www.abandonedireland.com/ Dartfield_House.html, accessed 20 Apr. 2011.

33 Paul Bew, *Land and the National Question in Ireland, 1858-82* (Dublin, 1978), pp 191-216; Philip Bull, *Land, Politics and Nationalism: A Study of the Irish Land Question* (Dublin, 1996), pp 88-110.

34 *Royal Commission on Labour*, report of Roger C. Richards, p. 49.

35 *Ibid.*, p. 21; *Report of the Royal Commission on the Land Law (Ireland) Act, 1881, and the Purchase of Land (Ireland) Act, 1885*, House of Commons, 1887, vol. xxvi, par. 12200-201.

36 CSORP, 1882/23402 and 1882/37691; *The Nation*, 25 Feb. 1882; *Roscommon Journal*, 24 Jun. 1882; *Roscommon Messenger*, 9 Sep. 1882; Fintan Lane, 'Rural Labourers, Social Change and Politics in Late Nineteenth-Century Ireland', ' in Lane and Ó Drisceoil (eds), *Politics and the Irish Working Class, 1830-1945* (Houndmills, 2005), p. 113-39.

37 *Roscommon Messenger*, 4 Mar. 1882.

38 CSORP 1882/36108.

39 *Roscommon Messenger*, 6 May, 16 Sep. 1882, 3, 24 Mar. 1883; *Roscommon Journal*, 3 Jun. 1882; 1901 census, household schedule of James Scott, Carns; *The Nation*, 18, 25 Feb.; 18 Mar.; 1, 8, 15 Apr.; 6, 27 May; 3, 10 Jun.; 1, 8 Jul.; 12 Aug.; 16, 23, 30 Sep. 1882.

40 L. Perry Curtis Jr, 'Landlord Responses to the Irish Land War, 1879-87,' *Eire-Ireland: Journal of Irish Studies* (Fall-Winter, 2003), pp 134-88.

41 *The Nation*, 8 Apr. 1882; *Roscommon Journal*, 6 May 1882.

42 *Roscommon Herald*, 20, 27 May 1882; *Roscommon Journal*, 3 Jun. 1882.

43 CSORP, 1882/37691; *The Nation*, 8 Apr. 1882.

44 *Roscommon Messenger*, 4 Mar. 1882, *The Nation*, 15 Jul. 1882.

45 CSORP, 1882/37691.

46 *Roscommon Messenger*, 9, 16 Sep., 23 Dec. 1882, 6 Jan. 1883.

47 *Freeman's Journal*, 25 Sep. 1882.

48 *Roscommon Messenger*, 9 Sep., 23 Dec. 1882.

49 *Ibid.*, 9 Sep. 1882. *Pro fidelibis defunctis*, which is part of a prayer said for the dead, translates 'For the faithful departed'.

50 *Roscommon Messenger*, 24 Mar. 1883, *Roscommon Herald*, 28 Apr. 1883.

51 *Royal Commission on Labour*, Wilson Fox report, p. 95.

52 *Roscommon Journal*, 2 Jul., 10 Sep. 1904.

53 Cunningham, 'Herdsmen around Loughrea,' pp 457-95.

54 *Western News*, 24 Jun. 1882.

55 CSORP, 1882/24208.

56 *Galway Express*, 15, 22 Jul. 1882.

57 *The Nation*, 24 Sep. 1881.

58 *Royal Commission on the Land Law*, 1887, par. 12200-202.

59 TNA, CO 904/16, Irish crimes records: Register of home associations: Memorandum as to the working of the Shepherds or Herds Association of County Galway WR,' pp 401/1-5.

60 *Royal Commission on Labour*, Richards's report, pp 21, 23.

61 Pádraig G. Lane, 'Agricultural Labourers and Rural Violence, 1850-1914,' *Studia Hibernica*, no. 27 (1993), pp 83-4.

62 Cunningham, 'Herdsmen around Loughrea,' pp 470-1.

63 *Tuam News*, 30 May 1884.

64 *Ibid.*, 27 Feb. 1885, 21 Aug. 1891; *Western News*, 19 May 1888.

65 *Galway Observer*, 5 Dec. 1891.

66 *Tuam News*, 13 Jul. 1894.

67 Divisional Commissioners and County Inspectors Reports (DCCI), CO 904/16, Information on Herds Association in Ballyvaughan and Ennis district, November 1892. For an account of the grazing economy in Clare, see Brendan Ó Cathaoir, 'Another Clare: Ranchers and Moonlighters, 1700-1945,' in M. Lynch & P. Nugent (eds), *Clare: History & Society* (Dublin: Geography Publications, 2008), pp 359-423.

68　*Tuam News*, 13 Nov. 1891.

69　*ibid.*, 12 Feb. 1892; *Western News*, 24 Jun. 1882.

70　*Tuam News*, 21 Jul. 1893. See also *Tuam Herald*, 22 May 1897.

71　*The Agricultural Labourer*, Wilson Fox report, p. 100.

72　*Tuam News*, 21 Jul. 1893, 19 Jul. 1895.

73　*Ibid.*, 8 Jul. 1892; Fintan Lane, 'Rural Labourers,' pp 139–35; Pádraig G. Lane, 'Agricultural Labourers and the Land Question,' in Carla King (ed.), *Famine, Land and Culture in Ireland* (Dublin: 2000), pp 105–9.

74　*Tuam News*, 6, 13 Jul. 1894.

75　DCCI, CO 904/58, Galway East Riding, Feb., Sep., Nov. 1895; CO 904/59, Jun.-Dec., 1896, Jan.-Jun. 1897.

76　DCCI, CO 904/69, Galway East Riding, Jan. 1900.

77　Inspector General's Monthly Confidential report, Box 2, Galway East Riding, Oct. 1899; DCCI, CO 904/71, Galway East Riding, Nov. 1900, CO 904/72, Dec. 1900.

78　Cunningham, 'Herdsmen around Loughrea,' pp 475–6.

79　*Western News*, 4 Jul. 1903; *Western People*, 14 Feb. 1903; 13 Feb. 2004; *Roscommon Journal*, 2 Jul., 10 Sep. 1904.

80　Anthony Varley, 'The Politics of Agrarian Reform: The State, Nationalists and the Agrarian Question in the West of Ireland' (unpublished PhD thesis, Illinois University at Carbondale, 1994), pp 96–286.

81　Forde *et al*, *Loughrea Folklore*, p. 255; Tom Glynn conversations.

82　Beatrice Bill Talbot & John Lenihan, *And That's No Lie* [memoir of Roscommon herd's son] (Cambridge, Mass: Houghton Mifflin, 1946), p. 53; Tom Glynn conversations.

83　Fintan Lane, 'Rural Labourers, Social Change and Politics in Late Nineteenth-Century Ireland', pp 113–39.

Chapter 8

1　Carla King 'The Early Development of Agricultural Cooperation: Some French and Irish Comparisons,' *Proceedings of the Royal Irish Academy* vol. 96, C, no. 3, pp 3–86.

2 Patrick Lynch and John Vaizey, *Guinness's Brewery in the Irish Economy, 1759-1876* (Cambridge, 1960).

3 J.J. Lee, 'The Dual Economy in Ireland, 1800-1850', *Irish Historical Studies*, viii (1971), pp 191-200.

4 Cormac Ó Gráda, 'Supply Responsiveness in Irish Agriculture during the Nineteenth Century, *Economic History Review*, 2nd ser. xxviii, pp 312-17.

5 S.H. Cousins, 'The Regional Variations in Population Change' in *Economic History Review*, xvii (1964), pp 301-21.

6 Michael Cuddy and Chris Curtin, 'Commercialisation in West of Ireland agriculture in the 1890s', *Economic and Social Review*, xiv, no. 3 (April 1983, pp 173-84.

7 Ciara Breathnach, *The Congested Districts Board of Ireland, 1891-1923* (Dublin, 2005), p. 11.

8 *Report on the Depressed Condition of the Agricultural Interest* [Richmond Report], Cd. 2778, HC 1881, xv.

9 Liam Kennedy, 'Traders in the Irish Rural Economy, 1880-1914' *Economic History Review*, 2nd ser. xxxii, 2 (May 1979), pp 201-10.

10 Cormac Ó Gráda, 'Seasonal Migration and Post-Famine Adjustment in the West of Ireland,' *Studia Hibernica*, 13 (1973), pp 48-76.

11 Ó Gráda, 'Seasonal Migration,' p. 57.

12 Desmond Norton, *Landlords, Tenants, Famine* (Dublin, 2006), p. 49-51.

13 Gerard Moran, 'Near Famine: The Crisis in the West of Ireland, 1879-82', *Irish Studies Review*, v, no. 18 (spring 1997), pp 14-21.

14 Anna Parnell commented that in any other country four relief agencies would cause duplication of effort and waste but in Ireland this was not the case as the competition between them would provide some check on corruption. Anna Parnell, *The Tale of A Great Sham* (Dublin, 1986), p. 58.

15 *The Irish Crisis of 1879-80: Proceedings of the Dublin Mansion House Relief Committee, 1880* (Dublin, 1881), pp 75-7.

16 *Report of her Majesty's Commissioners of Inquiry into the Working of the Landlord and Tenant (Ireland) Act, 1870, and the Acts Amending the Same* [C. 2779], HC 1881, xvii,1; *Royal Commission on the Land Law (Ireland) Act, 1881 and the Purchase of Land Ireland Act 1885* [C. 4969], HC 1887, xxxvi, 1.

17 Allen Warren, 'Dublin Castle, Whitehall, and the Formation of Irish Policy, 1879-92,' *Irish Historical Studies*, xxxiv, no. 136, pp 403-30.

18 He subsequently published accounts of his expeditions in *Narrative Describing the 2nd, 3rd and 4th Weeks of William Forster's Journey in the Distressed Districts of Ireland* (York, 1847) and *A Visit to Connaught in the Autumn of 1847* (1847).

19 See especially his article and pamphlet, 'Irish Emigration', *Nineteenth Century* (Feb. 1881), pp 694-714 and *Ought Emigration from Ireland be Assisted?* (London, 1882).

20 Rt Hon. Sir Edward Fry, *James Hack Tuke, A Memoir* (London, 1899), pp 197, 207.

21 J.H. Tuke, *The Condition of Donegal* (London, 1889), p. 45.

22 P.J. Perry, *British Farming in the Great Depression, 1870-1914, an Historical Geography* (Newton Abbot, 1974), pp 102-3.

23 *Freeman's Journal*, 9, 17, 20 Nov., 1, 5, 8 Dec. 1885. This was a return to its role in 1878 of raising consciousness about distress, carried out so successfully in 1878, with William O'Brien's series of articles entitled 'Christmas in the Galtees'.

24 Letter to the editor of the *Freeman's Journal*, 11 Jan. 1886; TCD, Davitt papers, MS 9609/2.

25 TCD, Davitt papers, MS 9545, Diary, 15 Jan. 1886.

26 Davitt relates that Fr O'Connor informed him that his jarvey was a souper and a temperance campaigner! TCD, Davitt papers, MS 9546/3.

27 TCD, Davitt papers, MS 9546, Achill, Jan. 1886.

28 *Ibid.*

29 *Freeman's Journal*, 28 Jan. 1886; also in TCD, Davitt papers, MS 9609/7.

30 *Freeman's Journal*, 1-4 Feb. 1886; also in TCD, Davitt papers, MS 9609/7-9.

31 The letter, dated 25 February, was published in the *Freeman's Journal*, 9 Mar. 1886. See also TCD Davitt papers, MS 9609/25.

32 *Hansard*, 3rd ser., ciii (8 Mar. 1886), cols 123-4.

33 Edward Fry, *James Hack Tuke: A Memoir* (London, 1899).

34 See Fry, *Tuke*, pp 236-41.

35 James Hack Tuke, *The Condition of Donegal* (1889).

36 *Irish World*, 26 Jun. 1886; in TCD Davitt papers, MS 9608.

37 TCD Davitt papers, MS 9436/2926, Account of receipts and disbursements audited by Koan & Co., Chartered Accountants, 23 Jul. 1886.

38 TCD Davitt papers, MS 9546/44. Notebook of Achill visit.

39   *Irish World*, 10 Jul. 1886; TCD Davitt papers, MS 9608/31. Tuke agreed that
     the money raised in 1886 had been squandered, and that no local board
     or authority was sufficiently honest to handle funds fairly or refrain from
     sharing in the spoil. See his letters to *The Times*, 20, 27 and 29 Jun. 1889,
     referred to in Ciara Breathach, *The Congested Districts Board of Ireland,
     1891-1923* (Dublin, 2005), pp 23-4.

40   Cable from Galway to the *Irish World*, dated 22 Jun. 1886; published *Irish
     World*, 26 Jun. 1886; TCD Davitt papers, MS 9608/31.

41   TCD Davitt papers, MS 9592. Western Islands Fishing Boat Fund bank
     book with the National Bank, Dublin. Davitt seems to have expended
     some of his own money in this and raised further funds through
     designated lectures in Britain and America.

42   TCD Davitt papers, MS 9436, J.J. Louden to Davitt, 14 Jul. 1886.

43   *Freeman's Journal*, 1 Sep. 1887; see also TCD Davitt papers, MS 9612/46
     press cuttings book.

44   TCD Davitt papers, MS 9548, diary 17-21 Jan. 1888 and 16 Mar. 1888;
     Freeman's Journal, 12 Mar. 1888.

45   See TCD Davitt papers, MSS 9426 and 9427, Achill disaster, 1894.

46   *The Times*, 2 Jan. 1886.

47   James Hack Tuke, *Spectator*, 6 Mar. 1886; quoted Fry, *Tuke*, pp 232-3.

48   A.J. Balfour, *Nationality and Home Rule* (London, 1913), quoted Andrew
     Gailey, *Ireland and the Death of Kindness: The Experience of Constructive
     Unionism, 1890-1905* (Cork, 1987), p. 3

49   Gailey, *Ireland and the Death of Kindness*, p. 311; see also, Catherine B.
     Shannon, *Arthur J. Balfour and Ireland, 1874-1922* (Washington, 1988), p. 54.

50   It is interesting to note that Balfour chose to remain on the Congested
     Districts Board after the change of government in 1892 when he ceased to
     be Chief Secretary, indicating a sense of commitment to it.

51   Warren, 'Dublin Castle', p. 429.

52   *Hansard*, 3rd ser. 25 Jul. 1890 [347] 896; 7 Aug. 1890 [348] 106; 11 Aug. 1890
     [348] 523; 15 Aug. 1890 [348] 1132.

53   British Library, Balfour Papers, MS 49827, Balfour to West Ridgway,
     15 May 1889; quoted in L.P. Curtis, *Coercion and conciliation in Ireland,
     1880-1892. A Study in Conservative Unionism* (Princeton, 1963), p. 357.

54   James Hack Tuke, *Condition of Donegal*, p. 41.

55   *Ibid.*, p. 44.

56   *Ibid.*, p. 41.

57   Quoted R.B. McDowell, *The Irish Administration, 1801-1914* (London, 1964), p. 220.

58   Margaret Digby, *Horace Plunkett, an Anglo-American Irishman* (Oxford, 1949); Trevor West, *Horace Plunkett, Co-operation and Politics: An Irish Biography* (Bucks, 1986); Carla Keating, 'Sir Horace Plunkett and Rural Reform,' (PhD thesis NUI, 1984).

59   Paul Bew, *Conflict and Conciliation in Ireland, 1890-1910: Parnellites and Radical Agrarians* (Oxford, 1987), pp 27-8; Carla King, 'The Recess Committee, 1895-6', *Studia Hibernica*, no. 30 (1998-9), pp 21-46.

60   Plunkett diaries, 18 Feb. 1897; NLI, O'Brien papers, MS 913/300-2, Davitt to O'Brien, undated.

61   John Hunter, *The Making of the Crafting Community* (Edinburgh, 1976), passim.

62   *Twentieth Annual Report of the Congested Districts Board* (Dublin, 1912), p. 12.

63   For more detail on these, see W.L. Micks, *An Account of the Constitution, Administration and Dissolution of the Congested Districts Board* (Dublin, 1925) and Breathnach, *The Congested Districts Board of Ireland*.

64   *Royal Commission on Congestion*, appendix to the *third report*, [Cd. 3414], HC 1907, xxxv, 384. Appendix xii, Memorandum of Horace Plunkett, para. 78.

65   Joanna Bourke, *Husbandry to Housewifery: Women, Economic Change, and Housework in Ireland, 1890-1914* (Oxford, 1993), p. 115.

66   *Fourteenth Annual Report of the Congested Districts Board* (Dublin, 1905), p. 33.

67   Breathnach, *Congested Districts Board*, p. 72.

68   *Hansard*, 4th ser. 13 May 1898 [57], 1248-9.

69   NAI, CO 904/68, Crime Special Branch, Confidential report of County Inspector for Mayo, Feb. 1898.

70   *Mayo News*, 16 Apr. 1898, reprinting letter of William O'Brien to the *Freeman's Journal*, dated 10 Apr. 1898.

71   His report is printed in the first *Annual Report of the Congested Districts Board, 1892*, Appendix E.

72   NLI, Horace Plunkett diaries, 23 Sep. 1891.

73 Micks, *The Congested Districts Board*, pp 144-7.

74 Raymond D. Crotty, *Irish Agricultural Production: Its Volume and Structure* (Cork, 1966), p. 89.

75 Fergus Campbell, *Land and Revolution: Nationalist Politics in the West of Ireland, 1891-1921* (Oxford, 2005), p. 24.

76 *Mayo News*, 29 Jan. 1898. From speech at inaugural meeting of UIL in Westport, 23 Jan. 1898; quoted in Heather Laird, *Subversive Law in Ireland, 1879-1920* (Dublin, 2005), p. 12.

77 TCD, Davitt papers, MS 9335/323: Morley to Davitt, 21 Oct. 1892. Unfortunately, Davitt's letters to Morley do not appear to have survived among the Morley papers in Oxford.

78 William O'Brien, *An Olive Branch in Ireland and its History* (London, 1910), pp 87-9; Sally Warwick-Haller, *William O'Brien and the Irish Land War* (Dublin, 1990), pp 152-6; Micks, *Congested Districts Board*, p. 103.

79 *Mayo News*, 29 Jan. 1898.

80 Gerard Moran, 'James Daly and the Rise and Fall of the Land League in the West of Ireland, 1879-82', *Irish Historical Studies*, xxix (1994), pp 189-207.

81 They were John McEvilly, Archbishop of Tuam, John Healy, Archbishop of Clonfert, John Lyster, Bishop of Achonry, John Conmy, Bishop of Killala and John Joseph Clancy, Bishop of Elphin.

82 *Irish People*, 7 Oct. 1899.

83 *Western People*, 24 Aug. 1912, quoted in William Keaveney, *The Land for the People: Robert Henry Johnstone & the United Irish League, a Story of Land Agitation in the Early Twentieth Century* (Dublin, 2007), p. 35.

84 L.P. Curtis, *Coercion and Conciliation*, p. 361.

85 Compulsory Powers Bill, 1898, 13, I, 373; H. Plunkett Diaries, 23 Feb. 1898; *Hansard*, 4th ser. 23 Feb. 1898 [53], 1446, 1448-50, 1471. Plunkett records supporting proposing a resolution in favour of compulsory powers as early as 1895, see Diaries, 10 May 1895.

86 Bew, *Conflict and Conciliation*, p. 43; TCD Davitt papers, MS 9460/3765 Davitt papers, O'Brien to Davitt, 22 Jul. 1898.

87 NAI, CO 904/68, Crime Special Branch, Confidential report of County Inspector for Mayo, Feb. 1898.

88 For example, on 26 Feb. 1898 he questioned Gerald Balfour about language used by M.J. Kelly, Crown Solicitor, in the petty sessions

court in Westport and supported a motion by Dillon to adjourn the House to call attention to it, *Mayo News*, 26 Feb. 1898. He also asked a question in the House on 11 March about information concerning a baton charge at Westport, referring to 'gross and unprovoked acts of violence on the part of a body of police at Westport'. *Mayo News*, 12 Mar. 1898. On 9 Aug. 1898, Arthur Balfour, under pressure from Davitt, conceded the principle of the need to increase the size of holdings as a means of tackling the problem of western distress; Bew, *Conflict and Conciliation*, p. 45.

89 *Hansard*, HC, 17 Feb. 1899, vol. 66 cc1347-404.

90 Donald Jordan, 'The Irish National League and the "Unwritten Law": Rural Protest and Nation-Building in Ireland, 1882-1890', *Past & Present*, no. 158 (Feb. 1998), p. 171; Philip Bull, *Land Politics and Nationalism*, pp 116-42; idem, 'The Formation of the United Irish League, 1898-1900: The Dynamics of Irish Agrarian Agitation,' *Irish Historical Studies*, xxxiii, no. 132 (November 2003), pp 404-23.

91 Laird, *Subversive Law*, p. 127.

92 William O'Brien, Diary, 14 Sep. 1898, published in *Irish People*, 16 Feb. 1907; quoted Bew, *Conflict and Conciliation*, p. 47.

93 *Royal Commission on Congestion*, eleventh report [Cd. 4089], HC 1908, digest of evidence, second appendix, xlii, vol. vii, p. 371, paragraphs 39305-9, evidence of P.A. Meehan.

94 Michael Davitt, *The Fall of Feudalism in Ireland, or the Story of the Land League Revolution* (London: Harper & Brothers, 1904), pp 663-4.

95 NLI, Horace Plunkett's diaries, for example, 16 Jul. 1898, 14 Mar. 1901.

96 Conor McNamara, 'The Revolution in East Galway, 1916-22' (PhD thesis, St Patrick's College, 2008).

97 *Royal Commission on Congestion, Third Report*, [Cd. 3414], HC 1907, xxxv, 384.

98 Micks, *op. cit.*

99 *Royal Commission on Congestion*, eleventh report [Cd. 4089], HC 1908, digest of evidence, second appendix, xlii, vol. i, p. 21, Evidence of W.L. Micks, paragraphs 181,183.

100 *Royal Commission on Congestion*, eleventh report [Cd. 4089], HC 1908, digest of evidence, second appendix, xlii, vol. i, p. 22, Evidence of W.L. Micks, paragraphs 462-3, 470.

101 Shannon, *Balfour and Ireland*, pp 56-7,

102 Crotty, *Irish Agricultural Production*, p. 84.

103 *Report of the Commission on De-Rating* (1931), p. 18; quoted Crotty, op cit, p. 91.

104 *Emigration Statistics of Ireland for the Year 1888* [C. 5647], p. 5, Table III showing by sexes the number of emigrants from each province and county from 1 May, 1851 to the 31 Dec. 1883, with the ratio of the population; *Emigration Statistics of Ireland, 1903* [Cd. 1489], p. 3, Table I, showing the number of emigrants from each province during 1901 and 1902, and the increase or decrease in the latter year.

SELECT BIBLIOGRAPHY

Beames, M.R., *Peasants and Power: The Whiteboy Movements and their Control in Pre-Famine Ireland* (Brighton, 1983).

Bew, Paul, *Land and the National Question in Ireland, 1858-82* (Dublin, 1978).

— *Conflict and Conciliation in Ireland, 1890-1910: Parnellites and Radical Agrarians* (Oxford, 1994).

Black, R.D. Collison, *Economic Thought and the Irish Question, 1817-70* (London, 1960).

Buckland, P.J., *Irish Unionism: The Anglo-Irish and the New Ireland, 1855-1922* (Dublin, 1973).

Bull, Philip, *Land, Politics and Nationalism: A Study of the Irish Land Question* (Dublin, 1996).

Campbell, Fergus, *Land and Revolution, Nationalist Politics in the West of Ireland 1891-1921* (Oxford, 2005).

Clark, Samuel, Donnelly, James S. Jnr (eds), *Irish Peasants: Violence and Political Unrest 1780-1914* (Manchester, 1983).

Clark, Samuel, *Social Origins of the Irish Land War* (Princeton, 1979).

Connell, K.H., *Irish Peasant Society* (Oxford, 1968).

Connolly, Sean J., *Priests and People in Pre-Famine Ireland* (Dublin, 1981).

Crossman, Virginia, *Politics, Pauperism and Power in Late Nineteenth Century Ireland* (Manchester, 2006).

Crotty, Raymond, *Irish Agricultural Production: Its Volume and Structure* (Cork, 1966).

Cunningham, John, *'A Town Tormented by the Sea'; Galway 1790-1914* (Dublin, 2004).

Curtis, L.P., *Coercion and Conciliation in Ireland, 1880-1892: A Study in Conservative Unionism* (Princeton, 1963).

Daly, Mary E., *The Famine in Ireland* (Dublin, 1986).

Donnelly, James S. Jnr, *The Land and the People of Nineteenth Century Cork: The Rural Economy and the Land Question* (London, 1975).

— *Captain Rock: The Irish Agrarian Rebellion of 1821-1824* (Dublin, 2009).

Gailey, Andrew, *Ireland and the Death of Kindness: The Experience of Constructive Unionism, 1890-1905* (Cork, 1987).

Geary, Laurence, *Medicine and Charity in Ireland 1718-1851* (Dublin, 2004).

— *The Plan of Campaign* (Cork, 1986).

Gray, Peter, *The Making of the Irish Poor Law, 1815-43* (Manchester, 2009).

Hoppen, K.T., *Elections, Politics and Society in Ireland, 1832-1885* (Oxford, 1984).

Jones, David Seth, *Graziers, Land Reform and Political Conflict in Ireland* (Washington, 1995).

King, Carla (ed.), *Famine, Land and Culture in Ireland* (Dublin, 2000).

— Michael Davitt (Dublin, 2009).

Lee, Joseph, *The Modernisation of Irish Society, 1848-1918* (Dublin, 1973).

Lucey, D.S., *The Irish National League in Dingle, County Kerry, 1885-1892* (Dublin, 2003).

Mokyr, Joel, *Why Ireland Starved: A Quantitative and Analytical History of the Irish Economy, 1800-1850* (London, 1983).

Moffitt, Miriam, *Soupers and Jumpers: The Protestant Missions in Connemara, 1848-1937* (Dublin, 2008).

Moran, Gerard, *A Radical Priest in Mayo: Fr Patrick Lavelle, the Rise and Fall of an Irish Nationalist, 1825-86* (Dublin, 1994).

Smith, William, and Whelan, Kevin (eds), *Common Ground: Essays on the Historical Geography of Ireland* (Cork, 1988).

O'Day, Alan (ed.), *Reactions to Irish Nationalism, 1865-1914* (Dublin, 1987).

Ó Gráda, Cormac, *Ireland: A New Economic History, 1780-1939* (Oxford, 1994).

— *Ireland Before and After the Great Famine: Explorations in Economic History, 1800-1925* (Manchester, 1988).

Ó Tuathaigh, Gearóid, *Ireland Before the Famine 1798-1848* (Dublin, 1972).

Shields, Andrew, *The Irish Conservative Party, 1852-68: Land, Politics and Religion* (Dublin, 2007).

Vaughan, W.E., (ed.) *A New History of Ireland, Volume V, Ireland under the Union I: 1801-1870* (Oxford, 1989).

— *Landlords and Tenants in Mid-Victorian Ireland* (Oxford, 1997).

Whelan, Irene, *The Bible War in Ireland: The Second Reformation and the Polarization of Protestant-Catholic Relations, 1800-1840* (Dublin, 2005).

NOTES ON CONTRIBUTORS

John Cunningham

John Cunningham is a lecturer in history at NUI Galway where he teaches courses on labour history, local history and modern Ireland. His current research interests include labour biography and the moral economy of pre-famine Ireland. His books include *'A Town Tormented by the Sea': Galway, 1790-1914* and *Unlikely Radicals: Irish Post-Primary Teachers and the ASTI, 1909-2009*. He is currently joint editor of *Saothar: Journal of the Irish Labour History Society*.

Carla King

Carla King is a lecturer in modern history at St Patrick's College, Drumcondra. She has published various works relating to the land question and Michael Davitt, including *Famine, Land and Culture in Ireland*; *Michael Davitt*; *Michael Davitt: Collected Writings, 1868-1906*; *Michael Davitt, Jottings in Solitary*; *Lives of Victorian Political Figures, Part II, vol. 4: Michael Davitt*; and co-edited with W.J. Mc Cormack, John Devoy's *Michael Davitt: From the*

Gaelic American, and articles on Davitt in scholarly and popular journals. She is currently writing a biography of Davitt's later life.

Pádraig G. Lane

Pádraig G. Lane taught history for many years at the Capuchin College, Rochestown, county Cork. His published work has focused on the plight of the marginalised in rural society including labourers and the rural poor, as well as aspects of land redistribution by the state in the nineteenth century. His has published works in both English and Irish, including *Ireland: Past and Present, Finíni Laoise* and *Éadbhard Ó Dufaigh*. He has contributed many chapters to important studies on various aspects of Irish rural history.

Donnacha Seán Lucey

Donnacha Seán Lucey is currently an IRCHSS Fellow in the Centre for Contemporary Irish History, Trinity College Dublin. His research interests include popular political organisation and state responses to poverty in nineteenth-century Ireland. His book *Land, Politics and Violence, 1872-86: The Case of Kerry* will be published in 2011. His previous study of the Land League, *The Irish National League in Dingle, County Kerry, 1885-1892* was published as part of the Maynooth Studies in Local History in 2003.

Conor McNamara

Conor McNamara is the author of numerous articles on the history of the west of Ireland in the nineteenth and early twentieth century. His first major book is a study of the Irish Revolution in Connacht entitled *Revolution in the West of Ireland: Galway, 1913-1921* and will be published in 2012. In 2009 he was awarded the National Library of Ireland Studentship for History and catalogued the Mahon Papers, one of the largest collections of landed estate papers in the state.

Miriam Moffitt

Miriam Moffitt is a graduate of NUI Maynooth where she held an IRCHSS post-doctoral fellowship. Her main research interest focuses on the history of the Protestant community in the west of Ireland and her most recent publications include *Soupers and Jumpers, the Protestant Missions in Connemara, 1848-1937* and *The Society for Irish Church Missions to the Roman Catholics, 1849-1950*. She currently teaches in St Patrick's College, Drumcondra.

Gerard Moran

Gerard Moran is one of Ireland's leading modern historians and teaches at the National University of Ireland, Maynooth. Much of his research has focused on the struggles of ordinary people in the west of Ireland and his books include *Sending Out Ireland's Poor: Assisted Emigration to North America in the Nineteenth Century* and *A Radical Priest in Mayo: Father Patrick Lavelle, the Rise and Fall of an Irish Nationalist*. He has also edited a number of important collections including *Galway: History and Society, Interdisciplinary Essays on the History of an Irish County*.

Andrew Shields

Educated in Ireland and Canada, Andrew Shields' research has focused on nineteenth-century Irish history. He has a particular interest in Irish political history in the mid-Victorian period and has taught history at a number of institutions, including the University of Sydney, the University of New South Wales and the Australian University. His first book, *The Irish Conservative Party, 1852-68: Land, Politics and Religion* was published in 2007. In 2009-10, he was a post-doctoral research fellow at St Patrick's College, Drumcondra, working on the archives of Archbishop Paul Cullen.

INDEX